RAINBOW**HANDBOOK**

HAWAI'I

The Islands' Ultimate Gay Guide

About the Author

Matthew Link is a writer, video maker, and kayaker living in South Kona on the Big Island of Hawai'i. A member of the National Gay and Lesbian Journalists Association, Matthew has contributed to the guides *Access Gay USA, Ferrari Gay Travel A to Z,* and *Fodor's* gay travel guides, as well as writing for numerous international magazines. He has also produced award–winning video documentaries on topics such as male prostitution, and HIV–positive Christians.

Spending his teenage years aboard his father's sailboat in and around the Pacific and Asia, he has at various times called Hong Kong, the Philippines, Palau, Papua New Guinea, Vanuatu, and New Zealand home. In addition, Matthew has traveled to India, Nepal, Mongolia, Finland, Brazil, Thailand, Spain, Estonia, and Russia. He now lives with Wayne, his partner of eight years, in a home on the slopes of the Mauna Loa volcano overlooking the wide Pacific.

RAINBOW**HANDBOOK**

HAWAI'I

The Islands' Ultimate Gay Guide

Matthew Link
Missing Link Productions
Kona, Hawai'i

First Printing November 1998
Second Printing May 1999, revised

Inclusion of an individual, business, group, or organization in this book does not indicate the sexual orientation of the party in any way, nor that the group or business encourages the specific affiliation or patronage of or by homosexuals, bisexuals, or transgendered people.

Although every effort has been made to ensure the accuracy of information, the publisher does not assume responsibility for any errors, omissions, inaccuracies, or travel problems due to information contained in this book. Opinions expressed are merely those of the author.

Cover design and book layout: Michael Aki

Cover artwork: *Warrior* by Douglas Simonson (copyrighted)

Printed in the United States of America by Missing Link Productions, P.O. Box 100-3, Honaunau, HI 96726. (808) 328-8654 www.rainbowhandbook.com

Link, Matthew.
     Rainbow Handbook Hawaii : the island's ultimate gay
guide / Matthew Link -- 1st ed.
     p. cm.
     Includes bibliographical references and index.
     "An insider's handle on gay Hawaii."
     Preassigned LCCN : 98-092014
     ISBN : 0-9665805-0-8

     1. Gays--Travel--Hawaii. 2. Hawaii--Guidebooks.
I. Title.

     DU623.25.L56 1998   996.904'41
                         QBI98-1170

Acknowledgments

This book is obviously the accumulation of many people's efforts and time, not to mention the enthusiasm and vital contributions of all involved. The gay and lesbian community in Hawai'i is held together by a handful of pioneering individuals with a vision, and if it weren't for these people who give of their time, money and energy, there would be little to put in a gay travel handbook.

My thanks go out to: Jack Law, John McDermott, Martin Rice, Douglas Simonson, Freddie Jordan, Frank Crouse, Gregg S. Gunter, Jon Fujiwara, Jason Yaris, Sue Aki, Michael Aki, Ku'umealoha Gomes, John Wilber, Kaholo Daguman, DeSoto Brown, Ama Joaquin, Carol Greenhouse, Dick Frazier, Ed Stumpf, Clem Classen, Scott Tambling, P.F. Buck, Doug Barret, Ryan Best, Barb Boodikins, Lori Paddock, Lorenzo Ross, Auntie Mary Green, and Lisa Jacob and all the great women at WHAF.

This book is dedicated to Wayne.

Warrior *Painting Copyright by Douglas Simonson.*

Contents

Contents

Author's Note

Having traveled to a hundred different places during my lifetime (and I'm not that old!), I've plowed through my share of dry, encyclopedic travel guides. I didn't care for the ones that seemed to be written by outsiders who hadn't a clue about the idiosyncratic *reality* of the place they were writing about. I always felt they missed the point that traveling (in contrast to touristing) is meant to be fun, or at least somewhat stimulating!

Gays and lesbians are traversing the globe in record numbers. Gay guide books are growing up to meet the demand, digging a little deeper than the bar/bathhouse/cruise spot mentality of the past. There are many things that separate us as gay, lesbian, bi or transgendered peoples: race, age, gender, nationality, income, beliefs, mind sets. But the underlying queerness is always a bond. And such it is with Hawai'i.

The reader should know that no company has paid to be in this guide. There are no advertisements. That way, you merely have *my* opinion on things, good or bad.

Although this guide is obviously written from a male point of view, it also includes nearly all information on Hawai'i's women– and womyn–oriented accommodations, tours groups, and organizations. The symbol ♀ has been added to women–owned businesses to distinguish them from the other listings.

A note on gay vs. gay–friendly establishments. What's the diff? Well, when called on it, no business in Hawai'i is going to tell you that they are gay–*un*friendly. Many straight businesses, especially B&Bs, go after the gay and lesbian market by adding gay–friendly to their listings. And many gay businesses have an overwhelming majority of straight paying customers. That's the beauty of life in Hawai'i – most everything and everyone is integrated. But what's a traveling homo to do? What is gay nowadays?

Well, to sift through all of it, I tried to include only gay or lesbian *owned, managed,* or *very gay–popular* businesses in the queer listings. All others get heaped into the not queer bin where they belong. Of these heterosexual ones, I tried to pick the funky, interesting, classy, or tasty ones – something that would appeal to the homo palate.

Since reality is constantly altering us and our world, by the time you have this volume in your little hands, a percentage of the information will be obsolete, out–of–date, or perhaps even down right contrary to what you read here. Sorry! You can help keep further editions of *Rainbow Handbook Hawai'i* current by sending in any alterations, updates, comments, bitching, or whatevers (however criticisms will be promptly shredded and burned!). I'll see what I can do about including them in upcoming editions for you.

I hope you find Hawai'i as fascinating and transformative a place as the Polynesians and explorers have before you.

Aloha!
Matthew Link
P.O. Box 100-3 • Honaunau, HI 96726

Artwork by Robert Lee Eskridge, ca. 1940
(DeSoto Brown Collection)

Where I live
There are rainbows
With life in the laughter of morning
And starry nights

Where I live
There are rainbows
With flowers full of colors
And birds full of song

I can smile when it's raining
and touch the warmth of the sun
I hear children laughing

In this place that I love

"Hawaiian Lullaby"

Preface

This book is about encountering Hawai'i. It is not like other places. Rules of far away continents don't apply or translate here. Hawai'i is her own, surrounded by thousands of miles of colossal ocean, proudly peaking up above the horizon like a hidden child. As with most foreign lands, the traveler must take her on her own terms. You'll find Polynesia here, as well as America and Asia and many other places. But they are all guests to the land. The islands themselves are strong and adherent, and have their own true song. Listen carefully and reverently. You might hear it.

Hawaiian Island Chain

Kaua'i

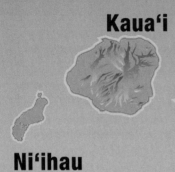

O'ahu

Moloka'i

Ni'ihau

Lana'i

Actual Geographical Layout

Maui

Kahoʻolawe

Hawaiʻi

CHAPTER 1

THE NITTY GRITTY

Fountain of Youth *by Douglas Simonson.*

State Facts for Trivial Queens

Hawai'i is nicknamed: "The Aloha State"	**Population:** 1,200,000 est.
State Flower: The Yellow Hibiscuss	**Highest point:** Mauna Kea at 13,796 feet/
State Bird: The Nene	4,205 m
State Mammal: The Humpback Whale	**State Motto:** *Ua mau he ea o ka 'aina i ka*
Land mass: 6,423 sq. miles/16,700 sq.km	*pono* ("The Life of the land is perpetuated in
fourth smallest U.S. state	righteousness.")

Visiting Hawai'i is not merely hopping off the jet with a lei wrapped around your untanned neck, sunscreen splattered on your nose and a cute bikini around your loins, then bolting to the pool side for your first of several pina coladas. You wish it were that easy! Oh no – Hawai'i demands much more of you than that.

Not only do you have all the hassles of getting anywhere (reservations, transfers, airports, taxi fare, ugh), but once you get here you're gonna have to figure out all the complex ins and outs about being a visitor in Hawai'i as well. The following load of information should get you nicely primed before you even set foot on the islands, so study hard.

Tell Me When You're Coming

Now when the heck are you gonna get here? Of course **tourist season** is year round, but mid–winter and early summer are when the retired snowbirds and the nuclear hetero families cram into Hawai'i, respectively. Late spring and especially the fall tend to be less frequented months, and room rates may drop during these months.

How *hot* will it be, you ask? If you're talking about the mercury, Hawai'i will rarely get into the high '90s at any time. Summer is between the high '70s to the high '80s (not a bad decade). Wintertime sees less than a ten degree dip from summertime. Cool northwesterly trade winds keep the climate temperate and consistent. On winter nights, it can dip down into the '50s, perfect for you cuddling queer honeymooners.

Given all this talk about **consistent weather** and all, be forewarned. Variations on any given island will occur a lot – and I mean a lot. Each island has a dry western side (leeward for you sailors) and a wet eastern side (windward). Between the wet and the dry sides, the weather can be like night and day (not darkness to sunshine, but arid desert to dripping jungle). To complicate things, *mauka* regions (up the mountain side) are cool: less three degrees per thousand feet. *Mauka* regions are rainier in general than the *makai* regions (down towards the water).

To complicate things further, different sides of the island usually have different rainy seasons. Fleeting rain showers that come and go before you realize it, called *blessings,* are common in Honolulu. And to complicate things to the point of no return, mornings may generally be sunnier than afternoons due to offshore and onshore breezes and cloud accumulation on the mountain tops.

Frosty Mauna Kea…It can even snow in Hawai'i, okay?

EAT THE MEAT

Hawai'i's populace ranks as the number one consumer group in the world for the mysterious canned meat product called *Spam*. It's been estimated that over 10,000 cans a day are opened by eager consumers in Hawai'i, and you will find more than one Spam cookbook on the shelves of island bookstores. One of the state's most popular snacks? The perfect hybrid of East and West: the Spam *musubi* (a rice cake with Spam filling, wrapped in seaweed – not popular in Japan!).

A case in point of all this madness is the Big Island where almost a *dozen* earth climates are represented, from monsoonal to periglacial. So like those Boy Scouts told you, Be Prepared.

What the Hell to Bring?

Obviously, Hawai'i is usually classified as warm even if you are from Miami, Manila, or Pago Pago. And guess what? **People dress casually.** Not just leisurely, but *casually*. For residents this means wearing a short–sleeved shirt is dressing up, and a tank top is dressing down (actually no shirt is dressing down). Unless you are here on stuffy Mainland business (and who would do that?), dress shoes, jackets, ties, even long–sleeved shirts are almost unheard of, even in Honolulu. High heels, formal dresses, and stockings are not usually worn by the feminine–inclined either. So leave those clothes and their uptight attitude behind. The most you will ever need are light slacks and an aloha shirt for the guys, a snazzy sun dress for the gals (in a nice restaurant for instance). Light materials are preferable, and dressing in "aloha wear" with bright island fabrics always looks classy. Shorts and nice shirt and sandals are the norm for most places. Cool, huh?

If I were you, I'd plan on **packing** at least some of the following: swim suits (a must, even if you don't know how to swim), shorts, shirts, a windbreaker, some kind of hat for shade, thick–soled tennis or hiking shoes (for the sharp lava rock), and yes, clean undies. A fanny pack or small backpack is also a good idea. Most sports equipment like masks and snorkels can be rented or purchased on the islands for a nominal price. Insect repellent and especially sun block are mandatory in Hawai'i. The sun on the islands is ferocious, and some Mainlanders go from fair to dangerously scorching red before you can holler *"careless pale face."*

A good Hawaiian dictionary and a copy of Rainbow Handbook Hawaii are also mandatory for your travels! You may want to complement these books with a respectable hetero guide like *Lonely Planet Hawaii* or *Hawaii Handbook,* available on the Mainland or in the islands.

Although Hawai'i is slightly more expensive for consumer items, everything from reef slippers to disposable underwater cameras to lava–lava wraps to water–based lube can be easily purchased here (we have Walmart, okay?). I would skimp on things like jeans and heavy jackets, although a light sweater might be handy for higher elevations. Packing everything in one carry–on bag is a good idea, since your clothes will be light and your check–in baggage may very well end up in Bora Bora.

What's Your Price?

As you probably figured, **Hawai'i is a pricey place to visit,** and living's not too cheap here either. Everything you see – clothes, cars, materials, most food items – have been shipped in. Their steep prices reflect inflated tariffs. But that doesn't necessarily mean that you need to sell your mother to have a good time in Hawai'i (although it never hurts).

Most superior **mainstream hotels** like the ones with the names Hilton, Four Seasons, and Sheraton plastered on them can easily run up to $400 a night and beyond into the stratosphere. They're perfect for those of you with annoying amounts of excess cash lying around. For the rest of us, most travel agents and package dealers will put you up in independent local hotels and chains, the biggest being Outrigger. The rate card price for these type of hotels may be any-where from $100 and up. However, if you're a clever miser you won't be paying the published price.

Hopefully your travel agent knew what they were doing and secured you an economical air/room/car deal. If not, there are a number of **discounts** you can haggle. These include AAA, entertainment books, certain weekday check–ins, fre-quent flyer points, senior discounts, and of course, nearly half–price *kama'aina* rates for locals (the catch is you need a valid Hawai'i driver's license). During times when a hotel has low occupancy, they may offer walk–in rates that slash the published price by a third. Some island timeshares present excellent room/car offers in exchange for viewing their property and asking if you are interested in purchasing.

Keep in mind that hotels in room–drenched Honolulu tend to be better priced than elsewhere in the state. Also, it's harder to get discounted rates in the busy winter months. Late spring and fall tend to be better for reductions.

For the gay or lesbian traveler, the humble **homo bed & breakfast** is the most highly recommended way to experience Hawai'i. Not only are you far from the maddening hetero crowd, you get to pick the brain of the built–in local gay information source (the owner). You are also a hundred times more likely to meet other gay travelers this way. And what you are getting for the cost of most

CAMP HAWAI'I–WOOD

With fake grass skirts, scantily clad "natives," primitive locales, and warbly "island" tunes, Hawai'i has been fertile ground for campy movie making on the grandest of scales. Hollywood, as always, has a way of gloriously distorting fact and fiction, and its flashy and **trashy exploitation** of the South Seas is no exception. Little thought or respect has been given to the Polynesian history, culture, or damage by Western influences. The exceptions are great historical films like *Hawaii, Mutiny on the Bounty,* and more recently, *Rapa Nui* starring Hawai'i's own beefcake Jason Scott Lee. *Au contraire,* Hawai'i and other tropical islands have merely served as an exotic Hollywood backdrop for the adventures of white people. And what a tawdry ride it's been:

Bird of Paradise (1932) Windward O'ahu impersonates "the island of Lani" in this story of a white man who runs off with an island princess. She, of course, ends up sacrificing herself into a flaming volcano at the end, something never practiced in Polynesia. In this pre–code classic, Dolores Del Rio does a topless "native" dance with a flower lei taped carefully across her perky bosoms.

Miss Sadie Thompson (1953) This W. Somerset Maugham tale of a sordid Honolulu "entertainer" on her way to redemption in Pago Pago is given the 3D musical Technicolor treatment, in this garish version starring Rita Hayworth. Shot mainly around the now defunct Coco Palms Resort on Kaua'i.

The Revolt of Mamie Stover (1956) Based on pre–WWII Honolulu red–light characters, the perpetually buxom Jane Russell plays the title role in this story of an ambitious Waikiki dance hall girl who becomes the "Henry Ford of harlotry," and amasses her fortune in island real estate.

Naked Paradise (1957) Exploitation king Roger Corman's entry into the South Seas genre, this convoluted plot about crooks using a charter boat to rob a pineapple plantation barely lives up to the film's promise of "Temptation and terror in a savage land of wild desire!"

Miss Russell demonstrating a mighty weak hula.
(DeSoto Brown Collection)

She Gods of Shark Reef (1958) Another one of Corman's glorious B pictures, the plot, if you can call it that, is about two shipwrecked survivors washed up on an isolated island inhabited only by women (a recurring dyke daydream). Shot back–to–back in Kaua'i with Naked Paradise.

Naked Paradise indeed!
(DeSoto Brown Collection)

CAMP HAWAII–WOOD ~ CONTINUED

Blue Hawaii (1961) This was the first of a handful of Hawai'i–made features for Elvis. Here he's the son of a pineapple plantation owner who becomes a tour guide for pretty girls in tight outfits, crooning the title tune made popular by Bing Crosby.

Gidget Goes Hawaiian (1961) This was the first sequel to 1959's *Gidget*, with a plot revolving around whether or not our heroine will give up her virginity to Moondoggie on Waikiki beach (I'll let you guess the outcome).

Goin' Coconuts (1978) A vehicle for big–toothed Donny and Marie Osmond, who are chased around the islands by crooks trying to swipe Marie's necklace. Guess what? The siblings get to yodel away in this one too!

When Time Ran Out (1980) In this, the cheesiest volcano flick of all time, Paul Newman and Jaqueline Bisset stay at a posh resort (the now homely Kona Surf on the Big Island) threatened by the worst *papier–mache* volcano and blue–screen tidal waves you have ever laid eyes on. Solely for film masochists.

The look of love: Winger and Russell.
(DeSoto Brown Collection)

Black Widow (1986) This film noir about a sexually ambiguous federal agent (Debra Winger) tracking a beautiful killer (Teresa Russell) to Hawai'i, has enough overt lesbian "subtext" to make it look like a sequel to *Personal Best*. Locations include the actual eruption site of Kilauea on the Big Island, spewing lava up 1,000 feet.

Joe Versus the Volcano (1990) A movie Tom Hanks would like to forget, this one includes every South Seas cliche on record: bizarre native rituals, natural disaster, and human sacrifice into a volcano (Pele never went for that in real Hawai'i!). Shot on O'ahu's North Shore, instead of the Big Island – where there *are* active volcanoes.

Exit to Eden (1994) Film critic Leonard Maltin called this asinine comedy a "strange cinematic catastrophe." It stars Rosie O'Donnell and Dan Akroyd as undercover cops on an S&M fantasy island ruled by a flustered dominitrix. Somehow based on an Anne Rice novel, and filmed at Lana'i's normally tasteful Manele Bay Resort.

B&Bs (anywhere from $25 to $250) is a lot prettier than the sometimes disappointing hotels in that price range. Most gay B&Bs have a quiet home–like atmosphere, and many offer pools or spas and wonderful natural settings.

If you are planning on staying longer than a week in any one spot, then check out **vacation rental** possibilities. There are more empty condos for short–term rent than you realize, and many island homes will lease out their downstairs or extra *'ohana* cottage for a reasonable fee. This works out especially well if you are traveling with a few people and don't want to be climbing up the walls of a tiny hotel room. A number of gay Hawai'i vacation rental agents are listed in this book.

Every island has some sort of youth hostel, and **camping** (no, not that kind) in warm Hawai'i is a favorable alternative to stuffy hotels too. Both county and state parks offer tent sites and at times, cabins with beds and kitchens. Many beaches offer decent camping an arm's length from the water. Just be sure to get a camping permit and not to tread on any local residents' toes. A great book for you outdoor types is *Camping Hawai'i* by Richard McMahon.

Restaurants tend to be pricey for what you get, especially in the more remote spots of the islands. Expect to pay extra for an ocean view too. Honolulu offers the full gamut of eateries, and fast food and plate lunch places can be found all over the state. Hearty plate lunches, which usually consist of an Asian–style meat, some vegetables or macaroni salad and two scoops of rice, are the food substance of choice for locals.

Oddly enough, it's hard to find Hawaiian restaurants that offer traditional island fare like *poi* or *lomilomi* salmon. Your best bet for these acquired treats is to head to a lu'au that has been recommended to you by a knowledgeable resident. Thai, Japanese, Chinese, Vietnamese, and even Indonesian restaurants are also abundant in Hawai'i. And there are always burgers and steak joints around for the true Mainlanders. Carefully prowl the regional island tourist publications for profitable restaurant coupons found within their folds.

Honolulu offers cheap and efficient island–wide **transportation.** The bus system can even get you to the North Shore for about a buck! But don't get excited. Everywhere else in the state, figure on renting a car to see or do anything. Taxis are a little pricey and hitchhiking is technically illegal, although you will spot a lot of people with their thumbs dangling out on the side of the road. Book your rental car well in advance of your arrival. Some outer island airports regularly run out of cars during busy spurts. And ask if they have free pick–up service to your hotel as well.

Doing Phone

Phone calls to the state of Hawai'i, it must be explained, all begin with the prefix (808). But you must also use this prefix whenever calling *between* islands. Hence, a long distance call.

For calls made *within* an individual island, you do not need the prefix. The calls are toll free from a private phone, twenty–five cents from a pay phone, and God knows how much from a hotel room. This unique system makes the Big Island the largest toll free calling area in the U.S. So go ahead – reach out and touch someone!

HAWAI'I'S FIRST AIDS FATALITY

According to the State of Hawai'i Data Handbook, Hawai'i's first AIDS causality was not a gay man, but an Asian woman fifty years of age. And it took place over twenty years ago! The unnamed woman was diagnosed with a mysterious illness in May of 1978, and succumbed in August of that same year. It was later discovered she had AIDS.

For A Good Time, Call...

Now that you know how to make a phone call, there are a number of gay tour agents on the islands to service you, so to speak. Getting a package deal to Hawai'i is the way to go. You get breaks on multiple nights at the same establishment, discounts on rental cars, and sometimes breakfast and activities thrown in as well. Some **tour operators** offer enticing discounts for island–hopping too.

Unless you just adore cities, try not to spend the bulk of your time on O'ahu. Each outer island has a distinct character, and merits its own separate trip for exploration. In fact, many savvy return visitors learn to skip Honolulu altogether and instead book direct flights to Maui, the Big Island, or Kaua'i. Think about staying put in one spot and getting to know it rather than madly taking in every single island in one trip.

Beechman Agencies offer air, room, and car packages for gay travelers to O'ahu and neighbor islands, as well as golf, bicycling, and discounts on activities. 2198 Smith Street, Honolulu, HI 96817. (888) BEECHMAN, 923-2433. aloha-net/~dig/beechman.html

Black Bamboo Guest Services is a well–established company on the Big Island that can help out with gay and straight accommodations, referrals, and car and activity packages for all the Hawaiian islands. P.O. Box 211, Kealakekua, HI 96750. (800) 527-7789, 328-9607

Hawaiian Hotels and Resorts is a chain of four oceanfront mainstream hotels on three islands that offer gay–friendly management and staff, as well as swimming pools, restaurants, and amenities. Their special packages and promotions are usually good value for multiple–night stays. (800) 22-ALOHA, www.HawaiiHotels.com

Pacific Ocean Holidays will find you gay–friendly hotels and B&Bs for all the islands. They also offer gay Waikiki vacation packages that include lodging, airport transfers, lei greeting, and gay–hosted welcome and orientation. Check out their inclusive island–wide web site at www.gayhawaii.com. P.O. Box 88245–PG, Honolulu, HI 96830. (800) 735-6600, 923-2400 www.gayhawaii.com/poh

Remote Possibilities is a lesbian–owned travel company on Maui that is dedicated to women's group travel in first class style. Their annual Maui Women's Week is an extremely popular package that includes luxury accommodations, adventure tours, golf, seminars, and socials. They also cover same–gender weddings, Europe and Alaska. 122 Central Avenue, Wailuku, HI 96793. (800) 511-3121, 249-0395 www.remotepo.com

What Tangled Webs...

Through the power of modern technology you can not *only* download dirty pictures, but also plan your homo Hawaiian wedding or meet that special local contact without every leaving the privacy of your own home! Most business web site addresses in this book are included with the actual listing, but here are some valuable queer Hawai'i sites to start you off:

www.hawaiiscene.com/gayscene – Hawaii Scene's Gay Scene. One–stop shopping for all gay info about Honolulu with some neighbor island info, links to web sites for gay bars, gay artists, gay travel companies. Extensive and well–detailed.

www.gayhawaii.com – Pacific Ocean Holidays Gay Hawaii Site. Online version of the Pocket Guide to Hawaii, with introduction and gay listings for each island, as well as complete list of links to gay businesses for the state. Helpful and popular.

www.islandlifestyle.com – Island Lifestyle Magazine online. Once the major gay Hawaii magazine in print, *Island Lifestyle* is now found only on the web. There are favorite links, covers and features from back issues, and links to the Gay Guide Hawaii. Will probably be expanded in the future.

Haole boys lapping it up at Queen's Surf.

www.discoveringhawaii.com/gayhawaii – Driving and Discovering Hawaii's gay pages offer some of the best information and photographs of beaches, abbreviated lists of accommodations, and highlighted maps for each island, but limited business listings.

www.ndhi.com/gg – New Dimensions Gay and Lesbian Guide to the Hawaiian Islands. Splashy online gay guide to the state, although not expansive in content. Includes weather, shopping, businesses, some accommodations, as well as free images.

www.maui–tech.com/glom – Gay and Lesbian 'Ohana Maui. Run by Both Sides Now, this snazzy web site will tell you of upcoming events for gay Maui, info

RIDING IN PARADISE

In August of 1998, Hawai'i sponsored the first statewide HIV bike ride fundraiser called The Paradise Ride. A joint effort between the AIDS services on each of the islands, riders from Hawai'i and the Mainland were required to raise at least $2,000 in pledges to be eligible. The four–island ride started in Hilo on August 8th and finished on O'ahu seven days later, covering over 350 miles. The ride was non–competitive, and riders could cycle at their own pace. The route covered some of the most gorgeous terrain in the state, including the Kilauea Volcano, the edge of the Na Pali Coast, and O'ahu's North Shore. Riders camped out at state parks and shared meals together, flying their bike and equipment from island to island. Local community support was strong, with volunteers providing support and Hawaiian entertainment for the riders, whose numbers could reach up to 500 in coming years. So what are you waiting for? Sign up and get your padded lycra butt on that hard little seat! Call (888) 285-9866 or check out the web site www.ParadiseRideHawaii.org.

on the Out in Maui newspaper, a sampling of gay businesses and organizations, and updates on the future gay and lesbian community retreat center.

www.RainbowHandbook.com – Rainbow Handbook Hawai`i. Put out by you-know-who, this site includes a state map leading to pages for each island, glossary, history, and gay business links, and Questions and Answers with the author. Order books online and vote for the next Rainbow Handbook!

www.aloha.net/~lambda – Gay Kaua'i Online. An up–to–date and instructive site for what's going on in queer Kaua'i, including The Lavender Pages, Malahini (Newcomer) Information, Hawai'i's Not–For–Profit Organizations and Support Groups, and Same–Gender Marriage News Archives. A must hit if you are going to Kaua'i.

www.tnight.com – Tropical Nights BBS. A laid back and friendly site for gay Hawai'i, with chat functions, personal classifieds, web services, cool links, and member's personal web pages. Mainly for Honolulu.

www.tnight.com/glcc – OUTLOOK newsletter by the Gay and Lesbian Community Center. Periodic text info on Honolulu gay events, politics, call for volunteers, dances and fundraisers.

www.global–aloha.com/qsbeach – Queen's Surf Official Homepage. Fun page of snapshots of regular sunbathers at Queen's Surf Beach in Honolulu, some complete with email addresses!

www.dinosaur.co.jp/amanda.html – Amanda's Shop Aloha. Offers an awesome collection of beefy island guys on cards, postcards, and calendars from different publishers, for purchase right over the net.

www.hawaiiscene.com/odyssey – Odyssey Magazine Hawaii. Gossip and info on club events, outer island gay listings, nightlife snapshots, and great reading like Freddie Jordan's famous column The Mouth. Sexy and fun.

www.Outspoken.com - Outspoken newsletter from Puna on the Big Island's snazzy site includes detailed resource listings for the both sides of the island, past issues for your reading pleasure, and cool gay Hawaii links.

Words, only words

Sadly, Hawaiian as a proper language became lost during the Twentieth Century. Younger generations have lost touch with the old island ways in English–dominated society, making for relatively few island residents who speak fluent Hawaiian. The language was banned outright after the Hawaiian monarchy's overthrow in the 1870's. It has only recently made a comeback. The privately–owned, purely Hawaiian island of Niʻihau is the last outpost in the world where Hawaiian is spoken as a first language, and English as a second.

The Hawaiian language has the shortest alphabet in the world with a mere twelve letters: the vowels A, E, I, O, U (with Latin pronunciation like vowels in Spanish or French) and the consonants H, K, L, M, N, P and W. A glottal stop mark ('), like the one used in this book, is used to denote syllable breaks. The glottal stop mark along with the long vowel macron are coming back into usage   to indicate proper Hawaiian pronunciation. When

An eyebrow–raising shop sign in Honolulu. (see vocabulary listing next page.)

you see a glottal stop, break up the sounds like in the word oh–oh.

With or without marks, Hawaiian can be daunting to try to pronounce for the uninitiated. Vowels tend to be clumped together, and some are technically pronounced differently on different syllables. Many vowels are slurred together in general speech anyway. Ass wy dem touriss buggahs 'ave such a har time, yeah?

Fortunately, the language is making a comeback in the state as a whole with popular Hawaiian language preschools. There, children are taught Hawaiian as a first language. Plenty of Hawaiian words will still creep up in local conversation and are widely used today. Here are some handy ones:*aloha* (ah-low-ha) – spirit of love and kindness, also hello and goodbye

'aina (eye-nah) – land

hale (ha-lay) – house

haole (how-lee) – Caucasian

heiau (hey-ow) – Hawaiian temple

kai (kigh) – sea

kama'aina (kah-mah-eye-nah) – long time island resident

kane (kah-nay) – male

mahalo (mah-ha-low) – thank you

makai (ma-kigh) – towards the ocean

malihini (ma-lee-hee-nee) – island newcomer

mauka (mao-ka) – toward the mountain

'ohana (oh-hah-nah) – family, close friends

pupu (poo-poo) – appetizers

pau (pow) – finish, end

wahine (wah-hee-nay) – woman

wai (why) – fresh water

For you sex pigs, these might come in handy:

hua (who-ah) – testicles

kohe (koh-hey) – vagina

lomi (low-mee) – rub (but *lomilomi* is proper Hawaiian massage!)

lua (loo-ah) – toilet

mahu (ma-who) – transvestite, or gay man in general

malo (ma-low) – traditional male loincloth

mane'o (ma-nay-oh) – turned on

okole (oh-koh-lay) – buttocks

puka (poo-kah) – hole (in general!)

ule (oo-lay) – penis

And for you stoners, this word might come in handy:

pakalolo (pah-kah-low-low) – marijuana

Pidgin

In Hawai'i, you will also hear lots of Pidgin, which is technically called "Hawaii Creole English." Pidgin has its roots in old plantation days where different nationalities needed to communicate with the white landowners and with each other. But it's not a language so much as local phrases and slang with a distinct island accent. It has evolved a long way over the years and picked up much street credibility. Pidgin is predominantly used by "locals" and some long–time *haoles*.

Proper Hawaiian and the informal Pidgin often overlap. Pidgin is colorful, fun, and usually hard to understand to the uninitiated. The worst is hearing a visitor clumsily attempt to say something in Pidgin or use a local accent, to the embarrassment of everyone involved! (Be sure to read the DON'T section.) So use these words as reference *only:*

"brah" – good friend (short for brother)

"bummahs" – bummer, too bad

"choke" – a lot of

"da" – the (as in "da store")

"fo' real" – really?

"grinds" – food

"howzit" – How's it going?

"junk" – lousy, shitty

"one" – used in place of "a" or "an"

"ono" – delicious, yummy (also used for people!)

"talk story" – converse, chat

"tita" – a rugged gal

"stink eye" – dirty look

"wikiwiki" – quickly, in a rush

I'll include these because they *sound* nasty:

"ass wy" – that's why

"beef" – fight

"buggah" – difficult thing or person

"hold ass" – a close call when driving your new car

"lesgo" – let's go

"mek ass" – make a fool of yourself

I'll include these because they *are* nasty:

"ala-alas" – the family jewels

"bambucha" – the family jewel, but only when BIG!

"lakas" – loins

"shi-shi" – pee-pee

"s'kebei" (skeh-bay) – dirty old man

And the honorary degree goes to:

"da kine" – loosely translated to English as "whatchamacallit." *Da kine* is the cornerstone of Pidgin. Without it, life would not function as known in Hawaiʻi. You'll want to use da kine when you're in one da kine bar and one da kine comes up to you and starts looking all da kine and you wonder if you should go to the da kine, but then you think da kine…

And Now a Word on Island Manners

Now, one thing most people agree on is that Hawaiʻi *is not* part of the U.S. Don't tell me about the Fiftieth State and all that; Hawaiʻi is a separate unique culture, apart from North America. As such, it merits its own social manners and customs. And you, as the inane visitor that you are, are bound to violate at least several social codes here, shaming your family for generations! Fortunately the local populace is aware of your impending blunders (as they have seen them all before), and luckily you have their aloha on your side. However, I wouldn't even think of doing any of these if I were you:

DON'T:

– Attempt to woo the island residents by how well you can **fake a local accent or talk Pidgin.** This has got to be the lamest thing visitors try, and you end up looking like an insulting fool (that's if you aren't one already).

– Leave your shoes on in the house or any personal human dwelling for that matter. You have now tracked in all kinds of dirt that Auntie must get down on her knees to scrub out, you Mainland fool! We don't care how bad your feet stink from all those stupid thick socks, boots and/or heels you wear over there. No shame, okay?

– Go to someone's house empty handed. Oh boy, if someone showed up at my door after I invited 'em over for grinds, and not even bring me one beer or one flower or anything, I would think that's one stingy *buggah* – no manners, eh? But of course my aloha would kick in and I would simply smile, then talk behind his back later.

– Act like you're from New York. I don't even care if you are from that place, change your accent, your religion, whatevers, but don't be acting like you in one big *wikiwiki* rush for everything and all arrogant and you need all dis and dat and everyone just so slow here and how do I get anything done. Oh boy, if you like that in Hawai'i you asking for one big beef, okay?

– Call anyone with a tan "Hawaiian." Almost everyone in Hawai'i could be classified as tan (except for those pink blotchy *haole* people), but guess what? This doesn't mean they are Hawaiian. They may have Hawaiian in them, but they could also be pure or mixed Samoan, Filipino, Tongan, Maori, Latino, African–American, Korean, Japanese, Chinese (do you want me to go on?) and proud of it. Hawai'i is classified as "mixed plate." Many Asian/Pacific Islanders in Hawai'i are simply called *locals*. Don't assume anyone's race without very nicely asking first. Then be prepared to explain your own in detail!

– Constantly refer to a gay man as a *mahu*. Although *mahu* is a term that can mean, well, fag, it more specifically and commonly is used to refer to local dudes in drag. If you made friends with one big guy with a deep voice named Butch who's all hairy and leathery and all that, I wouldn't really keep calling him a *mahu* if I were you (especially if you want something from him). Also, don't be calling your lesbo friends that either!

Some more mahu than others!

– Make fun of the island culture. Don't be minimizing the islands' history, satirizing the Hawaiian music on the radio, commenting on the idle lifestyle or acting like you know more of everything about Hawai'i than residents do. And for Pete's sake don't mock or parody a hula dancer in front of them, since a lot of those hula girls are big enough to give you one good *lickin'*, and not the kind of licking you're used to either!

DO:

– All the DOs are the DON'Ts backwards, okay?

CHAPTER 2

H O M O   H A W A I ' I

*"Gift of Water" by Shige Yamada in front of
the Hawai'i Convention Center.*

How are the Homos in Hawai'i?

Hawai'i. Just the word conjures up mystic waterfalls and hula dancers and sunshine and ocean and, well, lots of queer boys and girls trying to experience a Fantasy Island of tolerant peoples, liberal politics, and most importantly, thong bikini weather. As with most fantasy lands, **the reality** is tons more interesting and varied. Hawai'i at the end of the Twentieth Century is a land of mass tourism, budget cutbacks, high costs of living, cultural conflicts, racial pressures, unemployment, and economic uncertainty.

Now the good news: it is still an absolutely incredible place to encounter. The islands are filled with empty lava deserts, snow–capped volcanoes, huge valley systems, dripping rain forests, spectacular coral reefs, all thousands of miles from any continent. Hawai'i will always hold her magic. And she hides her secrets well. The traveler will need much time and maybe many return visits (not to mention an open heart) to truly get to know Hawai'i.

The islands host some of the most amazing people you will ever be privileged to meet on the planet. Naturally warm, generous, and kind, island residents are rightfully proud of their spiritually significant **heritage of "aloha."** Aloha is a word that does not merely mean hello and goodbye, but *love.* To live aloha simply means to live in the light, to do unto others as you would have them do unto you, to actively pursue love everyday. Aloha is the keystone of Hawai'i. It's the mystical attribute that draws people back to her shores again and again in search of its profound meaning.

Geographically limited and forced to rely on one another to survive, Hawaiians have always emphasized harmony and acceptance of individual differences. Everyone has a place in society. The Hawaiian culture has always been traditionally tolerant with its famous "hang loose" attitude. Subsequent immigrant groups for the most part have embraced this, making for a society where unique distinctions are celebrated and seen as beneficial.

This sense of *'ohana,* or a circle of close friends and family, includes gays and lesbians too. This is, after all, a culture where men are encouraged to wear flowers on their head and sing falsetto. With the 1997 Reciprocal Beneficiaries Act,

legally gays have some more rights than in many other parts of the U.S. The small handful of Waikiki street hustlers are usually allowed to carry on business, and many straights will pop up in gay restaurants or gay bars without a hint of embarrassment. In fact, almost all gay businesses around the state cater to both straights and queers.

Some visitors expect Hawai'i to be a homo holiday party heaven like Palm Springs, Provinceton, or Key West. Well, wrong! Only two small circuit party have ever occurred here. Hawai'i is actually more for the eco–adventure or honeymooning types. Many travelers with high expectations of a large and uniform gay scene in Hawai'i are usually disappointed.

Sunrise by Douglas Simonson.

Despite the attention Hawai'i gets for its liberal

THE RAINBOW

If you are from the Mainland, you may think Hawai'i is more gay–friendly than you ever dreamed when you spot all the usages of the rainbow around the state. Tons of business names have the word in their titles ("Rainbow Books," "Rainbow Vacuum Cleaners"). The colors are splashed on many buildings, the University of Hawai'i's famous men's and women's volleyball team (the nation's top) are called "The Rainbows," and the color spectrum appears on the background of the state's automobile license plates and driver's licenses. Even the state capital's official web site proudly announces, *"Welcome to the Rainbow Connection!"*

Sorry to burst your bubble, but as you probably figured out, the rainbow (*anuenue* in Hawaiian) does not have the same **homosexual connotation** in Hawai'i that it does in other places. In fact, the rainbow acts as an emblem for Hawai'i itself, since they are always popping up all over the state year–round. Maybe that's why queers and the islands attract each other the way they do!

Rainbows in ancient Hawai'i weren't always as joyous and gay. Spotting a rainbow could mean a sign of death, an impending separation of some sort, or bad luck during a journey. On the flip side, rainbows could also indicate the presence of high chiefs, and during child birth, the rainbow foretold of a blessed child.

politics and lifestyle, there are no huge gay parts of town, no all–gay resort areas, and relatively few gay island establishments to patronize. And as with a lot of small businesses in Hawai'i, many gay–oriented ones have a hard time surviving. The reasons could be isolation, island culture, and lack of community support. Ironically, it's probably also due to the fact that gays *are* more integrated into the general society here than in other places.

Still, the **actual attitude towards gays and lesbians** is and always has been a mixed bag. The reality is mixed, especially from island to island. It is safe to say a majority of residents don't really care if you're gay. But on the other hand, Hawai'i still has a strong family–based society with Asian influences. For many local gays and lesbians it's a "don't ask, don't tell" policy as far as being out, publicly or privately.

Into the Surf *by Raymond Hegelson.*

Some ethnic groups view coming out as bringing shame upon the whole family. Coming out on an island where everyone knows you since you were a kid may not even be necessary in the Mainland sense. For others, the family, the *'ohana,* is more important than one member's sexual orientation, and queers are integrated with aloha. For many Hawaiians no outing is necessary. You just are who you are, no explanation or gory details necessary, since forwardness has always been frowned upon in the Hawaiian culture. Many local gays and lesbians don't identify themselves with the mainstream gay world at all. Their race or heritage is a much more important trait than their mere sexual orientation.

This leads to a situation where many island residents never bother **coming out** at all. There are many stories of local men who enjoy having sex with gay men, only to remain in a heterosexual posture, never admitting to or fully living out their true tendency. It's common for these closeted men to remain living with their families, all the while pursuing guys on the side. Since they are not "muffy" (effeminate) types, they are not "gay." Of course this is a generalization, but one hears tales of even straight police officers keeping muffy or *mahu* lovers on the side for years.

On the Mainland, it seems "straight–acting" gay men are somehow more accepted within the cultural framework, while effeminate men are ridiculed and more of a threat to the hyper–macho society. In Hawai'i, the opposite probably holds true. Effeminate men are historically accepted within the Polynesian culture, and one finds many muffies happily integrated in Samoa, Tahiti, and other parts of the Pacific.

Mainland homos have been moving to the islands for decades, including a large wave in the '70s. Some are turned on by the warm culture and climate, others come for reasons of health or simply to escape the Mainland energy. A lot find that residing in the islands, with its high cost of living and limited opportunities, is a much different experience than *vacationing* on the islands, and a portion move back after a short stint.

Happy gays at play at the old Hula's.

Others stay, and migrating from large gay cities, these **Mainland transplants** have invigorated and organized the island's overall queer community, although white–washing it in the process. Separated from their own Mainland families for one reason or another, these *haoles* and other Mainlanders are more involved with politics and setting up an alternative gay society. The local born and raised don't feel the need to be as defiant in their gayness. Their focus is more on the *'ohana* and their own extended community.

The story is different from island to island and ethnic group to ethnic group. The saying is **"Everyone's a minority in Hawai'i."** Most people born on the islands are of mixed Asian, Pacific Islander, and/or European descent. Sadly, pure–blooded Hawaiians are few and far between, although there are a lot of people that are part–Hawaiian. Most non–white people get lumped into the category of "locals". However, locals may

> ## IT WAS THE SIXTIES BABY
>
> In 1963, the **Honolulu Advertiser** ran a three part article entitled "The Deviate," about the growing problem of homosexuality in the community. In 1964, there was an article about transvestites and the people who liked to watch them. Reference was made to a law passed that same year that required all men dressed as women to wear a card that said "I'm a boy" or "I'm a male." In 1967, there was another article about "The Strange World of Oahu's Different People," and in 1968 a piece about Hawai'i's so called loneliest citizens: "*Mahus Are People, Too.*"
>
> It wasn't until 1969 that the paper finally relented and ran a more positive article that suggested homosexuality was actually natural for some people.

still be proud of their Filipino, Samoan, or Japanese roots and practices. Thus, Hawai'i is classified as "mixed plate." A minority's distinct attitude towards gays can override the general consensus.

On islands outside of O'ahu, you will tend to find gays and lesbians coupled up or living with families. Honolulu presents more of a metropolitan gay singles scene. Many gays born and raised in Hawai'i turn towards Honolulu, with its freer anonymity, as "the Mainland." Many also take off to the continents and larger cities like Los Angeles, Las Vegas, and the San Francisco Bay Area to experience a Mainland "gay lifestyle."

Within the islands, **gay lifestyles can vary radically.** Being gay on O'ahu, with its openly homo beaches and bars, means a completely different thing than on rural Moloka'i, where wearing full–time drag is an acceptable way to be "gay." Gay communities between the islands don't interact much, except maybe through Honolulu. They usually have no clue what the others are even doing! Some visitors know much more about gay Hawai'i than gay residents do. This geographical isolation makes for a distinct mood on each neighbor island. It has been said that the Hawaiian Islands are like sisters, each with their own personality and character, which is mirrored in the gay communities.

Gays in Hawai'i still face the same **challenges** as anywhere. In some island

Cross–section of Hawai'i's gay world at AIDS Walk?

neighborhoods, towns, and beaches, gay or lesbian couples may not feel terribly welcome at all. P.D.A's (Public Displays of Affection) do not happen too often between gays, even in Honolulu. Gay bashing is not unheard of, job and housing discrimination happens, and undercover stings on cruise spots, with televising of the offender's face as a shame tactic, have also occurred. Although many local Christian churches accept openly gay members, there are those who don't fully understand or appreciate Jesus' example and teachings, and attack the gays they should be loving.

The question is: do queers overall have it better here than elsewhere? The answer is a conditional yes. Depends on who you ask. The first–hand interviews dispersed in the following pages will shed light on what it's like to be homo in Hawai'i on the verge of the next century. Without a doubt, Hawai'i will continue to be at the forefront of the new gay and lesbian dawning, showing the entire world what love and acceptance and *aloha* really mean.

Waikiki once upon a time.

Homos in Hawaiian History

Although most information about pre–contact Hawai'i was written *after* contact and thus shaded by the bias of foreigners, Hawaiians have a strong heritage of *mele* or chants that explain the olden times. It seems **sexuality in old Hawaiian culture** was treated as a loving, fluid part of everyday life. Like in the Psalms, it had a poetic characteristic. In the hula and *mele* you can still witness the exquisite form of sensuality that was part of a people who celebrated their sexuality. In fact, Hawaiians often named their genitals as a matter of course! There were also *mele ma'i*, or songs in honor of genitals, performed at events like the birth of a great chief.

Hawaiian **family structures** are and were collective and extended, unlike nuclear mom–and–pop Mainland families. Many related and unrelated aunties, uncles, cousins and *hanai* (adopted) family members merge together as an *'ohana*. According to tradition, first–borns were often given to the grandparents or others to raise. Mates were merely given the poetic label of *noho ai,* or "one to lay with." Private property in terms of marriage was unheard of. Although family lines were blurred in this way, genealogy was of utmost importance to the Hawaiians. Many old chants are solely information on lineage.

THE DEAD SPEAK

Certain eyebrow–raising passages of the **Cook expedition's journals** have long been overlooked by heterosexual scholars. In the early 1990s, Robert J. Morris made a concerted study of the logs from the ships *Discovery* and *Resolution,* which revealed some interesting tidbits on old Hawaiian culture. Among the juicy samples, drenched in Eighteenth Century views of decency:

From the log of David Samwell, ship's surgeon, 29th of January, 1779:

"Of this Class [*aikane*] are Parea [Palea] and Cani–Coah [Kanekoa] and their business is to commit the Sin of Onan upon the old King. This, however strange it may appear, is fact, as we learnt from the frequent Enquiries about this curious Custom, and it is an office that is esteemed honourable among them & they have frequently asked us on seeing a handsome young fellow if he was not an Ikany [*aikane*] to some of us."

From the log of Charles Clerke, second in command, March, 1779:

."...every Aree [*ali'i*] according to his rank keeps so many women and so many young men (I'car'nies [*aikane*] as they call them) for the amusement of his leisure hours; they talk of this infernal practice with all the indifference in the world, nor do I suppose they imagine any degree of infamy in it."

From Samwell's log of the 10th of February, 1779:

"He [Kamehameha] with many of his attendants took up quarters on board the ship for the Night: among them is a Young Man of whom he seems very fond, which does not in the least surprise us, as we have had opportunities before of being acquainted with a detestable part of his Character which he is not in the least anxious to conceal."

Old Hawaiian society was a **class system,** and the *ali'i* or royalty were believed to be directly descended from the gods. Thus, they had great mana or spiritual power. The bones of the *ali'i* were always hidden after death to preserve this *mana*. The commoners, or *maka'ainana,* were the farmers and fisherman and everyday workers, while the *kauwa* or slave class were marked by specific facial tattoos. The *kauwa* class was only allowed to live in certain designated areas. As you can guess, they were the ones routinely used for human sacrifices at the temples of the war god, Kuka'ilimoku, but never thrown into fiery volcanoes as Hollywood would like you to believe!

Many say that old Hawai'i was neither purely a heterosexual nor homosexual, but a **bisexual culture.** Same–sex relationships were evidently frequent, and many men and women had *aikane* or *punahele:* close friends or "favorites" that were at times involved sexually. No particular shame was associated with same–gender sex at all, and sodomy was not considered wrong. The words *ho'okamaka* and *moe aikane* were common terms used to denote same–sex relations. (They were obviously years ahead in politically correct terminology!) The more explicit way to put it was *upi laho*, which translates to something like testicle pressing, or literally "scrotum squirting."

The word *aikane* itself relates to a particular sexual relationship in old Hawai'i. It is a combination of *ai*, meaning to have sex with, and *kane*, meaning man. *Aikane* nowadays is used to mean "good friends," and most people don't realize what the word actually once pertained to.

Two guys working it out in old Hawai'i.
(Courtesy Bishop Museum)

***Aikane* relationships** between men in old Hawai'i are only recorded among the *ali'i* and high chiefs, but probably occurred between commoners as well. Royal *aikane* seemed to have been a whole rank of people who were granted special social and political status as a result of a sexual role (Clinton–esque?). Since the high *ali'i* had an obligation to mate with certain other royals, *aikane* were chosen voluntarily out of desire rather than duty. They were kept as exclusive concubines to the chiefs. Most *aikane* rose up from the lower ranks of royalty, and their sexual friendships with higher *ali'i* increased their *mana* and power.

Although *aikane* were usually young male sexual companions to the *ali'i*, they often had their own wives and children, and were not seen as less masculine in any way. *aikane* relationships didn't seem to be regulated by any "top or bottom" order, regardless of age or ranking. There were also female *aikane* (the word often occurs in the Pele goddess stories), but since women were subjugated in many aspects of society, it made for a stronger "guys only" club of royal *aikane* relationships that disregarded many women folk.

The *aikane* role seems to have been honorable and noble, and was not hidden at all. In fact, it was even boasted about to shocked European sailors. *Aikane* relations were talked about freely and often in Hawaiian culture, since they were an

An offering for Captain Cook.

important part of the royal hierarchy. These homosexual relationships had social value, and there are even ancient stories referring to *aikane* living together in great sacredness.

The first Europeans to set eyes on Hawai'i were aboard **Captain Cook's** vessel in 1779 (though there's historical evidence that Spaniards "discovered" the islands as early as 1627). When he first appeared, Cook was mistaken for the god Lono, but later he and the sailors showed themselves up for the mere humans they were.

The ship journals during this voyage described a culture that was ambiguously bisexual to Western eyes. Cook's men wrote aghast accounts of close, brotherly *aikane* relationships within the *ali'i* – "a shocking inversion of the laws of nature, they bestow all those affections upon them that were intended for the other sex" as one of the sailors put it. They recorded the kings of Maui, Kaua'i, and the Big Island all having their own *aikane*. There's even one account of chief Kalanikoa of Kaua'i asking if a certain young handsome European sailor would become his personal *aikane* for a little while, and he offered six valuable hogs to boot! It wasn't recorded if the lad said yes (but for six pigs, you decide!).

Although heterosexual historians don't like to mention it, the sailors' journals also record that the great unitor of the Hawaiian Islands, **King Kamehameha,** brought aboard one young *aikane* while traveling on Cook's ship. According to tradition, some children were raised specifically to become *aikane* of the chief. Scholars figure the king also had male *aikane* in his household (in addition to his two wives and numerous courtesan women – what a stud!), as well as intimate *aikane* relationships with high–ranking male ministers.

In fact, some scholars profess that Kamehameha himself was a "favorite" of King

The revered King Kamehameha I.

Kalaniopu'u. There are sketchy details of a jealous rivalry between Kamehameha and another of the King's *aikane*, Palea, which ended in Kamehameha's favor. The trouble–making Palea is often credited with setting up a theft incident during Cook's stay in Kealakekua Bay on the Big Island. The incident led to mistrust between the formerly neighborly Europeans and Hawaiians, and finally led to Cook's attempt to kidnap King Kalaniopu'u for ransom of the stolen boat. A large skirmish ensued and Cook was beat and stabbed to death in the conflict.

Cook's death didn't stop other European voyages to Hawai'i, including Captain Vancouver's. The knowledge of war technology the outsiders brought was closely studied by Kamehameha. He eventually took control of the Big Island and conquered the entire island chain by brute force.

Did the fabled King have any sexual preference, or was he merely following old Hawaiian customs by having *aikane*? We'll probably never know. For Hawaiians, it's an irrelevant point, since these kinds of sexual lines have little meaning or purpose. But the *aikane* tradition didn't end with King Kamehameha. Historical rumor has it that his grandson, **King Kamehameha III** (1815-1854), had his own *aikane* too.

Besides the tradition of *aikane*, another notable queer aspect of the Hawaiian culture is the **mahu**. Transvestism was, and still is, frequent in parts of Polynesia, where men choose to don women's apparel, grow up as a girl and even become a wife of another man, perhaps one of several, sometimes even cutting his/her thighs to "menstruate" (talk about cramps!). Some traditions tell of a male, usually a younger brother, being compelled to take on the feminine role of family caretaker and keeper of traditions when a suitable daughter is lacking. *Mahu* in old Hawai'i referred to either an effeminate male or a masculine female, someone who took on the opposite gender's role. Whether or not that meant homosexuality was not important. They held a necessary role in the *'ohana* and were not outcasts.

Nowadays the word *mahu* usually refers to a local male transvestite or an effeminate man, who is primarily gay and non–white. At times it's also used simply to mean any gay man, even a "butch muffy," or a "fag" from the Mainland. *Mahu* is now seldom used for women, and there's really no Hawaiian word for lesbian (sorry ladies).

Dancing dandies of old.

Despite aspects of an inclu-

sive, *'ohana*–like society, pre–contact Hawai'i was still a vigorous and potent culture. Society was strictly regimented by the *ali'i* in the form of **kapu (taboo) laws.** For instance, stepping on the king's shadow was grounds for execution, as was failing to kneel or prostrate in his presence. Kapu laws, however arbitrary, kept everyone in check and the often–warring chief's societies running somewhat smoothly.

Interestingly, the fall and winter months were usually designated as a time of peace and planting, with wars commencing after February. It's been said that *mahu*s were sometimes encouraged to follow the warriors into battle; not to fight, but to fill the female role while the men were away from their homes for so long.

Women often had same–sex relations while men were away at war. There are also accounts of women sometimes taking on the traditional male role of warrior and accompanying their men in battle. These Hawaiian Amazons were called *wahine kaua,* or battle women (shades of Xena?). They asked to be warriors, and the men obligingly trained them in this traditionally masculine occupation. They were seen as nothing terribly unordinary, and they would return to their family life after war.

Between men and women, there were many *kapu* laws and social mores. Women couldn't fish or even touch men's fishing equipment (early signs of "penis envy" paranoia?). Women couldn't eat certain kinds of fish, pork, coconuts, or even bananas (p.e. again!). Women had it tough no doubt – the only compensation being that older women were looked very highly upon. They could become honorary *kupuna* or elders, setting down the laws of a region. Some recorded rare instances tell of women being given the male role of priest from birth and becoming *na kaula wahine,* or women–prophets.

Some specific *kapu* may have worked to the homo's advantage. One edict was that after seven or eight years of age, men could only sleep in the men's house while women slept in the women's house. This law was practiced by King Kamehameha himself. Men and women couldn't even eat together, only with members of the same sex (talk about bonding!). However, there are occasional accounts of apparently *mahu* men being allowed to eat and sleep with the women as one of them.

BUMP AND GRIND

The Hawaiians' straight–forward views on sexuality are reflected in the ancient *mele ma'i*, or genital songs, usually in honor of an *ali'i*. The Hawaiians respected the procreative abilities of sex and revered them. The following Polynesian *mele* (a name chant for Kaualiliko'i) is performed as a *hula 'ōhelo*, or reclining dance, in which the suggested motions are most vital to the meaning.

Tu 'Oe *(You Are Erect)*

Ae, Tu 'oe, tau 'oe, tu'i tele la
Tu 'oe, tau 'oe, tu'i tele la!
'Awe, 'awe, 'awe, 'awe, 'awe, 'awe la!
'no ta mea, ta mea nui la!
Ti'o lele, ti'o lele, ti'o lele la!
Kaualiliko'i, liliko'i, tu'i tele la!
Ho'i iluna la!
Ha'a ilalo la!
Ho'i iluna la!
Ha'a ilalo la!

Indeed, You are erect, you place it, hit liquid
You are erect, you place it, hit liquid!
Tentacle, tentacle, tentacle, tentacle, tentacle, tentacle!
The thing is mean, the big thing!
Thrust out, thrust out, thrust out!
Kaualiliko'i, liliko'i, hit liquid!
Return up!
Go down below!
Return up!
Down below!

The eating *kapu* was finally abolished when King Kamehameha II sat down for some royal "grinds" with his mother, **Queen Ka'ahumanu,** in 1819, effectively ending the whole *kapu* system altogether. It's speculated the strong–willed queen wanted to crush the powerful *kahuna* or priest class in the process.

With the fall of the *kapu* system and the coincidental arrival of **missionaries** shortly after in 1820, many old customs slowly became extinct. Although it's easy to pick on the oppressive missionaries for the obvious destruction they inflicted upon the Hawaiian culture (not to mention the custom of wearing lots of clothes!), the good ones did set up hospitals and schools for the islanders. They also helped create the first Hawaiian alphabet and written language. Their adversaries, the

The big kapu breaker: Queen Ka'ahumanu.

whalers, made prostitutes out of the women and displayed less concern for the native born. Of interest, Hawaiian beliefs and Christianity somewhat overlap. The Hawaiian creation myth closely mirrors the one in Genesis. The Hawaiians also believed in a great god Lono who would return to Earth, and in the loving and forgiving high god Kane, to whom all life was sacred.

During this time of cultural upheaval, many *mahus* were involved in carrying on the outlawed hula dance and chants clandestinely. Even today, many gay men are *kumu hula* (mentors of hula) and hula dancers, and are respected for their talents and creative abilities. As always, the queers keep the arts and culture alive throughout history!

Homo Hawai'i Politics

Going to the Chapel

Hawai'i is seen as an amazingly open and liberal state, which it often is and sometimes isn't. Since it was the first state to legalize abortion and ratify the Equal Rights Amendment, Hawai'i seems like a natural environment **for the legalization of same-gender civil marriages.**

Traditional Hawaiian fisher-dude in malo. *(Courtesy Bishop Museum)*

The irony is that Hawai'i has a fairly politically indifferent gay community, rural and traditionalist voters state wide, and an island culture that discourages forwardness and "boat-rocking." Add to this the tremendous national backlash against same-sex marriage, both in the media and in other states' legislatures, and you can see why the road has been a long and bumpy one, filled with enormous blocks.

The whole same-gender marriage *thing* began in December of 1990, when three homo couples (two lesbian and one male) applied for marriage licenses at the

Honolulu City Hall. They were – you guessed it – denied a couple months later. Attorney **Dan Foley** filed a suit on their behalf, which became known as the **Baehr vs. Miike case.**

The case was ultimately appealed to the State Supreme Court, which ruled in favor of the gay couples in 1993. In the court's opinion, the state was refusing to grant marriage licenses (and thus marriage rights) due to the gender of couples applying. Technically, the sexual orientation of the couples had nothing to do with it. The Hawai'i State Constitution is probably the most human rights–oriented state constitution in the U.S., and strongly prohibits discrimination based on gender.

Although this amazing ruling was handed back down to a lower court and did not

Hawai'i cover boy Dan Foley.

become law, it made headline news around the globe. Thus began the **backlash** against "Hawai'i's gay marriages." State legislatures across the U.S. scrambled to pass laws and change constitutions limiting marriage to one man and one woman. And of course, good ole' Billy Clinton signed something much later called the Defense of Marriage Act to make sure no one would have to recognize what little Hawai'i had done. Or what everybody *thought* it had done.

In retaliation to the Supreme Court's 1993 ruling, the Hawai'i legislature abruptly passed **Act 217** in the spring of 1994. The act asserted that procreation was the basis for marriage. This was despite the fact that procreation had been taken *out* of the statute in 1984 as discriminatory against the elderly and disabled. The act was widely understood as ineffective and unconstitutional. Two other attempts to amend the state constitution were killed in legislative committees.

One interesting thing that Act 217 did was to create a Commission on Sexual Orientation and the Law. The commission looked at marriage rights and privileges, and heard public testimony and examined many witnesses. In late 1995, after studying the overwhelming evidence, the commission recommended full marriage benefits for same–gender couples.

In late 1996, when the ball was relayed into his lower court, **Judge Kevin Chang** finally ruled that there was no compelling state interest in *not* issuing marriage licenses to same–gender couples. That monumental decision technically allowed same–gender marriage in Hawai'i. But of course the Department of Health refused to issue licenses. Judge Chang granted a stay, which meant it went back to the State Supreme Court!

FRED WANTS BARNEY

Matt Matsunaga

Matt Matsunaga is legislator of O'ahu's Ninth Senatorial District and co-chair of the state's Senate Judiciary Committee, and he has been **a strong voice** for the advocacy of same–gender marriage in Hawai'i. He's even appeared in a couple Honolulu Gay Pride parades. Matt's father, Spark Matsunaga, was a beloved U.S. Congressman and Senator, and Matt himself was voted Best Legislator by a local magazine in 1997. Although he has at times played political hot potato with the marriage issue depending on the legislature's mood, he has said this about the same–gender marriage battle:

"We recognize that the public wants to decide whether marriage should be between one man and one woman; but why would anyone want to deny fundamental civil rights on the basis of sex? The due process and equal protection clause in our State Constitution clearly prohibits discrimination or denying a person's civil rights based upon race, religion, sex, or ancestry."

Or, as he succinctly put it in 1994 for the Ricki Lake crowd: "If Wilma is permitted to marry Fred, but Barney may not marry Fred, then, assuming that Fred would be a desirable spouse for either, Barney is being disadvantaged because of his gender."

That's all fine and dandy, but what about poor Betty?

In the meantime, a very watered–down form of same–sex marriage was passed on July 1, 1997, called the **Reciprocal Beneficiaries Act** (quite a mouthful). It gave only sixty out of 400 benefits that married people enjoy. The license is technically a legal document between two unmarried people (a mother and son could get one). It covers important areas of insurance, worker's compensation, hospital visits, survivorship rights and survivorship benefits. And it must be said it is better than most Domestic Partnership laws in effect locally and regionally around the U.S. However in actual usage, the R.B. Act has proven to be quite toothless, with many challenging its very function. Many say the license is not worth the paper it's written on.

One thing that appeals to Mainland gays is the fact that one does not need to be a resident to obtain an "R.B." license. It could also prove beneficial for insurance policies and estate planning in other states. Regardless of all the legal this and that's, gays have been flocking to Hawai'i for years to get "married" anyway, and many island business are set up primarily for executing your fabulously illegal same–gender union.

THE LONG HARD ROAD TO HUMAN RIGHTS

Homosexual acts done in private were decriminalized in Hawai'i in the early '70s. In 1975, Hawai'i's first homosexual protection bill was introduced in the state legislature. It was passed by the House but rejected by the Senate. In 1977, it was reintroduced but died in committee, and in 1978 a **gay rights** amendment to the state constitution was also killed. It wasn't until 1992 that a law prohibiting job discrimination based on sexual orientation was finally passed by the state legislature (and it's about time!).

So where does same–sex marriage stand now? **The State Supreme Court was expected to rule** on Judge Chang's verdict in favor of gays in early 1998. This would have been the final ruling **and** whatever the outcome, it would stick. The Hawai'i Supreme Court, who has already ruled in favor once, would have no choice but to abide and allow same–gender couples the right to marry. However, The Supreme Court held off on its ruling. It was decided that this sensitive civil rights issue should go to unprecedented popular state-wide vote in November instead. The results were disastrous.

Mainland money on both sides of the issue began pouring into humble Hawai'i. The group **Save Traditional Marriage** began their assault on Hawai'i's media with distasteful TV and print ads, including one with mock tourists explaining why they won't visit Hawai'i if it passes, to one of a child reading a same-gender marriage book and asking disturbing questions. **Protect Our Constitution** was on the other end, itself criticized for linking the issue to abortion and sweeping the homosexual aspects of the issue under the rug. Sign-waving along Hawai'i's streets, a quaint island tradition during election time, at times turned into ugly yelling matches. Could this be the land of Aloha?

Needless to say, the vote against same-gender won by a landslide (68% to 32%). Many island gays and lesbians who had long felt safe and sound in Hawai'i began to question their stand on the islands. Conservative groups announced a victory of common sense and denounced those who called them "homophobic". Queer visitors thought twice about their next

Taking it to the streets during '98 campaign.

HAWAIIANS AND HIV

According to *Ke Ola Mamo* (the Native Hawaiian Health Care System), Hawaiians and part–Hawaiians are **diagnosed with AIDS and HIV proportionally higher** than any other Asian or Pacific Islander group in Hawai'i. In fact, more than twice the rate of the next highest Asian/Pacific Islander group, the Chinese. From 1986–1995, the number of Hawaiians with AIDS jumped up 157 percent, compared with 99 percent for the state's population as a whole. Prevention efforts have focused on innovative education with Hawaiian values in mind, and better access to health care for Hawaiians, who have one of the lowest health profiles in the nation.

visit.

So is Hawai'i now really that gay-*un*friendly? Why didn't same-sex marriage pass? It could have been the strong presence of the Mormon and Catholic churches on the islands, the elderly age of the average voter, or the fact that Hawai'i had fought with the issue for so long even liberal voters became sick of it. Or it could have been that same-gender marriage was just to radical for modest Hawai'i to tackle.

Either way, Governor Ben Cayetano has dedicated himself to passing a strong **Domestic Partnership bill** in place of gay marriage in 1999 (although it will not include adoption and custody rights). The former gay marriage advocates have transformed into the group Equality Hawai'i, and the DP outcome has yet to be realized. And the fight continues.

Sign of the times.

Sovereignty (Onipa'a)

History has not been kind to the Hawaiians. Their culture has been subverted, their population decimated, their land taken, their monarchy overthrown, and their language nearly lost. Through years of foreign diseases and intermarrying with immigrant races, there are less than a few thousand full–blooded Hawaiians left. Most live on the privately–owned island of Ni'ihau. Not unlike the Native Americans, **Hawaiians have become strangers in their own land.** However, unlike American Indians, Hawaiians are *void* of rights to ancestral lands, economic autonomy, college tuition funds, and most importantly, they have no right to organize their own nation like Native American nations on the Mainland.

Na Mamo O Hawai'i

Ku'umeaaloha Gomes

Ku'umeaaloha Gomes is a professor at the University of Hawai'i at Manoa, where she teaches a class on gays and lesbians in Hawai'i. She is also the founder of *Na Mamo O Hawai'i* **(Hawaiian Lesbian and Gay Activists).** She regularly holds anti–oppression workshops on interrupting oppressive behaviors. Although a big part of her work is about the sovereignty issue for native Hawaiians, Gomes explains her group is multi–issue. "We wanted to show that the same–sex marriage issue is not just about middle–class, white transplants to the islands, but also about people that are born here, in our family."

The issue of heterosexism is also a factor for Hawaiians as well. "We as native Hawaiians who are gay do not want our Hawaiian community to become our colonizers, and prevent us from our equality in society…Na Mamo O Hawai'i is trying to be the bridge between the Hawaiian and the gay communities. That's what makes me so tired!"

Gomes' view is that **heterosexism, sexism, racism, and classism** are all inter–related, and must be tackled as a whole. "The gay communities and the Hawaiian movement need to interact. The native people are the most oppressed here, with no right to self–government, and the gay community cannot isolate the issues…For a lot of residents, they have come here as gay people into this place, and they have to realize that the native Hawaiians are their hosts. You should know the history and understand it, and celebrate the culture."

Most importantly, Ku'umeaaloha stresses you to ask, "If I'm going to participate in this, what am I going to give back to the Hawaiians? These people are sharing their culture with me, do I stand up for them, or stand back from it? What do I do to keep these people and their culture alive?"

In 1993, Mr. Bill Clinton signed an official apology on behalf of the American businessmen who overthrew Queen Lili'uokalani in 1893. It acknowledged the deprivation of the rights of Native Hawaiians to self–determination. This was due to the fact that the Hawaiian people never did officially and voluntarily relinquish their claim to sovereignty. The United Nations also recognizes this fact. This has helped fuel the islands' sovereignty movement, which is now focused on retribution and compensation for ceded lands.

Most residents of Hawai'i favor a **"nation–within–a–nation"** framework for the Hawaiian people. The state has tried to hijack the movement with bills influenced by financial institutions, that only make it harder for poor Hawaiians to make mortgage payments on homestead land.

Most sovereignty activist groups seek only to have a council of native Hawaiians consulted to approve all land transactions in the state. A handful of groups advocate real secession from the United States, causing much controversy within the haole community. The movement is growing, and is a potentially divisive issue in the coming century.

NI'IHAU

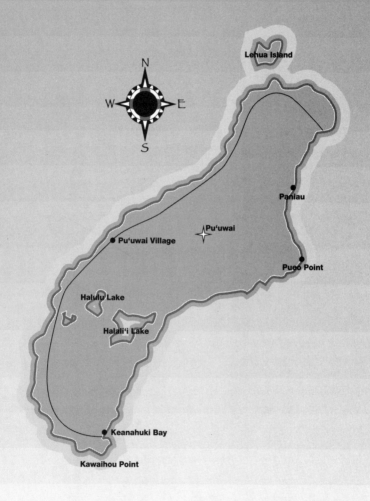

Kaulakahi Channel

Lehua Island

N
W   E
S

Paniau

Pu'uwai

Pu'uwai Village

Pueo Point

Halulu Lake

Halali'i Lake

Keanahuki Bay

Kawaihou Point

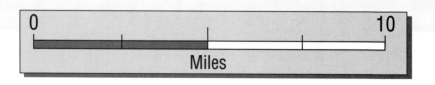

0   10

Miles

CHAPTER 3

N I ' I H A U

The quiet solitude of undisturbed Ni'ihau. (Hawaii State Archives)

Island Facts for Trivial Queens

Ni'ihau is nicknamed: "The Forbidden Island"
Island color: White
Flower: Pupu
Land mass: 70 sq. miles/182 sq. km

Population: 230 est.
Highest point: Paniau at
1,250 feet/381 m
Rainfall: 19 inches/48 cm

The only island on earth where Hawaiian is spoken as a first language. Site of Hawai'i's largest lake, Halali'i, at 841 to 865 acres (depending on the rain).

Why Bother?

The answer to the question of whether or not to visit the island of Niʻihau is *Don't even think about it.* It's not that this arid, desert isle doesn't hold any intrigue. Bought by Eliza Sinclair in 1863 for $10,000 (what a deal!) and completely controlled by the Robinson family ever since, life on Niʻihau is simple and untamed. There are no telephones, no restaurants, no movie theaters, no paved roads and relatively few trucks or cars. Everyone is employed by the Robinson's ranch, so no rent is necessary. An old WWII landing craft acts as the island's sole supply ship.

The catch to all this quaint tranquility (and it's a whopper) is that no outsiders are allowed to visit Niʻihau. It is completely closed off to non–residents, save for restricted helicopter flights to specific uninhabited spots. Hence the nickname "The Forbidden Island." Residents of Niʻihau, a majority of who are full–blooded Hawaiian, are allowed to visit the other islands, but cannot bring anyone back with them. When a Niihauan marries an outsider, they are rarely allowed to return (talk about tough love!). This compound–like system means a dwindling population due to younger people leaving for more modern lifestyles. But the exclusive paternalism of the Robinson family has allowed for an uniquely Hawaiian culture to flourish, far from the over–paving and commercialism of other parts of the state.

The Robinson ranch could obviously make a better profit by selling the island outright, for assumably a bit more than the $10,000 they paid for it. They have evaded this option despite grave financial concerns due to extremely high taxes imposed by the state. Even a future deal with the military (which will lease parts of the island for – get this – rocket launching) will not seem to cure Niʻihau's economic woes. Whether this last outpost of Hawaiiana will survive the 21st century completely unscathed, or succumb to modern market pressures, is anyone's guess.

Niʻihau in a Mac–nut Shell

The north shore of Niʻihau looks out on to the crescent–shaped Lehua Island. On the island's north–west shore is **Keawanui,** a stunning three and a half mile stretch of beach. A lot of Niʻihau women spend time (they got a lot of it) creating the intricate **Niʻihau lei necklaces** from seashells washed ashore on the island's beaches. The delicate jewelry is coveted throughout the islands. The one main dirt road on the island runs along the island's western spine, where Niʻihau's main village **Puʻuwai** sits about mid–point. The town is the center of the island's ranching operations, with stone walls built up around the houses to keep out the grazing animals. South of Puʻuwai are two large lakes, Halulu and Halaliʻi, which can dry up to puddles during rough droughts. The dirt road ends at Keanahaki Bay on the southern tip of the island.

Things for Homos To Do (well, actually anyone)

Ni'ihau Helicopters and Safaris offer pricey tours for people interested in setting eyes on Ni'ihau. The short flights take off from Makaweli on Kaua'i, in a seven–passenger helicopter owned by the Robinson Family. A majority of the three–hour tour takes place on land. Depending on the weather the chopper lands at two sites, a beach on the north shore and Keanahaki Bay in the south, avoiding Pu'uwai where people live. Snacks are provided or you can bring your own lunch and freely picnic and beach comb at these remote spots. Pleasure hunting tours for sheep and wild boar can also be arranged. Call 335-3500.

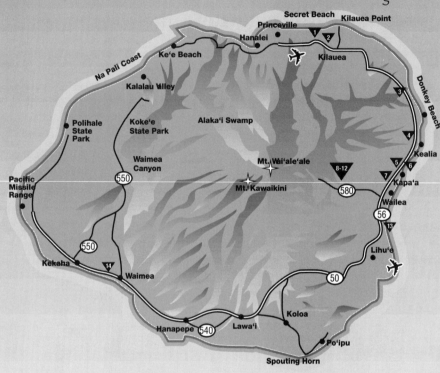

KAUA'I

Secret Beach · Kilauea Point
Princeville
Hanalei
Ke'e Beach
Na Pali Coast
Kalalau Valley
Koke'e State Park
Alaka'i Swamp
Polihale State Park
Waimea Canyon
Mt. Wai'ale'ale
Mt. Kawaikini
Kilauea
Donkey Beach
Kealia
Kapa'a
Wailea
Pacific Missile Range
Kekaha
Waimea
Lihu'e
Koloa
Hanapepe
Lawa'i
Po'ipu
Spouting Horn

0 ————— 10
Miles

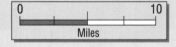

KAUA'I'S Gay and Lesbian Accommodations

1. Pali Kai Bed and Breakfast
2. Kalihiwai Jungle Home
3. Mahina Kai
4. Rainbow Valley Vacation Rental
5. Anuenue Plantation B&B
6. Mahina
7. Royal Drive Cottages
8. Aloha Kauai B&B
9. Hale Kahawai B&B
10. Mohala Ke Ola
11. Kauai Waterfall B&B
12. Kealoha Rise
13. Kaha Lani
14. Ole Kama'ole's Beach House

CHAPTER 4

K A U A ʻ I

The astounding Na Pali Coastline.

Island Facts for Trivial Queens

Kauaʻi is nicknamed: "The Garden Island"	**Highest point:** Mt. Kawaikini at
Island color: Purple	5,243 feet/1,598 m
Flower: Mokihana	**Rainfall:** 21 inches in Waimea/53 cm,
Land mass: 552 sq. miles/1,435 sq. km	85 inches/216 cm in Princeville
Population: 56,000 est.	

Kauaʻi is the geologically oldest of the major islands. Its Mount Waiʻaleʻale has been classified the wettest place on the earth with a killer average of 444 inches a year. Kauaʻi has more miles of sandy beach (nearly 40) than any other Hawaiian island. The state's largest beach is 15 miles from Polihale to Kekaha. Kauaʻi was the first island explored by Captain Cook in 1778.

Why Bother?

Kaua'i is what a lot of people fantasize about when they think of Hawai'i. It's full of huge empty beaches, lush river valleys, exotic rainforests, jagged cliffs with long thin waterfalls, and an overall primordial feeling – basically your postcard Hollywood version of Paradise. Come to think of it, Hollywood *has* exploited the place a little! *South Pacific, Jurassic Park, King Kong, Blue Hawaii, 10, Hook, Outbreak, 6 Days 7 Nights*, and the Hollywood artistic cinematic triumph *Throw Mama from the Train* were all shot here, as well as lots of stupid TV shows (a redundant phrase?). So you probably have seen Kaua'i, you just never knew it. Now is your chance to see it for real, without a Hollywood filter.

In 1992, Hurricane Iniki hit and nearly devastated Kaua'i, leaving hundreds homeless and the island in shambles. Redevelopment of Kaua'i's tourist infrastructure has been a long hard road since then. However, it usually ranks as the number one favorite Hawaiian island on travelers' lists.

Tourism here tends to be less flashy and more eco–friendly than on O'ahu and Maui. More emphasis is put on the dramatic outdoors and slower lifestyle, rather than mega–resorts. Having said that, the areas of Po'ipu in the south, Kapa'a on the eastern coast, and Princeville in the north feel like the tourist magnets they are.

Most of Kaua'i's queer community lives north of the Wailua River, especially up along Highway 580 in the Wailua Homesteads. A bulk of the gay bed and breakfasts are found around here. The gays and lesbians are extremely well organized and cohesive on Kaua'i compared to the other islands, with frequent potlucks, movie nights at people's homes, camp outs at Polihale Beach, and bonfires at Kealia Beach which visitors are more than welcome to join (fresh faces always needed). It has been

Resident queers on a boat outing.

said that on any given holiday the gay crowd is putting on some kind of event.

Lambda Aloha is the leading bi, transgendered, lesbian, and gay community organization, and sponsors the men's beach bonfire and is politically active. Be sure to check Lambda Aloha's info number (823-MAHU) for upcoming events before you get to the island. Malama Pono, the

Kaua'i AIDS agency, is also heavily involved with activities and puts out a darn informative newsletter. The women at Mango Mama's (see listing) freely give info on lesbian events, parties, and community listings as well, or call the new women's info maintained by Hui 'O Wahine at 245-0505.

There is no totally gay bar on Kaua'i, but Secret Beach and especially Donkey Beach attract a social gay crowd. The rainbow flag is proudly flown at many of the gay outdoor community events too. Kaua'i also has a gay coffee club, a gay swamp tour, and the gay–popular Mokihana cultural festival in September. The men's and women's communities are solid and friendly, so try to get involved during your time here!

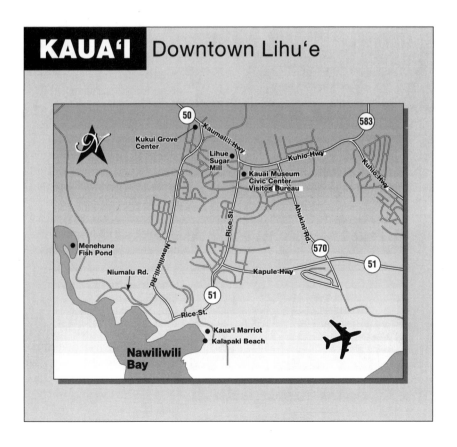

KAUA'I Downtown Lihu'e

This Town

Lihu'e is a grown up plantation town with some interesting architecture and a local business feel to it. There's not much here to turn on the tourists who usually head out to the resort areas and skip the town (it ain't no Vegas). Lihu'e is still the main point of entry for most visitors to Kaua'i, and the seat of county government. A **sugar mill** operates right next to town, near the junction of Highways 50 and 56, and the sticky but calorie–free smell of molasses can hang in the air on certain days. The mill's fate will probably follow the other closures in the state's sugar industry.

Stroll just up from the highways' junction along Rice Street heading east. A few doors down is a Spanish stucco–style main post office. On the north side of Rice Street sits the oval Civic Center building, and a few doors down from that, the

Selling orchids at the Kauai Museum.

Cocks hanging out in Lihu'e.

Kauai Museum. Housed in a black lava rock exterior, this museum offers an excellent and in depth overview of Kaua'i's and Ni'ihau's history. Inside, awaiting the curious are everything from illustrations of Kaua'i's extinct volcanoes, missionary quilts, necklaces made out of braided human hair, *koa* bowls, and photos of every ethnic group on Kaua'i. If you haven't had your fill, you can ask for a re–entry pass for another day! And don't forget to check out the orchid sale every Friday on the front lawn.

This area of Lihue's **downtown** is generally quiet and stoical, with a white–columned county building, a couple of monuments to Japanese and Filipino immigrants, and chickens casually hanging out on the wide lawn in front. (You'll spot these perky birds everywhere on Kaua'i, since the island has no mongooses to steal the

HAWAI'I'S FAIRIES

The **menehune** are Hawai'i's race of legendary little people who live in the islands' mountains. The little buggers are credited with creating marvelous engineering feats throughout the islands, such as irrigation ditches, fish ponds, and temples, which are especially noticeable on Kaua'i. They build quickly and swiftly, often in one night, possess magical powers, and are super–cute to boot. Archaeologists agree that the intricate style of construction of *menehune* works, as well as their distinct markings, bear no resemblance to works done by ancient Hawaiians. A more boring explanation is that the name menehune was given to the first migration of Tahitians to the islands by subsequent arrivals from the south. *Manahune* means "outcast" in Tahitian, and elsewhere in old South Pacific it referred to a servant class of laborers. Fairies or construction workers? I'll let you decide…

eggs.) A helpful **Hawai'i Visitor's Bureau** office sits nearby on Umi Street.

Heading east on Rice Street in your car, you will pass some shopping plazas and end up at the edge of Nawiliwili Bay. This is where the **Kauai Marriott** stands on the nice, if brief, Kalapaki Beach. Restored after Hurricane Iniki, the Marriot sports a two–acre reflecting lagoon, lovely grounds, and probably the largest swimming pool in the state with a 26,000–square foot surface. Slink into **Duke's Canoe Club** for some good fish and viewing of the volleyball players on the beach. At the adjoining parks, old–timers hang out under the ironwood trees to gulp beers and "talk story."

The road loops back uphill and becomes Highway 58. If you turn left on Niumalu Road you'll drive past the commercial port. Keep following the signs for the **Menehune Fishpond Lookout.** The road curves up to a vista point along the bend of the Hule'ia Stream. A perfectly preserved aqua culture pond sits far below, evidently built by the legendary race of fairies (see sidebar), with a view of the hills beyond.

If you head west back on Highway 58, keep your eyes peeled for the **Grove Farm Homestead** on the right hand side of the road. A two–hour tour on Mondays, Wednesdays, and Thursdays

The pond that Hawai'i's fairies built.

takes you through a preserved farm house from 1800s plantation life. The Wilcox family's canes, hairbrushes, and even clothes (no undergarments, please) are on display throughout the rooms. Two housekeepers have their hands full dusting all the furniture, baking cookies, and making mint iced tea for the tour groups that saunter through (reservations required, 245-3202). For you mall addicts, at the end of Highway 58 is the large **Kukui Grove Shopping Center,** with department stores, a cineplex, and a monolithic, empty feel.

Kaua'i in a Mac–nut Shell

Working north from Lihu'e on the scenic Highway 56, turn *mauka* (mountain side) at Highway 583 (Ma'alo Road) to experience the **Wailua Falls.** TV–addicts will instantly shout out "da plane! da plane!" when they see the eighty–foot falls, since they were used in the opening credits of *Fantasy Island.* The cliffs once acted as a diving platform for daring chiefs, but seems they lost a few along the way, since a sign now proclaims "Slippery rocks at top of the falls. People have been killed."

Back on Highway 56 going north, you will pass a golf course and then the **Lydgate Beach Park,** with a pleasant grassy area and a long narrow beach. This was once the site of a *pu'uhonua* or place of refuge for *kapu* law breakers, and I guess it still is, since it's said to be a risky cruise spot as well.

Further on Highway 56, you will drive over the **Wailua River,** where cattle–barges of tourists make the pilgrimage up to the **Fern Grottos.** A band plays Elvis' Hawaiian Wedding Song as you are hauled up river to see the fern–covered cave, which may or may not be worth the effort; you'll see a lot of people kayaking on the river instead. Right after the river mouth, the defunct **Coco Palms Resort** pops up on your left. Too bad it's closed indefinitely due to damage from Hurricane Iniki, since it holds a perfect spot for a same–sex wedding. The small outside chapel on the grounds was built for the Rita Hayworth musical *Miss Sadie Thompson* in 1953.

The fantasy falls of Wailua.

Here, take a left up Highway 580 for views of the winding river, and check out the *heiau* (Hawaiian temple) remains, as well as the **'Opaeka'a Falls** on the opposite side of the road. This highway takes you up into the residential Wailua Homesteads. The road ends at the beautifully peaceful **Keahua Arboretum** where you could take a dip (non–skinny) in the cool mountain stream, complete with a rope swing!

Going down the windy Wailua river.

Back on Highway 56, a little ways up and you're in the resort area of **Wailua.** This area blends right into **Kapa'a** as you head north, creating Kaua'i's main tourist universe of shops and restaurants. Since Kaua'i has no complete circle–island highway, the backtracking of cars around here gets mighty cramped at certain times, making for rush hour in paradise. On the ocean side of the highway is the **Coconut Plantation** development, which includes a handful of hotels, the best being the

The outline of the Sleeping Giant.

Kauai Coconut Beach Resort (see listing). There's a low–key outdoor shopping mall with funky souvenir shops and eateries next door. Be sure to check out the views of the **Sleeping Giant** on the nearby mountain ridge from around here – living or more like dead proof of what happens when a large man eats too much *poi* at a lu'au, or so the legend goes.

Once you exit the town of Kapa'a heading north, the crescent–shaped **Kealia Beach** pops up on your right. This splendid spot is the site of the men's and women's community bonfires. Further north past sugar cane fields is the island's main gay nudey spot, **Donkey Beach** (see listing). The beach is past the 11 mile marker and not visible from the highway.

Further north, you'll go through the scattered village of **Anahola.** The road floats past rich green pastures, some stunning mountain towers and unhurried countryside on your way to the village of Kilauea. Stop for a super smoothie at the lesbian–owned **Mango Mama's** (see lsiting) on the side of the highway just before Kilauea. There's also the **Guava Kai Plantation Visitor's Center** for anyone who is just dying to know more about this tropical fruit.

Take Kolo Road through the town to Kilauea Road, and half a mile later you will be at the **Kilauea Point National Wildlife Refuge.** The point makes a picturesque site for humpback whale watching in the winter months, with a 1913 lighthouse, thrashing waves, and an emerald sea completing the postcard picture. The refuge is a haven for many nesting birds such as albatross, nenes, and red–footed boobies (!).

Back on the main highway, just before the 24 mile marker is the first turn–off for Kalihiwai Road, along which you will find the parking lot and trail to **Secret Beach** (see listing). Further on the highway, a bridge curves over the pretty Kalihiwai Stream and soon the Princeville Airport is on your left. On your right pops up a swanky golf course that looks like it was imported from some smug place in France.

Turn at the signs for Princeville, and a manicured road will take you over 11,000 acres of ornate statues, fancy townhouses, and then arrive at the posh **Princeville Hotel.** For you interior decorator types (you know who you are), take a gawk at the maaarvelous lobby, with dripping chandeliers, tapestries, pillars, fountains, and marble floors. Immense windows face the striking Makana mountain peaks. The range is still referred to as Bali Hai ever since Bloody Mary sang to them here in *South Pacific.* The weather may be wet and mushy all winter long, but the out–of–this–world views and luxury island setting definitely compensate any of nature's shortcomings.

The crescent of Hanalei Bay.

Just past the Princeville turn–off there's a shopping center, and across the road is the **Hanalei Valley Lookout.** The bird's eye view from here looks on to the lush patches that produce two–thirds of Hawai'i's commercial taro. The valley acts as a national wildlife refuge as well. The road winds down the valley to the tourist town of **Hanalei.** Casual and laid back despite the tourists, the village fea-

Sons and Lovers

On Kaua'i in the late 1930s, Robert Allerton and his lover John Gregg Allerton began to transform a 100-acre estate in the jungle into an amazing garden showplace. The estate was originally started by Queen Emma, the wife of King Kamehameha IV, as a royal vacation spot in the 1870's. Robert and John spent twenty years planting rare and beautiful varieties of flora on the lush property, sometimes scouring islands in the South Pacific for certain species. Today the **Allerton Estate,** along with the adjoining National Tropical Botanical Garden (332-7361), is one of the premier botanical gardens in the country, with sweeping gardens, reflecting pools, and comely statues. However, most tourists are told Robert Allerton and his *son* developed the property, not his homosexual lover. This is because Robert legally adopted the younger John with some strings pulled by Robert's prominent family in Chicago. The result being John officially changing his name to John Gregg Allerton.

The Allerton Estate.

tures an old school house converted into a shopping plaza along the main road. Some nice beach parks line the town's crescent bay. As you leave Hanalei, the **Waioli Mission House Museum** is on your left. Built by the Alexanders (who didn't fancy the thatched hut they were residing in), the house holds some interesting early 1800s furnishings and woodwork and the best part is the admission, which is free.

The road out of Hanalei is gloriously winding and serene. It crosses many one-lane bridges where you must take polite turns yielding (no New York driving here). These bridges along the highway have been kept narrow for a purpose: to frustrate big development, and it's worked. You'll twist past many island homes and peek-a-boo beach coves. No self-respecting queer will pass up the chance to pull over at **Lumaha'i Beach** (not well marked), and follow in Mitzi Gaynor's footsteps to "wash that man right out of my hair." The water here is often dangerous for swimming, but it's a nice beach for exploring and well, singing.

Off the highway past the micro-town of Ha'ena is the **Maniniholo Dry Cave,** an

The stunning Ke'e Beach.

Once bustling, now tranquil Kalalau Valley.

eerie football–field sized cavern acting as a perfect refuge from the North Shore's drizzle. The highway tends to get more cluttered with tourist cars as you go along, but stop to compare the dry cave to the gaping pools of the wet cave along the same side of the road.

At the end of the highway is the legendary **Ke'e Beach,** a popular snorkel spot laid out exquisitely at the beginning of the **Na Pali Coast**. A rocky trail up the western end of the beach takes you to a famous hula *heiau* ruin. It was here where hula apprentices had to swim across the shark–infested waters and chant above the roar of the ocean at the temple to become teachers – talk about apprenticeships! It was also here that the volcano goddess Pele had a "hot" affair with the local stud prince Lohiau in his abode nearby.

Many tourists end up at Ke'e Beach to try their luck at the slippery **Kalalau Trail.** The trek begins here and ends up eleven miles later at the magnificent Kalalau valley – but only for the strong–thighed! A shorter jaunt on the Kalalau Trail will quickly give you gorgeous views of the coast line and take you to the **site of Lohiau's home.** If you keep on trucking, two miles later you'll hit **Hanakapi'ai Beach,** attractive but famous for its drownings! Regardless, it makes a nice day hike, and permits can be obtained to camp in the further valleys, including the fairy–tale perfect **Kalalau Valley.** No matter how you do it, the Na Pali Coast *must* be seen – whether you choose helicopter, raft, or foot. It is one of the most astonishing and stirring valley regions humans can visit on the planet. Home to many Hawaiians up to the 1800s, the area has few inhabitants now. In this century, there have only been some bootleggers, one gun–toting Ko'olau the Leper, a hermit doctor who resided in caves there in the

'50s, and some slightly smelly hippies that were finally driven out in the '70s. So go ahead and explore – the coast is now clear! (Although there is a guy back there who now declares himself the mayor . . .)

Rewinding your way back down the coast to civilized Lihu'e again, head south on Highway 50, you will find the **Kilohana Plantation** just beyond town. This 1930s Tudor–style mansion has been restored as an upscale shopping spot. The bedrooms, closets, and even toilets and bathtubs of the former home act as store displays for artwork, antiques, clothing, and handicrafts. There are over thirty–five acres, a working farm, a restaurant called **Gaylord's** (see listing), and a poofy Clydesdale–drawn carriage for rent to round out the picture.

Past Kilohana keep your eyes out on the left hand side of the road for **Queen Victoria's Profile.** Scan the top of the Hoary Head Mountains to the left and don't worry if you have no clue whatsoever to where it is – you aren't the only one. A few miles later is the *makai* (ocean side) turn–off for Highway 520, heading south towards Po'ipu. You'll pass through a long **tree tunnel** of swamp mahogany along this stretch of road, which will lead you to the cozy plantation/tourist town of **Koloa** – site of Hawai'i's very first sugar plantation in 1835.

Heading south on Highway 520 out of Koloa, three miles later is the arid resort area of **Po'ipu.** If you head west on Lawa'i Road after you pass the Po'ipu Plaza, you will see the visitor's center for the **National Tropical Botanical Garden** and **the Allerton Estate.** Here they pick you up for a tour of one of the premier botanical gardens in the country, located near the town of Lawa'i, developed by Robert Allerton and his lover John Gregg Allerton (see sidebar). Just past the visitor's center is the queerly named **Spouting Horn blowhole** (hmmm . . .). When the ocean rushes into a lava tube below, a moaning/groaning sound emits that is said to be a giant lizard trapped inside. A large expulsion of white ocean also discharges to the delight of the tourist throng. And like most spouting horns my eyes have seen, this one's reputation at times exceeds its actual performance.

Head back east into Po'ipu to find the scenic **Po'ipu Beach,** which was ripped

Waiting to exhale: Spouting Horn.

The Grand Canyon of the Pacific.

apart by thirty–foot waves and 220–m.p.h. winds during Hurricane Iniki in 1992. It was the hardest hit spot in all of Kaua'i. Still, it's a great stretch of beaches intermittently interrupted by rocky points, with some of the best swimming and bodysurfing on the island. A long line of rebuilt condos and hotels, including Hyatt and Sheraton, elbow each other along the sunny coast line.

Back on Highway 50 past Lawa'i is the village of **Kalaheo,** a sleepy old settlement descended from Portuguese fishermen and cane workers. The scenic point after the 14 mile marker offers a deep view into **Hanapepe Valley** and the red cliffs beyond. A large chunk of the land in these parts is owned by the Robinson family, the ones who count Ni'ihau island among their possessions. Following is the little town of **Hanapepe,** a ways off from the main highway. The village looks so much like the Australian outback that they filmed *The Thorn Birds* here. A few miles further is the sparse overgrown rock remains of **Russian Fort Elizabeth,** built as an alliance between a group of Russians and Kaua'i's king to overthrow Kamehameha, which of course never happened.

Soon you will hit the largest town in west Kaua'i, **Waimea.** This was the site of Captain Cook's first landing in Hawai'i, and you'll know it by the statue of the *haole* dude on the side of the road. A handful of cute shops and businesses line the highway. If you are around here in February, try to catch the annual **Waimea Town Celebration** (see events listing). Turn up Menehune Road next to the Waimea fire station to behold the **Menehune Ditch:** a three–foot wide, watertight aqueduct built by the legendary race of little people (did someone say fairies?).

The next sleepy town west is Kekaha. From here, take Highway 550 to wind your way up to **Waimea Canyon.** The road twists and turns a zillion times as your ears pop open, and the foliage goes from barren to forested as you ascend. The chunk of land you see sitting in the ocean from here is the all–Hawaiian island of Ni'ihau (read that chapter!). The first major canyon view-point you hit, **Waimea Canyon**

Wonderfully huge Polihale Beach.

Lookout, is the grandest one. The more than 3,000–foot views will make you feel as dizzy as a blonde! When you peer down at the gold and maroon vertical walls, terraces, and winding crevices below, you will know why Mark Twain dubbed it with the perfect marketing slogan "Grand Canyon of the Pacific."

Keep on heading up the road, and you will be in the **Koke'e State Park.** Here you'll find a snack bar and a gift shop full of cool Kaua'i stuff. Adjoining is a small museum of flora, fauna, and weather displays that includes a nasty continuous video of Hurricane Iniki ripping the island apart.

For you nature lovers, over forty–five miles of hiking trails start from around here, and don't you turn your car around yet. The road goes past the stunning Kalalau Lookout to magnificently end at the **Pu'u O Kila Lookout.** Both of these vista points gaze down into the magical Kalalau Valley, which looks like something out of an artist's dream. The sheer green walls and tall rock spires reach magnificently towards the heavens. This is where they finally decided *not* to build a continuous highway to the North Shore to create a circle–island road. One look at the arduous cliffs, and you'll see why.

Backtrack your way down to Highway 50 and go northwest along the beach–rimmed highway, where you'll spot the Pacific Missile Range military compound. Nicely ask the man in uniform for permission to visit the wide **Barking Sands Beach,** named after the sound the sand supposedly makes when the wind hits it just right. But why even bother? A little further up is the *makai* (ocean side) turn–off for **Polihale Beach.** A dirt road leads you through sugar cane fields to one of the most stunning beaches in the state. This remote, amazing length of sand and dunes is bordered on one end by rugged sea cliffs. The next annoying human thankfully feels a long ways away. Almost always sunny and empty, this is the beach you've always dreamt about. But don't even think about swimming when the water is turbulent: there are no hunky lifeguards to save you here!

Tell Me When You're Coming

The **Waimea Town Celebration** in February (338-9975), formerly the Captain Cook Fair, happens in the southwest corner of Kaua'i. The fair includes canoe and foot races, kiosks, cotton candy, pig–on–a–spit, games, and lots o' beer – can't get more island style than that! All to help commemorate the landing of that white guy on Kaua'i (later to be killed on the Big Island). **The Japanese Obon Festival** runs on weekends from mid–June to August at various temples and monasteries around the island. Festivities involve drumming, kimono–clad participants in graceful circular dances, and launching of boats stocked with food and paper lanterns to light the way to the Buddha Land of Peace. The nine–day **Mokihana Festival** (822-2166) in late September attracts a lot of local gay participation and spectators, with games, story–telling, lei making, and in particular dance – and a lot of it. The ending night with an outdoor hula competition in Kekaha is a hands down favorite for locals and tourists alike. The **Malama Pono annual fundraiser** (822-0878) for Kaua'i's AIDS organization is held in early December, with a silent auction and *pupus* (island appetizers) in a ballroom setting.

Queer Pages ⚥

Lambda Aloha Newsletter is published four times a year and informs of homo potlucks and meetings, and offers an events calendar and direction to the men's bonfire. For more current updates, call their gay info line at 823-MAHU, or check out their extensive web site at aloha.net/~lambda. P.O. Box 921, Kapa'a, HI 96746. 822-7171

Things For Homos To Do ⚥

ABBA Taxi & Tours is run by the hospitable Michael, a Kaua'i resident for over twenty years. He will take you and up to six others in a mini–van for personalized tours of gay beaches, restaurants, and/or points of beauty on Kaua'i. Michael custom designs each trip to your tastes, charged by hourly increments. He's also happy to do pick ups and drop offs at the airport and hotels for other "family members." 639-2222

Holy Union Commitment Ceremonies are performed for same–gender couples by the serene Dawna Su Maria. By having the individuals write their own vows and pick their own style of private or public ceremony, Dawna encourages the couple's hearts to "talk to each other." Sites can include a sacred Hawaiian temple or other holy places on the island. She also provides blessings and spiritual counseling as part of the union, and she oversees the bisexual network group on the island. 821-1690 ♀

Men's and Women's Community Bonfire is the unqiue queer thing for the traveling homo to do on Kaua`i. Originating from casual get-togethers on Lydgate Beach, the bonfires have evolved into a men's community event that happens every Friday (weather permitting - call the guys at 822-7171 and if no answer, head to the beach!). Go right at the 10 mile marker, and you'll see the fire just north of the river on the picturesque Kealia Beach to roast weenies. As night falls, you can sit around and "talk story" and hobnob with the local gay community. Sometimes there is a small handful of people, and sometimes a whole town shows up. Be sure to bring your own hot dogs - buns are happily supplied! The women's cozy and sociable bonfire takes place on the third Friday of the month (check with the 245-0505 hotline), also at the southern end of Kealia. Either way, be sure not to miss 'em!

Swamping with the Swamp Stud is a unique adventure led by the friendly and tattooed Frank, through the high–elevation Alaka'i swamp near the North Shore. A gorgeous trail takes you through different ecosystems of native Hawaiian plants and birds, with beautiful look-outs and a partly boardwalked path. The set piece is the swamps, full of cool "clean" mud, perfect for rolling around and wrestling in. A nearby river acts as a natural bath, and this full–day adventure is not to be missed for the seekers of something unusual! 2916 Pala St. #14, Lihu'e, HI 96766. 246-0041

Letting it All Hang Out ◈

Donkey Beach, despite its curious name, isn't called that for its size but for the fact that donkeys from a nearby sugar plantation used to graze along its shores.

North of Kapa'a on the eastern coast, look for the 11 mile marker and park at the second gated dirt road on your right. You won't see the beach from the highway, but walk down through an old cane field and ironwood trees and you'll see the sand on your left. There are usually some surfers here, and a selection of nudists and homos or both. The northern end is usually more gay and weekdays can be sparse people–wise. Some low trees line the back of the beach, which generally tends to have more sand in the summertime. Car break–ins are frequent, and swimming's not so good, but with the serene, remote feel to it all, who's complaining? The down side is that Mainland developers have bought the adjoining land, so future "clean ups" of the beach could occur.

Secret Beach is big, even bigger than Donkey! Go to the 23 mile marker on

Highway 56, and turn right on towards the ocean on to Kalihiwai Road. Turn right again at the first red dirt road, and park at the end, where you will see a handful of other cars. A worn trail begins here, made up of incredibly slippery steps that steeply descend all the way to the beach. A wide stretch of sand nestled in a cove, there's often a small waterfall half way down the beach that can be used as a fresh–water shower. The Kilauea Lighthouse is visible in the distance, and the foliage bordering the back of the beach brings very welcome shade. Secret Beach attracts an alternative crowd of surfers, belly boarders, nudists and gays. All would be fine expect that the Edith Crabbit–style neighbors have been bitching about all the bare buns, so the beach is getting less nude and less gay in the process. There could be future crackdowns here, so beware!

Place to Put Your Head ⟡

For Sure Queer

Aloha Kauai Bed & Breakfast is nestled up the Wailua Homesteads on Highway 580. The owners (who used to manage Hamburger Mary's on Maui) offer three rooms in their home overlooking the Wailua River valley, with views of the nearby mountains as well. There's a small clothing–optional pool, and the clientele is strictly gay. A reasonably priced pool house is also for rent, and complimentary sunset refreshments are served in the South Pacific decor living room. 156 Lihau Street, Kapa'a, HI 96746. (800) 262-4652, 822-6966 www.eskimo.com/~borg/alo-hakauai.html

Anuenue Plantation Bed & Breakfast is a modern five–acre estate away from

the noise of traffic and surf. Owners Harry and Fred offer three spiffy, comfortable guest rooms in their newly–built, tasteful home. A separate cottage also resides on the property, and every room has wide open panoramas of the sky and ocean and mountains, including a perfect shot of the world's wettest, Mount Wai'ale'ale. There's a guest lounge/library, and wellness and human growth seminars, music, and dances frequently

occur in the windowed ballroom. P.O. Box 226, Kapa'a, HI 96746. (888) 371-

7716, 823-8335 www.anuenue.com

Hale Kahawai Bed & Breakfast is a serene retreat for both men and women, a

short walk from the picturesque 'Opaeka'a Falls and Poliahu Heiau (Hawaiian temple). Overlooking the Wailua River gorge are three guest rooms plus one studio with kitchenette and open beams. Surrounding are lush tropical gardens including a golden bamboo grove and lots of flowers and exotic palms. There are expansive sun decks and a garden hot tub illuminated by Tiki torches to soak in. Tom and Arthur will tell you how to find their favorite sea turtle spot near by. 85 Kahawai Place, Kapa'a, HI 96746. 822-1031 www.members.aol.com/bandbkauai/index.html

Kaha Lani is a scenic group of condos above the cliffs of gay–popular Lydgate Beach, surrounded by green fields and hills. Dave and Bruce rent out their tidy and tastefully decorated apartment while on the Mainland. It's on the top floor, with one bedroom and one and a half baths, and views of miles of beach. A quiet, modern atmosphere close to both Lihu'e and Kapa'a. (800) 565-2648, 822-5216 www.members.aol.com/selectdave/index.html

Kalihiwai Jungle Home is the upstairs of a luxurious home, directly overlooking

an incredible jungle view, with the mountains behind. The 1,100–square foot unit has a marble bathroom with jacuzzi bathtub, marble fireplace, kitchenette, and verandah with a swinging hammock for those nice long afternoon siestas. Thomas is your amiable host downstairs, who can help you out with local info and show you where the path to the nearby secluded beach is. P.O. Box 717, Kilauea, HI 96754. 828-1626, 828-0070 www.hskauai.com/kvp/jungle

Kauai Waterfall B&B offers a private waterfall on the lush grounds, which border the Wailua River State Park. A large pool and five–person hot tub are on the premises, and the rooms are light and comfortable. Large sunbathing decks overlook the nearby mountains. Continental breakfast is served amid the porcelain and crystal collection, and your host can also make tour arrangements for activities around the island. 5783 Ha'aheo Street, Kapa'a, HI 97646. (800) 996-9533, 823-9533

Kealoha Rise is a gay–owned vacation rental comprised of a main house and cottage in the cool hills above Kapa'a. The contemporary house has two luxurious

RAINBOW HANDBOOK

A MIXED COMMUNITY

Barbara & Janie
Owners of Pali Kai Bed and Breakfast

"Kaua'i has a really mixed community, and everyone knows one another. Visitors are always welcome to any function – that's why we sponsor the 823-MAHU number. You can't say you don't know what's going on, and it couldn't be easier to get involved."

bedrooms, a formal dining room, custom tiled bathrooms, full gourmet kitchen, den, and a fireplace. The cozy cottage has one bedroom, full kitchen, and an open living/dining room, and both houses have large private lanais looking on to immaculate tropical gardens. 6085 'Opaeka'a Road, Kapa'a, HI 97646. (415) 834-9195 www.gleep.com/users/kealoha

Mahina is Kaua'i's guest house for gay and straight women. The sound of the waves lull you to sleep from the beach right outside the door, in this comfortable and affordable lodge centrally located in Kapa'a. There are three bedrooms and a shared bath, kitchen, and living areas, and an overall healing atmosphere of friendship. Gay owner Sharon can fill you in on local happenings and will make you feel like Mahina is your island home. 4433 Panihi Road, Kapa'a, HI 96746. 823-9364 www.naturalhawaii.com/membersites/mahina ♀

Mahina Kai is an artist's former blue–tiled Asian–Pacific villa. Its name means "moon over the water." You can sip tea around a gorgeous Oriental *koi* pond atrium, or bask by the outdoor lagoon swimming pool surrounded by elegant Japanese gardens. The two–acre property also includes banyan trees and Royal Hawaiian palms. Personal paintings and art adorn the three Japanese–inspired rooms, complete with *shoji* sliding doors, and there's also a separate two–bedroom apartment. Gay popular with straight ownership. P.O. Box 699, Anahola, HI 96703. (800) 337-1134, 822-9451 www.paccww.com/mahina/mahina.html

Mohala Ke Ola is a serene gay–owned guest retreat with four reasonably–priced private rooms. Plenty of peace and quiet is offered by the surrounding state forest. Awesome mountain and waterfall views encircle the pool, hot tub, and sunbathing deck, and be sure to take advantage of the on–site *lomilomi* Hawaiian massage, Reiki, or acupuncture. Hiking to Secret Falls &

Sleeping Giant is possible from the house, and kayak and bicycle rental is offered. A tropical breakfast is served by the warm and friendly owner Ed, who offers you his knowledge of the island and environment. 5663 O'helo Road, Kapa'a, HI 96746. (888) GO-KAUAI, 823-6398 www.waterfallbnb.com

Ole Kama'ole's Beach House (Ole the Barefoot's Beach House) are two new cottages fronting a black sand beach just three miles from the mouth of Waimea River. The bright roomy interiors sport open beams, ceiling fans, and oil paintings, and sleep up to six. Breakfast groceries are supplied by the gay caretaker who lives on the property, and the whole place couldn't be more private. You can catch a glimpse of Ni'ihau from the spacious windows and deck, as well as surfers at the point nearby. 8663 Kaumuali'i Highway, Kekaha, HI 96752. (800) 528-2465, 337-9113 www.virtualcities.com/vacation/hi/k/hik17v2.htm

Pali Kai Bed & Breakfast offers a remarkable 360–degree view of the North Shore and three mountain ranges from its hilltop perch. Every window looks out on to an incredible view, whether it be mountains, waterfalls, or ocean. Every comfortable room has cooking facilities and well–stocked refrigerators. A hot tub, a brand new lap pool, and nearby hiking trails to beaches are all available. For even more privacy, check out the 1,000–foot cottage built on the hillside. The clientele is almost purely gay and lesbian, and the very helpful owners Janie and Barbara will supply you with beach chairs, boogie boards, and snorkeling gear. A treat to visit. P.O. Box 450, Kilauea, HI 96754. (800) 335-6968, 828-6691 www.palikai.com ♀

Rainbow Valley Vacation Rental is run by Ken and Dennis who rent two family–style rooms on the side of their large secluded home with shared baths, a downstairs living room, and a large kitchen. Each quiet room has its own entrance, small refrigerator and microwave. The property offers spectacular sunset views of the coast above Kealia Beach, where gay community bonfires are held. P.O. Box 3936, Lihu'e, HI 96766. 822-4155

Royal Drive Cottages are tropical bungalows offering peace and privacy, just south of Kapa'a in the hills above Sleeping Giant Mountain. Situated on a private drive, the grounds are lush and cloistered, with fruit trees for the guests' picking. Cottages come with kitchenettes and garden views. Owned and operated by a gay man and a lesbian, the cozy establishment caters to both genders, and the on–site hosts offer guests their knowledge of hidden Kaua'i and other islands. 147 Royal Drive, Wailua, HI 96746. 822-2321 www.planet-hawaii.com/royal ♀

CALL ME BASHFUL

Ed Stumpf
....
Acupuncturist, owner Mohala Ke
Ola Bed and Breakfast

"The local Asian and
Polynesian bashfulness
makes Kaua'i a great
place for someone as shy
as me. It's a mellow place to be gay."

Non–Dorothy Digs

Princeville Resort was originally dubbed "the prison" by locals who weren't thrilled at the originally dark and inward structure. Completely gutted and renovated in 1991 at something close to a 100 million dollars, the hotel holds the plum spot on Kaua'i's North Shore. Every room looks on to an immense and perfect view of Hanalei Bay. Although the weather is a bit unreliable, the spectacular setting, golf course, shops and restaurants make up for it, not to mention the posh furniture, fountains, statues, and marble floors. Not for the budget traveler! 5520 Kahaku Road, Hanalei, HI 96714. (800) 826-4400, 826-9644

Kauai Coconut Beach Resort is a large, cement–looking structure that is actually quite clean and comfortable. The hotel is adjacent to the scenic but not–great–swimming Waipouli Beach, sitting amid eleven acres of coconut trees. There are 309 plantation–style rooms, a forty–foot waterfall cascading into a reflecting pool, a spa, restaurants, and a full–on authentic lu'au to boot (which can be viewed from the hotel parking lot for you cheapskates). The gay–friendly staff will not ask who's the man and who's the woman when you check in. P.O. Box 830, Kapa'a, HI 96746. (800) 222-5642, 822-3455

Bar Crawl ◆

Not Queer but Oh Well

Tropix (formerly called Sideout) is along the main highway in Kapa`a. A small and sports-style bar under queer ownership, it's a mixed place where different genders and orientations show up to slam 'em down. There are some seats fronting the street, windows opening all around, a big screen satellite TV, plastic chairs, and a mixed atmosphere of locals and lost tourists. The place has evidently risen above its seedy beginnings.

Lambda Aloha Pride Pins available here. 4-1330 Kuhio Highway, Kapa`a, HI 96746. 822-7330

Eating Out

Happy for Gays

Eggbert's, at the Coconut Plantation Marketplace in Waipouli is half gay–owned, and omelet connoisseurs appreciate their egg specialty dishes. Their Eggs Benedict comes in five styles and two sizes, with their world–famous Heavenly Handmade Hollandaise. Breakfast is served all day and dinner has recently been added to the menu as well. General manager Gordy has been a restaurateur in Kaua'i for over twenty years, when the island "didn't know what an omelet was!" 4-484 Kuhio Highway, Kapa'a, HI 96746. 82-BERTS (822-3787)

Mango Mama's Fruit Stand Cafe is a tropical fruit and smoothie stand, right along the highway in Kilauea, just before the 23 mile marker on the *makai* (ocean) side of the road. Owners Liz and Brie proudly proclaim they have the best smoothies in Hawai'i, and their no sugar, no syrup concoctions like Kaua'i Creme (banana, coconut, passionfruit and guava), with optional organic spirulina or bee pollen, will make you a believer. The stand has local baked goods, date bars, ginger snaps, and fresh vegie sandwiches on whole grain bread. Liz also acts as info central of local women's events and happenings. Highway 56 at Ho'oku'i, Kilauea, HI 96754. 828-1020, 245-0505 home1.gte.net/lizbrie/home.htm ♀

Not Queer, but Oh Well

Beach House is affiliated with A Pacific Cafe on O'ahu and Kaua'i. This classy restaurant, surrounded by condos, offers drop–dead views of the ruby sunset, the ocean, and surfers from its popular bar and dining area. The atmosphere is clean, modern, and yes, gay–friendly. *Pupus* like Salmon Firecracker and Grilled Fish Nachos adorn the menu, as well as entrees ranging from Sauteed Duck Breast with White Peach Ginger Glaze, or Mysteriously Aromatic Indonesian Giant Shrimp. 5022 Lawa'i Road, Koloa, HI 96756. 742-1424

INTERNATIONAL HAWAI'I

Kímo Lauer

Photographer

Born and raised on O'ahu, Kimo is a photographer for a number of magazines including *Detours* and the covers of *Odyssey*, as well as the official photographer for the Miss Universe pageant. Having studied at the Honolulu Academy of Arts and lived in Los Angeles, his work is characterized by high fashion. His bold black and white portraits feature intriguing models, many of whom are local residents and first–timers in front of the camera. Kimo explains, "I'm trying to bring more high–profile, international work into Hawai'i, to invigorate the local scene." 3731 Kanaina Avenue, #249, Honolulu, HI 96815. 737-1371 www.hawaiiscene.com/lauer

INTERNATIONAL HAWAI'I – CONT.

Caffe Coco calls itself an art gallery/espresso bar/caffe and no one is apt to disagree. Housed within a restored wooden plantation home with a gravel parking lot in front, the funky eatery has photo montage table tops, local art on the walls, outside garden seating, and a tin roof. There's an antique and collectible shop next door. Breakfast (turkey sausage omelet), lunch (Thai noodle salad with peanut dressing), and dinner (spinach fettucine with ahi and roasted tomatoes) are served with tons of daily specials to boot. All produce is local and fresh and every dish tastes gourmet. Also offered are daily tasting of their homemade jams and salsa, live music on the weekends, and the gay coffee club meets here on Saturday evenings. 4-369 Kuhio Highway, Wailua, HI 96746. 822-7990

Gaylord's is located within the grand Kilohana Plantation Tudor mansion, now transformed into an upscale artsy shopping complex. The restaurant's courtyard vistas look over the sprawling lawns, lending to the plantation ambience of the property. Named after a member of the prominent Wilcox family (I didn't include it just because it sounds queer, okay?), the menu offers dishes like lamb with exotic chutneys and grilled duck with mango sauce. Gorgeous setting and tasty food. Off of Kaumuali'i Highway (50), just south of Lihu'e. 245-9593

Spending the Gay Dollar $

Remember Kaua'i is a shop owned by Charlie and Darryl and Sam (yes, you read that correctly). Located in the lobby of the picturesque Outrigger Kauai Beach Hotel north of Lihu'e, the little shop holds many interesting items of jewelry and Kaua'i memorabilia. There are carvings, framed pictures, pocket knives, and Asian art, as well as the must–have Lambda Aloha Pride Pins. The same owners run one of the souvenir booths at Spouting Horn near Po'ipu. 4563 Kuli Road, Lawa'i, HI 96765. 245-6650

You've Got A Friend

AA Alternative Lifestyles meets Sunday nights at St. Michael's Church in Lihu'e. Call Bill at 245-1770.

Aloha Movie Nights for men and women happen on alternating Saturdays. Call Jason at 245-5939.

Bisexual Network is a local supportive group that meets regularly. Call Dawna at 821-1690.

The Coffee Club is an informal mixed social group that meets at the Caffe Coco in Wailua on Saturday nights. Call Jim at 822-1017.

Lambda Aloha Organization Freedom Network runs the gay info line at 823-MAHU, with calendar updates and a brief directory. Extensive listings at www. aloha.net/~lambda

Malama Pono is the HIV service agency for Kaua'i in Kapa'a, with an informative newsletter of community

SOMETHING SPIRITUAL

Jason Yaris

Education/Volunteer Coordinator at Malama Pono AIDS Agency

"I grew up right on the beach near Waimea, then I left for O'ahu, but I returned to take advantage of this island's beauty. This place is home, and I feel protective of this island. There's something spiritual about the sunsets here. I never get tired of it."

events. 822-0878. www.planet-hawaii.com/malamapono

Queer–themed videos
(co–ordinated by Lambda
Aloha) are periodically on
broadcast Ho'ike, Kaua'i's
Public Access Channel 12. You
can access their interactive
video bulletin board before or
after broadcast hours by calling 246-3600.

WELCOMING GAYS

Martin Rice
Political activist, co-founder of
Lambda Aloha

"We have such a welcom-
ing, inclusive community,
and we're always happy
to see visitors."

Women's Events calender is available from Hui `O Wahine at 245-0505, and
include monthly breakfasts, potlucks, bonfires, and movie nights.

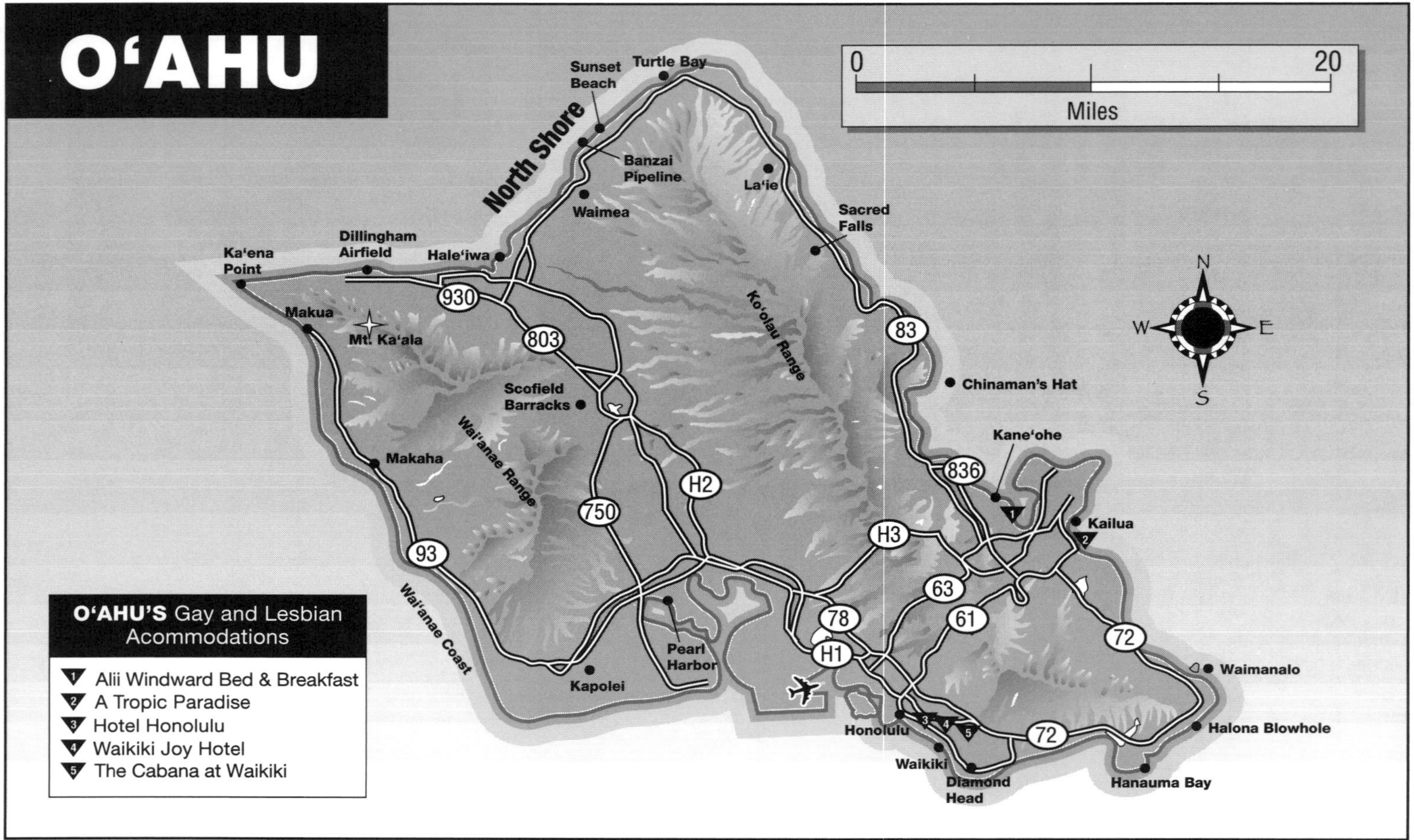

O'AHU

O'AHU'S Gay and Lesbian Acommodations

▼ 1 Alii Windward Bed & Breakfast
▼ 2 A Tropic Paradise
▼ 3 Hotel Honolulu
▼ 4 Waikiki Joy Hotel
▼ 5 The Cabana at Waikiki

Miles

0   20

North Shore

Ka'ena Point
Makua
Mt. Ka'ala
Dillingham Airfield
Hale'iwa
930
803
Makaha
Wai'anae Range
Scofield Barracks
93
Wai'anae Coast
Kapolei
750
H2
Pearl Harbor
Waimea
Banzai Pipeline
Sunset Beach
Turtle Bay
La'ie
Ko'olau Range
Sacred Falls
83
Chinaman's Hat
Kane'ohe
836
H3
63
61
78
H1
Honolulu
Waikiki
Diamond Head
3 4
5
Kailua
2
72
72
Waimanalo
Halona Blowhole
Hanauma Bay

CHAPTER 5

O ‘ A H U

Diamond Head standing stoically behind Waikiki.

Island Facts for Trivial Queens

Oʻahu is nicknamed: "The Gathering Place"	**Highest point:** Mt. Kaʻala at
Island color: Yellow–orange	4,003 feet/1,220 m
Flower: Ilima	**Rainfall:** 25 inches/64 cm in Waikiki,
Land mass: 597 sq. miles/1,552 sq. km	158 inches/401 cm in Manoa Valley
Population: 870,000 est.	

Over 75% of the state's population lives on Oʻahu. It's the site of the only *inter-state* highways in Hawaiʻi, and the only royal palace on U.S. soil, the ʻIolani Palace. The longest river in Hawaiʻi is the Kaukonahua Stream at 33 miles.

Why Bother?

It's painfully obvious that O'ahu is technically classified as *the beaten path*. Waikiki as a word has become synonymous with tourists – not just hundreds, but thousands of 'em, streaming off jets from colder and less welcoming origins around the globe. Sheer concrete reaches towards the clear sky, horns honk above sounds of the soft beach, and steep dark green mountains stand quietly in the background.

Honolulu was a thriving new gay mecca in the '70s, where recently liberated fags and lezzies flocked to the carefree beaches and accepting society. Waikiki was seen as new and exotic then, but twenty years down the line with mega–construction, traffic jams, and hoards of straight vacation–package families, the charm is a bit tarnished. Although nowadays gay travelers may be bolder to explore more off–the–track locales, Honolulu still serves as a central destination on your way to the neighbor islands or on to Asia. For singles, it has the only real gay nightlife in the state. Cozy couples are more emphasized on the quieter neighbor islands.

Once explored, the city of Honolulu reveals some surprising treasures outside the tourist ghettos. It's full of international architecture, scenic campuses and churches, funky restaurants, eclectic shops, and an astonishing mix of East and West in its peoples and outlook. Access to beaches, hiking trails, bike paths, and lush valleys is extremely easy in this metropolis in paradise. So don't just sit your butt on the beach all day!

For homo tourists touching its warm shores, Honolulu can present a dilemma. There's plenty of social tolerance, sun–kissed shiny bods, and let's–have–fun attitude, but quite a limited gay world to run around in. This is despite the number of tourists and the fact that a huge chunk of Hawai'i resides here. The last couple of years have seen a number of gay businesses close or move out of the former queer magnet of Kuhio Avenue. This splintering of Honolulu's gay district has meant the loss of synergy within the city's community. A new, equivalent gay area has yet to pop up in its place.

Silent auctioneers at the Gay and Lesbian Cultural Festival.

In addition, the state's main gay newsmagazine for almost a decade, *Island Lifestyle,* printed its last issue in August of 1998. The owners blamed financial concerns for the folding. Add to this the fact that many gays born and raised in Honolulu often head to the Mainland to really come out (and not to mention for higher paying jobs), and you understand the lack of queer cohesiveness compared to other U.S. cities.

Regardless of all this, Honolulu has been quite the queer pioneer. The *oldest* gay university organization in the U.S. is the *Gay and Lesbian 'Ohana* at UH Manoa. The Metropolitan Community Church, *Ke Anuenue O Ke Aloha,* is over a quarter century old, as is the local gay support group that meets on the roof top of the Hotel Honolulu. The community also holds a fancy Gay and Lesbian Cultural Festival in the summer. There are men's and women's choruses, an annual gay tennis tournament, gay boat cruises, and gay Lutheran, Mormon, and Catholic groups. And of course, Honolulu has been at the trailblazing forefront of the same–gender marriage movement in this country.

MELTING POT
 **David Waters**
Former owner of the Centaur Zone
"It's a real melting pot here: you see Japanese, Swedes, surfers, hapa haoles, Asians, straight people, gay people – everyone is co–habitating together in Hawai'i. It makes for a great people–watching crowd."

Honolulu is one of the most gay–friendly cities you'll likely encounter, with few gay bashings, a gay–positive state government, and a generally cordial hetero populace that will treat you and yours with warmth and respect.

Once you crawl out of the city that dominates the island, the rest of O'ahu is neat and despite the growing suburbs, fairly rural. On all coasts O'ahu has some of the finest surfing and white sand beaches in the state, as well as dramatic mountains and jagged cliffs. There are lots of hidden natural attractions worth spending a couple days or more to discover, so kick off your shoes, put on your sandals, and hang loose.

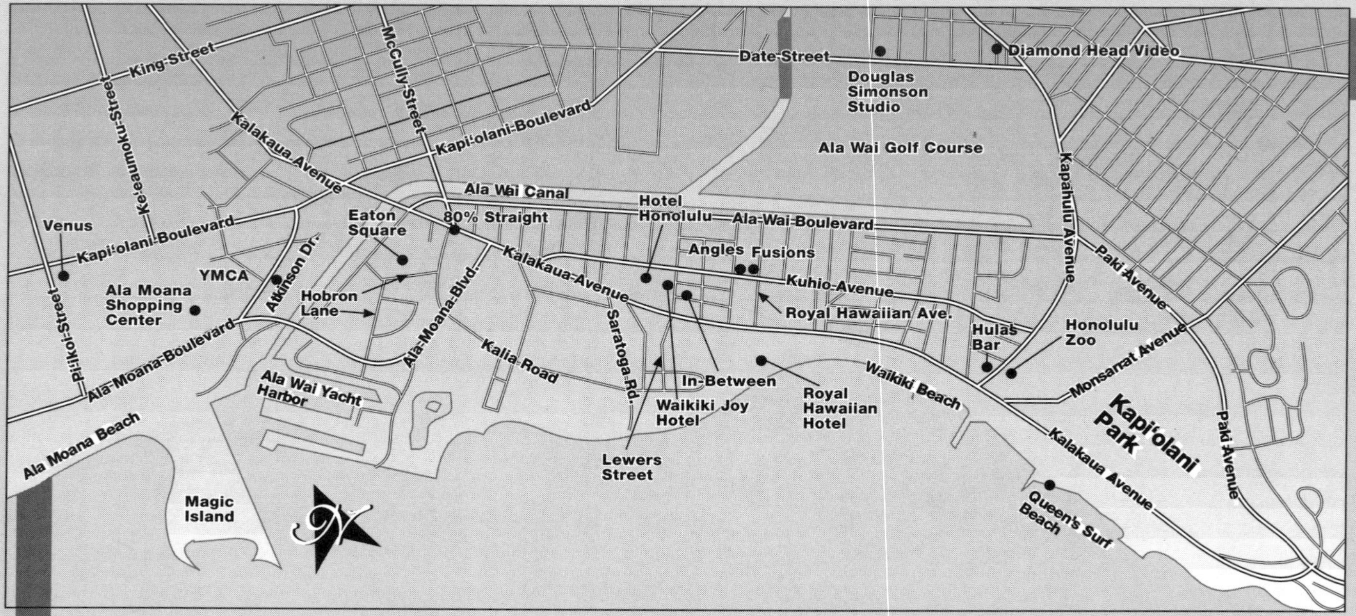

OʻAHU Waikiki

Paki Avenue

Kapiʻolani Park

Honolulu Zoo

Monsarrat Avenue

Kalakaua Avenue

Queen's Surf Beach

Kapahulu Avenue

Paki Avenue

Diamond Head Video

Douglas Simonson Studio

Ala Wai Golf Course

Date Street

Hula's Bar

Waikiki Beach

Kuhio Avenue

Royal Hawaiian Ave.

Royal Hawaiian Hotel

Angles Fusions

Ala Wai Boulevard

Honolulu

Hotel

Ala Wai Canal

In-Between

Waikiki Joy Hotel

Lewers Street

Saratoga Rd.

Kalakaua Avenue

80% Straight

McCully Street

Kapiʻolani Boulevard

Kalia Road

Ala-Moana Blvd.

Eaton Square

Hobron Lane

Atkinson Dr.

Ala Wai Yacht Harbor

Magic Island

YMCA

Ala Moana Shopping Center

Keʻeaumoku Street

Kalakaua Avenue

King Street

Venus

Kapiʻolani Boulevard

Piʻikoi Street

Ala Moana Boulevard

Ala Moana Beach

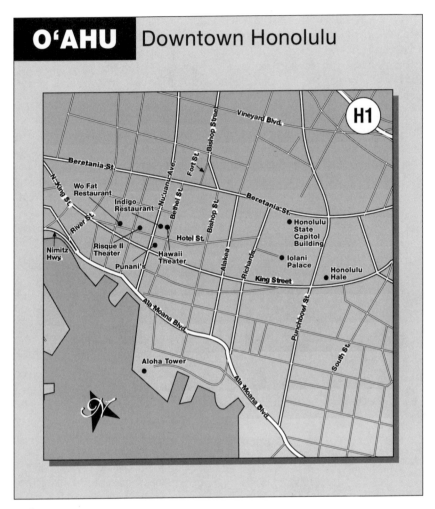

This Town

Waikiki refers to the long stretch of cement and steel along one of the world's most justifiably famous beaches. This is where most tourists (gay, straight or totally confused) congregate. The area of Waikiki is roughly outlined on the west and north sides by the Ala Wai Canal, and on the east side by the Honolulu Zoo and Kapi'olani Park.

Waikiki is Tourist Heaven and Tourist Hell, and can appear as an incredible, natural Pacific setting or a tacky concrete shopping mall. It is a mountain range of distinguished and undistinguished hotels and shops crammed along a mile of pristine white sand with a perfect series of smooth ocean swells. The jagged crater of Diamond Head overlooks it all. The peaceful yet polluted **Ala Wai Canal** acts as a city moat where you may spot canoe paddlers practicing. Remember the opening to **Hawaii Five-0** in the '70s, with the late Jack Lord looking cool standing on top of one of the Waikiki buildings? Well, there could be twice as many there now.

Nearly all established gay nightlife in Hawai'i happens in Waikiki, so be sure to get your fix here! The traditional **gay center** was up until recently a unique stretch along Kuhio Avenue between Kalaimoku Street and Lewers Street. The block was given relatively inexpensive rent for decades by the benevolent gay landowner Bob McGoon, who also owns the gay–friendly Eaton Square mall. Market pressures finally won out, and the funky Kuhio block of old shops and buildings was sold to make way for a modern shopping center (as if Waikiki needs another one).

The concrete jungle: Waikiki.

The original home of the famous **Hula's Bar and Lei Stand** (see listing) stood on the west end of the block. Nestled under a majestic banyan tree for nearly a quarter of a decade, it was a Honolulu icon, along with adjoining bars Trixx and Treats. The new home for Hula's (see listing) has opened across the street from the Honolulu Zoo on Kapahulu. It's on the second floor of the Grand Waikiki Hotel, with large windows overlooking the tranquil park. Since Hula's has always been the epicenter of Hawai'i's gay universe, other homo businesses are anticipated to sprout up around it in time.

The old Hula's entrance off Kalaimoku.

The only truly gay accommodations in Waikiki, the **Hotel Honolulu** (see listing) still stands solemnly on the east

A PIONEER

Tracy Ryan

A political pioneer of sorts, Tracy Ryan ran for the State Senate in 1996 as a Libertarian candidate. Her platform included the legalization of prostitution, marijuana, and same–sex marriages, as well as less government and less taxes. What made Tracy a trailblazer was the fact she is a **transgendered person,** and legally a female. Honolulu's gay community supported her bid, with many transgendered and transvestites helping organize fundraisers for her. A few days before the election, certain opponents ran a smear campaign against her in the Honolulu Star Bulletin, stating that she was "this transgendered man," even though she never hid the fact during the campaign. Regardless, Tracy went home with 31% of the vote – a very high percentage for the local Libertarian Party.

end of the Kuhio block. The hotel has been recently remodeled, and the gay-owned **Waikiki Video** stands right around the corner. And the twin homo bars of **Angles** and **Fusion** are spitting distance down the street. Many of the other gay businesses in the area closed down in the late '90s in expectation of the inevitable, and were not able to reopen elsewhere. Hawai'i's gay and lesbian community is still reeling from this giant loss, and the relentless paving of Honolulu continues!

The main faggy beach in Waikiki, **Queen's Surf** (see listing) is not far down the road from the location of the new Hula's on Kapahulu. It's a major social spot for the bikini–clad beach crowd. Further east around the point lies the gay –popular **Diamond Head Beach** as well (see listing).

Eaton Square, an enclosed courtyard–style group of buildings located in a section of northwestern Waikiki, also acts as a small gay enclave. A Waikiki rarity stands next door to it: an indispensable validated parking garage. Eaton Square has a couple of "private clubs" for men and the **Michelangelo** bar (see listing), albeit a bit hidden from the main streets. More gay businesses may pop up here in the future;

Stud at Queen's Surf.

Gay–friendly Eaton Square.

time will tell.

Now that the gay world is randomly sprinkled throughout Honolulu, get on your walking shoes since you will be doing a lot of trekking between Eaton Square on Ena Road to Fusion on Kuhio to Hula's on Kapahulu, not to mention to other bars like **Venus** or **Punani's** (see listings) located outside of Waikiki!

The city of Honolulu is by no means merely Waikiki. Head over the Ala Wai Canal on Ala Moana Boulevard, and you'll be out the clutches of Waikiki and in the grasp of the **Ala Moana Shopping Center.** Huge and monolithic, this multi–tiered monument to consumerism is Hawai'i's finest, and was the world's largest mall when it opened in 1959. Shops and department stores of every size and shape await your wad of tourist cash.

Across the street on Atkinson Drive is the **YMCA,** which harbors a spanking new gym. On the other side of the boulevard is the **Ala Moana Beach Park.** It's a pleasant beach where you may find the odd gay (so to speak), but it's mainly popular with local families who don't even want to deal with crowded Waikiki beaches. Further west on Ala Moana is the trendy **Ward Center,** with restaurants including **A Pacific Cafe** (see listing). Further on Ala Moana you will hit the conspicuous **Aloha Tower,** whose ten stories can be scaled for decent views of the city. Tourist cruise ships still dock here as in the olden days, and the area around the tower has been transformed into a tidy shopping plaza.

Many visitors completely bypass the **historic downtown** area, which is the general area tucked between King and Beretania Streets, behind the Aloha Tower. The district holds many architectural and ethnic wonders. The **'Iolani Palace** off of King Street is the only royal palace in the U.S. The impressive building was erected by **King Kalakaua,** known as the Merrie Monarch for his

Towering Aloha.

DEAR DIRTY DIARY

Honolulu's gay grand hotel.

The Hotel Honolulu has been *the* gay hotel in Honolulu since its opening almost a decade and half ago. Although nearby gay businesses have been razed, the hotel is still going strong with a fresh overhaul and new renovations. In the relatively short time span it's been open, the "Gay Liberation" movement has evolved tremendously, and the guest books left in the rooms of Hotel Honolulu act as a sort of random, confidential chronicle over this era.

Each occupant staying in a particular room in turn spilled their guts (almost literally!) on to the worn pages left for others to read. The books record happy drawings of rainbows, multi–page essays on relationships, stupid and hilarious poems, addresses and phone numbers left for contacting, vivid narrations of dark drug trips, recountings of sad and remorseful vacations, and of course pages of *blow by blow* sexual escapades acted out on the hotel's beds, floors, sinks, counters, balconies — some so excruciatingly descriptive you feel like calling the maid for a major spring cleaning before you sit anywhere. At press time, the ultimate fate of these chronicles when the hotel closes is unknown. But the memories of the Hotel Honolulu will live on forever in these volumes for generations to come. After all, aren't we all just one of this week's guest stars on *Fantasy Island?*

fab parties. Sadly, it was also the site of his sister **Queen Lili'uokalani's** imprisonment after American businessmen overthrew her in the late 1800s. They set up the Republic of Hawaii without U.S. government backing, but the federal government came in and snatched up the islands a few years later anyway. The palace was the state capitol all the way up until 1969, and was restored in the late '70s to its original splendor. The grand throne room features the original thrones of king and queen, and the Douglas fir floors around the palace are so polished that visitors must wear cute little booties over their shoes for the forty–minute public tours.

Just north of the palace is the current **State Capitol Building**. Looking some-

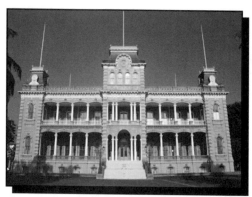

Home to queens and kings: 'Iolani Palace.

Slumming it up on Hotel Street.

thing like a '60s public library, it includes a four–story atrium, a courtyard paved with Moloka'i sand, two domes meant to represent volcanoes, and water surrounding them to represent islands (you'll get it if you look closely enough). It still looks a bit grungy despite a recent renovation, and the public is welcome sit in on Senate and House of Representatives sessions January through April, that's if you really feel like spending your vacation listening to politicians! Check out the strange squat statue of the revered Father Damien standing in the front of the building.

If you want to see what a *real* queen looks like for a change, check out the **Queen Lili'uokalani statue** between the palace and the State Capitol Building. In her hands, the monarch is holding a copy of a revised Hawai'i constitution and the hymn *Aloha 'Oe* (both of which the very intelligent woman penned), and the *Kumulipo,* the Hawaiian chant of creation.

From the statue, stroll up to the beginning of **Hotel Street**, which winds its way through the hustling financial and banking district of Honolulu. Just before you see two dragons on either side of Hotel Street, turn right up Bethel Street to check out the newly renovated **Hawaii Theater**. Art films and frequent gay and lesbian presentations are shown here. Once you pass those dragons on Hotel Street, you'll know by the old–fashioned store fronts, Vietnamese and Filipino eateries, and cluttered Asian supermarkets that you have entered colorful **Chinatown.**

This is where Hotel Street quickly degenerates into the splendid abode of video peep show parlors, transvestite prostitutes, and raunchy drug dealers (you may or may not feel right at home). This area has traditionally been on the seedy side, and

DO GAY GUYS SURF?

Ryan Best

An indigenous Hawaiian sport, surfing (like football and other heterosexually–dominated sports) is highly eroticized by gay men. The rippled young bodies carrying surfboards out into the waves is a favorite fantasy in gay images. But how does the reality hold up? Are there actual surfers who identify themselves as gay, and how do they fit into this unique world of men?

Ryan Best, who lives and surfs on O'ahu, writes software in his spare time. Originally from the Mainland, he's surfed in Hawai'i waters for years. "I've told people in gay bars that I'm a surfer, and their eyes kind of glaze over, like *Wow!*" he explains. Has he seen many other gay surfers? "Sometimes I see guys eyeing me out in the water, and it makes me wonder," he explains. "There have been other times I recognize surfers in gay bars. It's frustrating for me because there are all these good looking guys out there on the waves, but for the most part they won't risk it . . . the surfers know that there's cruising at some of the beaches, but they usually won't venture in. As far as local resident surfers being out, at least in a Mainland sense, it doesn't happen too often. I have one other gay surf buddy and he's pretty closeted."

Ryan describes Hawai'i as a very tolerant place, but ironically, due to its size many people don't feel free to come out since everyone knows them. "A lot of the time it's an understood thing, and people don't need to tell everyone they're gay. **But the surf world can be homophobic,** even paranoid about it at times. I tried to start a group of gay dedicated surfers and I barely received any calls. You figure the amount of surfers out there, you know there has got to be a lot of gay ones."

True, it was hard to find many other gay surfers to interview. Beyond a lesbian who owns a surfing school on Maui for tourists, the horizon was empty. But I did hit upon Scott, who is also out and originally from the Mainland. "I don't surf all the time, but when I do go out, I go with my two other gay buddies. We just kind of do our own thing, and the other surfers can think whatever. You know, it's like, *'Eh? Boddah you?'* If you got a problem, my friend is twice your size!' "

Ryan also took a gay friend out surfing once, and the guy began singing Broadway show tunes from his surfboard! "That didn't go over too well to say the least." Even without many out–of–the–closet surf comrades, Ryan still hits the waves regularly. "To be out there with it quiet, away from cars and cellular phone and everything, it's just you and the ocean. There's a certain peace to it all that can't be duplicated any place else."

once included the district dubbed "Hell's Half Acre." It was actually worse off during World War II and thereafter, when numerous brothels serviced the men in uniform. The pink–painted Armed Forces YMCA nearby was a notorious cruise spot, since WWII was quite the peak of free sex in Honolulu. Numerous clean–ups of Chinatown have been instigated over the years, including a current high–tech one complete with video cameras. But it seems the area still reverts back to its old perverted self regardless.

On Nuʻuanu Avenue in Chinatown, one block up from the Hawaii Theatre, you will find some art galleries as well as **Punani's** and **Indigo** (see listings). A little further up you can slum it up at the skanky **Risque II** theatre (see listing). Top it off with a meal at **Wo Fat,** Hawaiʻi's oldest restaurant at the corner of Hotel

Chinatown's Wo (not Wow) Fat Restaurant.

and Maunakea Streets with an exterior that resembles a Chinese temple.

Along Maunakea Street are many **lei stands** where aunties sit around and string some of the best garlands of fresh flowers found on Oʻahu. It's a welcome scent in all the noisy commotion. The whole artsy, ethnic area of Chinatown is attracting more and more of a homo crowd recently, so keep your gaydar well tuned.

O'ahu in a Mac-nut Shell

One worthwhile trip out of Honolulu is up the Pali Highway, right behind Punchbowl Crater. This road takes you up the green **Nu'uanu Valley,** where many of Hawai'i's royalty are buried at the **Royal Mausoleum.** Many historic homes of various architectural interest line this four lane highway, and about half way up on the south side of the road is the driveway to **Queen Emma's Summer Palace.** A few bucks forked over to the Daughters of Hawai'i, who lovingly restored and run by the place, and you can walk through the affluent interior. There are large *koa* wood four-poster beds, royal feather plumes, and paintings of the *ali'i* adorning the walls. There are also a side building where you might catch quilters at work and a nice gift shop with Ni'ihau shell work, cards, trays, quilted pillows, and other take-me-homes.

Continue up the highway, and before you enter the first tunnel follow the signs for the **Nu'uanu Pali Lookout.** You, standing next to every other tourist currently on O'ahu, will behold an impressively wide view of the windward coast. The towns of Kane'ohe and Kailua are sprawled out before you, with sharply carved cliffs swinging downwards. The sheer drop-off is where King Kamehameha infamously forced nearly 400 of the island's warriors over the *pali* (cliff) to plummet to their deaths far below, securing his victory over O'ahu.

Douglas Simonson's painting of the Nu'uanu Pali battle.

Head out of Waikiki towards the east on Monsarrat Avenue, and you'll hit **Diamond Head.** Arguably the most famous landmark in the Pacific, this extinct volcano was named by a group of stupid British sailors who mistook the calcite crystals they found

Where tourists and fish meet: Hanauma Bay.

POLYNESIAN HERITAGE

Kawika Trask
....
Owner of Punani's

"Being gay is part of the Polynesian heritage. There are *mahus* all over the South Pacific and honey, everyone's got a muffy in their family! They're the ones who take care of the family, look after the kids. Maybe no one talks about it, but they're accepted."

there for gems. The Hawaiians call the crater Le'ahi instead. Tons of visitors take the time to drive up past the Kapi'olani Community College and through the tunnel into the crater, where you can hike up through military shelters and ramparts to vista points. The absolutely splendid 360–degree views of southeastern O'ahu offer a gorgeous perspective of the city.

Drive out of Honolulu eastward on the H–1, and the road will become narrower and change into the Kalaniana'ole Highway (72), then lead past **Hanauma Bay.** Only ten miles from the city, this arid cove offers good snorkeling for the throngs, and I mean throngs, of eager tour buses that flock here. Take some sturdy shoes and hike out to the point on the left side of the bay (about fifteen minutes) to the attractively named **Toilet Bowl.** A must for you scatologists, this formation in the rocks allows for swimmers to sit inside a large cavity as the sea water rushes in and then flushes you back out like, well, a turd.

About a mile further east on Highway 72 is the **Halona Blowhole** (not what you're thinking), which you can see from the lookout parking lot. Down to the right is **Halona Cove,** where that horny beach scene between Burt Lancaster and Deborah Kerr took place in *From Here to Eternity.* Look inland along the highway and to make out the **Koko Crater,** which tradition tells us is the imprint left by the vagina of Pele's sister Kapo (what a woman!).

Making your way around Makapu'u Point, you'll spot where people pull over to hike out to the pretty lighthouse on the point. You will soon pass Makapu'u Beach with the cheesy **Sea Life Park Hawaii** nearby. Although touristy, the park offers pleasant aquariums and dolphin shows. Check out the two islands offshore: the bigger one is Manana (Rabbit) Island, named not only because it appears as a sitting rabbit but that hundreds of the varmints live on it too.

Heading north from here you will pass some ranching country and a polo club. Then you'll spot the longest continuous stretch of sand on O'ahu, the nearly four and a half mile–long **Waimanalo Beach,** famous for its rental car break–ins. If you're lucky, the *pali* (cliffs) along this coast will be void of clouds, offering dramatic vistas of weather–worn fingers of green cliff rising out of the sea.

LOCAL BOY MAKES IT BIG

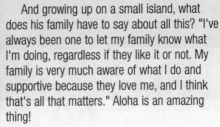

Tony West

For those who get off on porn trivia scraps, you will be happy to know that Hawai'i has produced some regional talent – namely in the form of **cute local boy Tony West.** Born and raised on O'ahu, Tony left the island for stardom in L.A.'s gay porn world, starring in a number of projects including *Sharp Shooters,* where he was hog–tied in long johns and gagged with a bandana (there's no accounting for art). Tony explains, "In gay porn it's always black or white, and I'm considered the gray area. I'm Asian, but don't look it, even though I'm proud to be Japanese. Most gay porn emphasizes only big corn–fed white boys, topping some little boy like, well, like me!"

And growing up on a small island, what does his family have to say about all this? "I've always been one to let my family know what I'm doing, regardless if they like it or not. My family is very much aware of what I do and supportive because they love me, and I think that's all that matters." Aloha is an amazing thing!

For you addicted one–handed fast–forwarders, check out these titles for a taste of porno Hawai'i (most featuring only big corn–fed white boys with bad tans): *High Tide* by Falcon, *Hawaiian Illustrated* and *Hawaiian Dreams* by All Worlds Video, *Hawaiian Desire* by HIS video, and of course, you guessed it, *Dallas Does Hawaii* from Bacchus.

The highway then wanders into the bedroom community of **Kailua,** known for its excellent year–round windsurfing and swimming beach. **Kane'ohe,** once famous as the site of the island's mental hospital, is now another suburban sprawl just north of Kailua. Here you will find the **Windward Bed and Breakfast** (see list-

Byodo-In with the Ko'olau mountains behind.

Whooping it up at the PCC in La'ie.

ing). The new H–3 highway that also leads into this area is said to be the most expensive freeway ever built, and many residents tried to thwart its construction for years. This scenic stretch of freeway–on–pillars is also shaping the windward coast of O'ahu into a major crowded strip–mall satellite city, just like how they do it on the Mainland!

North out of Kane'ohe on the Kahekili Highway is the beautiful Valley of the Temples, which is home to the Japanese temple of **Byodo–In.** This stunning replica of a 900 year old building in Uji, Japan is open to the public. The site makes a dramatic image with the verdant Ko'olau Mountains looming behind. If you choose instead the coastal Kamehameha Highway out of Kane'ohe, you'll notice a somewhat less cultural sight offshore: **Coconut Island** was used for the opening credits of *Gilligan's Island.*

Inching your way up the windward coast, the highway winds around some lush landscape, past the Kualoa Beach Park and **Chinaman's Hat** (Mokoli'i). If you still have those sturdy shoes, it's said the 500–yard walk out to this scenic island can be accomplished at low tide. Further north are some deep valleys including the **Sacred Falls State Park.** This park offers a great hour and a half trail that is unfortunately renowned for washing out hikers with flash floods.

The green landscape opens up to the town of **La'ie**, the Mormon heart of Hawai'i. Hate 'em or love 'em, this freshly–scrubbed clan has built, among other things, the **Polynesian Cultural Center** and the Brigham Young University campus nearby. A lot of the Pacific Islander college students work at the PCC, demonstrating authentic crafts and dances from numerous island groups. But the overall corny Hollywood atmosphere of the place, not to mention the outrageous admission price, is enough to make you think twice about entering. Still, it remains one of the major tourist attractions in Hawai'i, so up to you.

Yummy! Yummy!

Past La'ie you will find the only major resort on O'ahu outside of Honolulu, the uneventful **Turtle Bay Hilton,** with a couple of Arnold Palmer–designed golf courses nearby. Along this part of the coast keep you eye out for the popular **shrimp trucks,** where motorists pull aside to chow down on the little critters, lunch–wagon style. Past the town of Kawela is the notorious **North Shore,** with some of the best and most intense surfing on the entire planet. You'll understand why surfing originated in Hawai'i when you witness the monstrous, multi–story walls of water plummeting the coast line every winter.

Die hard experts hit the surf along **Sunset Beach** and **'Ehukai Beach,** the latter being home to the infamous Banzai Pipeline. Loads of surfers and their admirers park along the highway to watch the death–defying display. The most popular of the North Shore beaches is **Waimea Bay Beach Park** further south, and parking is typically tight. Waimea holds the record for the biggest waves ever surfed in a competition: over thirty–five feet. Each December is the Triple Crown tournament, where surfers from around the world vie for prizes in the six–figures.

For other suicide shows, head up the nearby **Waimea Falls Park** where cliff divers hurdle sixty feet into a waterfall pool five times a day. The park charges a good fee for all this adrenalin, and also offers dances and demonstrations. Exquisite gardens line the valley, which used to be settled by hundreds of ancient Hawaiians.

Taking the plunge at Waimea Falls Park.

Surf capitol of Hawai'i: Hale'iwa.

A few miles further is **Hale'iwa,** the main town on the North Shore, filled with surfers and wanna–bes, not to mention those pesky tourists. There are plenty of eateries in shopping malls along here, and be sure to stop by **Matsumoto's** tin–roofed general store for some of the best shaved ice (Hawaiian snow cones) that the islands offer. The county gives **free surf lessons** as well as windsurfing, sailing, and canoe lessons from September to May at the Hale'iwa Ali'i Beach Park in front of town.

Head west on Highway 930 from here, and there's not much along the coast except scenic, rugged mountains and the **Dillingham Airfield.** It's here where cool glider rides and sky diving are offered to the public (call 677-3404 and 637-9700 respectively for info). The nearby **Mokule'ia Army Beach** is popular with personnel and their brats. The road dead ends at Ka'ena Point. A railway once joined this area with the western Wai'anae Coast, but it was washed out in the tidal wave of '46. This stretch of road is called the Farrington Highway, as is the other section around the point.

LOTS OF WANNABES

Coco Chandelier

Honolulu's celebrity drag queen

"Everyone shows up to our shows: straight people, co–workers, and lots of wanna–bes! People like it when I emcee, since I gossip and talk shit about everyone…Drag is probably more socially acceptable here, since Hawai'i is so kick back about everything."

Backtrack on 930, then head south through central O'ahu and the military town of Wahiawa, better known as home to the **Scofield Barracks**. It is said to be the largest permanent army post in the U.S. If you like military culture (there's a strange phrase), you can get tattooed at the parlors and beat up at the bars here. Take Highway 750 south instead of lugging it on H–2, since the former offers views of pineapple and corn fields at the feet of the Wai'anae Range.

OUT IN PARADISE

Media is a powerful tool for education and influence, and one the gay world is slowly beginning to take into their own hands. *Out in Paradise,* **Hawai'i's only gay, lesbian, bisexual & transgendered TV show,** is viewed in O'ahu on Channel 52 on Sunday nights at nine. It's a mixture of politics, personalities, revelations, and the various sexual tease (to keep the viewers happy).

Originally called *Out and About,* the name changed when the pioneering John McDermott took over as producer in '94, creating over thirty one–hour shows about the gay community, shot by a skeleton crew on a bare–bones budget. Ironically, heterosexual viewers make up nearly all of the show's audience. John explains, "I have more straights calling up being supportive of the show than gays in the community. Amazingly, there's been only one really negative call over all this time." The modest show was one of the first to cover new AIDS drugs, local military same–sex scandals that went nationwide, and the on–going struggle for same–gender marriage in Hawai'i. For the future, John hopes to eventually air the show on the neighbor islands as well, "So we can have some cohesion in the community, and support what each other are doing."

When you hit H–1, head west and it becomes the Farrington Highway (I hope you're looking at a map). It takes you past Barbers Point and what is being dubbed O'ahu's "Second City," **Kapolei.** The area is being primed as the next mini–metropolis outside of Honolulu. The highway then heads north along the hot and dry **Wai'anae Coast,** which many local folk of Hawaiian, Samoan, Tongan and other Pacific Islander descent call home. Although there have been some resorts erected here, the locals aren't famous for extending gobs of aloha to the nosy tourists. Behind the highway are eloquent valleys winding their way along the shore line. Surfing is also big here, and the **Makaha Beach Park** holds annual long board competitions in February.

Venturing past Makaha a few miles, there's the once–sacred **Kaneana Cave,** where *kahuna* (priests) used to perform rituals in the cave's

A scenic, shadowy day at Makua Beach.

HONOLULU'S HOOKER HISTORY

It's been said that ever since the first Europeans arrived on Captain Cook's vessel, Hawai'i has known prostitution. The first European sailors paid for a night with a Hawaiian woman with one iron nail. By the 1800s inflation had kicked in: half an hour cost a whopping $1.50. Thus, an excellent way to spread venereal and other diseases, which led to great sickness and death in the local population, was formed.

Queer writer W. Somerset Maugham spent some time in Honolulu in 1916, where he visited **the infamous district of Iwilei.** This area had been set up as a walled legal red–light district of sorts. Maugham described in detail desolate streets full of garish houses with blaring gramophones, where Japanese and American prostitutes would expose their breasts to passers–by. Eighty years later, Iwilei is now home to Honolulu Community College and the Hawai'i Children's Museum!

Miss Sadie gets down with the boys.
(DeSoto Brown Collection)

One lady of Iwilei, evicted by police from her work place when the district was finally shut down, climbed aboard the ship Maugham took to Pago Pago in late 1916. Maugham never even spoke to her on that voyage, but this boisterous sex worker became renowned as the basis for his famous short story *Rain,* later made into three Hollywood film versions and a Broadway show. The actual name of that unknown shipmate? None other than *Miss Sadie Thompson.*

Before World War II, many women in the sex trade became quite wealthy and prominent on the island, exemplified by Jane Russell in the movie *The Revolt of Mamie Stoker.* During WWII the prostitution industry boomed, as well as free and easy homosexual cruising on the beaches and parks. Although it was a financial heyday for the happy hookers, the gals had it rough. By rule of the police chief they couldn't own property nor automobiles, they couldn't marry military personnel, they couldn't dance, visit golf courses, sit in the front seat of taxi cabs, visit neighbor islands, or phone or wire money to the Mainland without the madam's permission (talk about tough love!). Regardless, **Hotel Street** in old downtown blossomed as *the* place to get laid for servicemen – a deserved reputation that spread throughout the Pacific wartime theater. In the film *From Here to Eternity,* set at Schofield Barracks, the effervescent Donna Reed played a somewhat coded WWII Honolulu hooker hankering after real–life queer Montgomery Clift.

Nowadays, you will find many female streetwalkers near the tourist centers on

HONOLULU'S HOOKER HISTORY – CONT.

Donna and Monty eyeing one another.
(Desoto Brown Collection)

Kalakaua Avenue in Waikiki, strolling around looking for trouble. Their male counterparts sometimes hang out on Kuhio Avenue, and guess what? Many are straight and on drugs – surprise, surprise. Hotel Street still holds its crown as Sleaze Central, with its video arcades and drug dealers, but with a '90s twist: a good number of the prozzies down here now have a big surprise taped tightly up between their legs for potential customers to discover. Let's see Donna Reed try to top that!

inner chambers. Now beer drinkers and graffiti artists do the same. Further north is the **Makua** area, with a picturesque and often empty white sand beach, site of Lahaina for the filming of *Hawaii* in 1966. Sadly, Hawaiians living in the area were forced out of their settlements when the U.S. military took over the beautiful valley for bombing practice. The road dead ends again soon after, with Ka'ena Point in the distance. If you're really into it, hike the unshaded yet pleasant trail a few miles around this bend, which makes up the western–most tip of the island.

On your way back to the rat race of Honolulu, you will go through **Pearl City** and more proverbial mega–shopping centers. Do your patriotic and tourist duty by stopping by **Pearl Harbor** off Highway 90 and wait forever for the free boat ride that takes the *millions* of annual tourists to the **USS Arizona Memorial.** Built over the visibly sunken ship, the memorial is a rather reverent affair, with oil from the vessel still oozing up to the water's surface. The average age of the Arizona's casualties was a mere nineteen years old (talk about chicken!). There's also a submarine museum, and the newly added **USS Missouri,** on which the Japanese signed their surrender.

Memorial as tourist trap: USS Arizona.

All of Hawai'i on display at Bishop Museum.

On your way back into town, don't forget to stop at the remarkable **Bishop Museum** for a stirring gaze into life in Hawai'i. It's right off the H–1 freeway near the turn–off for the Likelike Highway. An amazing, expertly organized museum full of mechanical displays and interactive exhibits, there are revolving subjects on everything from Polynesian exploration of the Pacific to the newly–restored Queen's Carriage in the Kahili Room to Japanese cultural contributions to ancient Hawaiian artifacts. If you don't see it at the Bishop, it never happened!

Tell Me When You're Coming

In mid–February, Honolulu is the home of an annual international gay and lesbian tennis weekend tournament, the **Aloha Tennis Open** (834-6656), which enjoys good turn out from the community. The annual **AIDS Walk** around

Making a splash at Gay Pride.

Kapi'olani Park is in mid–March (521-2437), and receives a lot of hetero involvement as well. **Gay Pride** is a rather small affair in June compared to other Mainland cities. This could be due to the fact that lots of gay residents hop on a plane to L.A. or San Francisco for their June pride fix (Honolulu's happens the third weekend in June). However, Honolulu's Pride celebration is growing each year, with 500 participants at last count. The Gay & Lesbian Community Center (951-7000) puts together a prominent parade from Ala Moana Boulevard to Kapi'olani Park, with related festivities at bars and hotels.

The **Honolulu Gay and Lesbian Cultural Festival** (941-0424 ext. 18), which incorporates **The Adam Baran Gay & Lesbian Film**

Festival, (named after the late VJ at Hula's), happens after Pride in August. The festival offers an array of queer happenings, such as drag musicals, poetry slams, queer comedians, key note speakers, dance performances, and of course lots of gay and lesbian cinema with an Asian accent, shown at the Hawaii Theatre and throughout town. Honolulu is famous for her hometown enchantresses: there are a number of annual drag pageants, the biggest being **Universal Show Queen** (593-1416) in April or May (depending on the mood), packing 'em in at the mainstream Ilikai Hotel. **The AIDS Dance–a–thon** is put on by Pacificare (521-0344), and the boogying happens in late September at the Dole Cannery Ballrooms. **Halloween** is a surprisingly large public street event, with men in drag and tourists galore packing the sidewalks of Kalakaua Avenue. The city hasn't gotten to the point of closing off the street to traffic, so sauntering the few blocks through masses of bodies may take up a good chunk of the evening.

> ### LOHA LAMBDA WEDDINGS
>
>
>
> ### Scott Tambling
> Minister for Aloha Lambda Weddings
>
> "When even the tough women cry during their wedding ceremony, we know we've done a good job. An element of grace comes down when we're administering vows – a God–felt sensation of a spiritual union. We do marriage in the eyes of God, and it's a blessing to have that opportunity."

Queer Pages ⚓

Da Kine is the new gay publication for Hawai`i that took the place of the now-defunct Island Lifestyle magazine. The professional, snazzy layout includes local gay news, calendar of events, columns, and state-wide listings. Don't leave Hawai`i without one! 2410 Cleghorn St. #2302, Honolulu, HI 96815. (808) 923-7378

Odyssey is a local mag that covers the bar and club scene, with party pics and great gossip columns, and this is where you'll at long last locate the photographic escort ads. Check out their snappy web site too. 1750 Kalakaua Avenue, Suite 3247, Honolulu, HI 96826. 955-5959 www.hawaiisecene.com/odyssey

The Pocket Guide to Hawaii is published three times a year by Pacific Ocean Holidays, and its handy pages include street maps of gay Honolulu, coupons for gay vendors, and coverage of neighbor island businesses. P.O. Box 88245,

Honolulu, HI 96830. 923-2400 www.gayhawaii.com

Things For Homos To Do ✥

Aloha Lambda Weddings offer one–stop shopping for your same–sex (although technically illegal) marriage, with packages on Oʻahu and other islands that can include valet, tuxedos, and honeymoon. Ceremony sites range from chapels to rainforest valleys to botanical gardens. 2979 Kalakaua Avenue, Suite #304, Honolulu, HI 96815. (800) 982-5176, 922-5176 global-www.aloha.com/gaywed.htm

Lambda Travel Hawaii offers help with local gay–friendly accommodations, as well as personal hike, bike, scuba, or fishing tours on Oʻahu by the personable Scott. 2979 Kalakaua Avenue #304, Honolulu, HI 96815. (800) 982-5176, 922-5176 www.global-aloha.com/lambda.html

Leis of Hawaii have gay–friendly airport greetings by two hunks with leis (or two babes), and offer limousine service, activity reservations, and more. (888) 534-7644, 732-7134. Check out their jam–packed web site at www.leisofhawaii.com

Men Au Natural of Hawaii host biweekly nude social events, including bay cruises from Waikiki and "weenie–roast" BBQs on dry land, with visitors always welcome. P.O. Box 235426, Honolulu, HI 96823-3507. 591-3826 www.tnight.com/maka/manoh

Rainbow Charters offer gay whale watching, snorkel, sunset cocktail, or commitment ceremony cruises from Waikiki. Captain Gaelyn and her friendly crew will let you take the helm of the spacious forty–foot sailboat, which is comfortable for two to eight people. P.O. Box 75422, Honolulu, HI 96836. 943-2628 (943-BOAT). ♀

Taking the Plunge is a queer–owned and operated underwater tour guide service. They offer a wide spectrum of diving opportunities, from intro dives to night dives to multiple–day underwater photography classes to shipwreck exploring to expert wall dives! 922-2600, 941-5497. ♀

Thing for Homos to See ✥

Douglas Simonson Studio carries work by the native Nebraskan who has been a mainstay of the Honolulu arts scene for over fifteen years. He is now internationally known for his male nudes, mainly of strapping young Asian and Pacific Islander men. Works are priced anywhere from $25 to $25,000, and Simonson is happy to arrange private showings at his Date Street studio. 4614 Kilauea Avenue #330, Honolulu, HI 96816. 737-6275 www.douglassimonson.com

Gay and Lesbian Community Center Library is staffed by volunteers and open for visits whenever the office manager is in (call first). Monday evenings are when the tiny but proud library offers readers gay and lesbian magazines and reference material from around the world. Don, the helpful librarian, will also answer any burning questions you might have on local gay life. Book and magazine donations accepted. Located at the YWCA. 1566 Wilder Avenue, Honolulu, HI 96815. 951-7000

Honolulu Academy of Arts includes thirty galleries displaying world–renowned European and American Masterpieces, a permanent Oriental collection, and the best of Hawai'i's art. There are over 33,000 pieces in all! Queer artists like Paul Gauguin and Georgia O'Keefe are represented, as well as frequent exhibits that include Andy Warhol and Frida Kahlo. The handsome tile–roofed building opened as a museum in 1927, and the landscaped courtyards are filled with tropical plants and sculptures. New York architect Bertram Goodhue designed the structure, which is a blend of Hawaiian, Oriental, and Western styles. Donation requested. 900 Beretania Street, Honolulu, HI 96814. 532-8700

Risque II Theater, located on Chinatown's seedy Hotel Street, should have been named Risky Theater (you will know why when you see the crowd on the street). Downstairs is your basic straight and gay 24–hour porno shop, made complete by video games and pinball. Ten bucks gets you upstairs to the male–only gay theater, which is really a smelly sex club/bathhouse–type of set up, only without the baths (although there are a couple of scummy showers). Large dark rooms with videos and smaller rooms with locks – you get the idea. 32 North Hotel Street, Honolulu, HI 96813. 545-2891

Letting it All Hang Out ◆

Quiet morning at Queen's Surf.

Queen's Surf Beach – what could be more perfectly named? This is the main gay beach in Honolulu, actually an eastern–most section of Waikiki Beach. It's near the grand yet currently abandoned war memorial Natatorium (just past where Kapahulu Avenue meets Kalakaua Avenue). Here's where tourists and *kama'aina* gather in the sand and on the grassy lawn,

HONOLULU'S BARFLY HISTORY

Back in the swinging '70s, Honolulu's **most infamous gay bar** was named the Blow Hole, bordering Kapiʻolani Park on Kapahulu Avenue. Guys would come in off the beach at Queen's Surf, strip down at the bar, and jump into the Blow Hole's large warmed pool, which would be jam–packed by evening's end. The bar and dance floor were on the ground floor of a now–defunct hotel, and in true Waikiki fashion, a grocery store now sits where this Honolulu gay landmark once thrived. As one '70s survivor describes it, "It was a wild and crazy time, just after the hippy era of sexual revolt, and even when you went to the bathroom, people were mighty free with their hands. People are a little more respectful of each other now!"

Another popular Honolulu dance club, especially with the young crowd, was The Tomato. The Lava Bar, another homosexual hang out, did business in the same building that gay–owned but straight–dominated The Wave now resides, and near that was the popular Gay Nineties. **Ryan Idol** got his start dancing at Fusion and the now–closed The Answer. Another popular spot was The Balcony. The Steamworks, on the old Kuhio block, was the busy gay bath from the 70s up until the 90s when it finally closed.

If you go back far enough, the big gay bar in the '50s and '60s was called The Clouds, on Kapahulu off Kalakaua. It was frequented by the *creme–de–la–creme* discreet queer community of the time, but went downhill by the '70s. And The Wagon Wheel, near the formerly gay Kuhio block, was gayish even in the '40s.

History, as always, does indeed repeat itself: in the same proximity to where the ghosts of The Blow Hole and The Clouds dwell, Hula's now operates on the same street overlooking Kapiʻolani Park, a stone's throw away from Queen's Surf.

Speedo bulges protruding towards the sun and all eyes a–gawking. There's a new pavilion built behind the beach, near where you'll see some old–time queens playing bridge in bikinis. The volleyball areas on the grass are where gay groups play on Sundays and Wednesdays. There's usually a collection of local families having their picnic *grinds* as well. Check out the local gang of beach bums at www.global-aloha.com/qsbeach, the official web site of Queen's Surf.

Diamond Head Beach is the other gay beach area in Honolulu besides Queen's Surf. Take Kalakaua Avenue east until it merges with Diamond Head Road, below the famous crater. Walking access is from the main road, down steep cliffs to a rocky shore line, or better from the small off–shoot road before the cliffs called Beach Road. The narrow strip of sand around the point is at times more nude than others, especially under the lighthouse. Here alcoves and rocks act as a natural protectorate for the you're–my–endless–love–for–ten–minutes brand of male bonding. Lots of surfers and windsurfers frequent this area too, and it's always a good idea to not be too bold. Many cars park on the other side of Diamond Head Road, where the vertical paths heading up the crater are for those who are agile and feeling drastic enough to cruise them.

Place to Put Your Head

For Sure Queer

Ali'i Windward Bed and Breakfast is also located on the windward side of O'ahu overlooking Kane'ohe Bay, thirty minutes from Honolulu. This cozy B&B offers two bedrooms: the Victorian Room and the Circus Room, filled with antiques and teddy bears. Both have private baths, and there's a pool with views of Kane'ohe Bay. You've got the run of the house, and afternoon tea is included! 46-251 Iki'iki Street, Kane'ohe, HI 96744. (800) 235-1151, 235-1124

A Tropic Paradise is a modern, elegant home in Kailua on the windward coast that offers a locale literally steps away from the beach. Friendly owners Ken and Alex provide beach mats, towels and coolers. The three Asian and Polynesian decorated bedrooms are private and large, and there's a waterfall beside the tropical pool and spa. There are ocean and mountain views, cathedral ceilings, and a private entrance to the second floor suite. 43 Laiki Place, Kailua, HI 96734. (888) 362-4488, 261-2299. 1.gte.netdarreld

The Cabana at Waikiki is a brand new, relaxing gay inn off Kapahulu Avenue, not far from Hula's and the beach. The four-story property is gay-owned, and its fifteen units are light and decorated in vintage Hawaiian. Each suite has a secluded lanai, and some also have full kitchen and living areas. Guests are offered an intimate tropical verandah to meet and mingle, as well as a whirlpool, and complimentary continental breakfast and parking is included. The friendly staff will be happy to help you out with local gay info. Cartwright Street, Honolulu, HI 96815. (877) 902-2121

Hotel Honolulu borders the old gay block on Kuhio. Its recent renovations have helped the gay old hotel, which is conveniently centrally located in Waikiki. After fifteen years, it's still one of the only outright gay lodging in Honolulu. The downstairs is filled with foliage and caged tropical birds cackle as you check in. All rooms come with private bathroom, kitchenette, and private lanai. Spend the extra money for the front deluxe units facing the quiet dead end street. The staff are cordial, and join their gay group on a dinner cruise of Waikiki Bay on Wednesday and Friday nights. 376 Kaiolu Street, Honolulu, HI 96815. (800) 426-2766, 926-2766 www.lava.net/~hotelhnl

Waikiki Joy Hotel is owned by the Aston chain, with a gay–friendly management that is advertising to the homo market. A premier, ninety–four room boutique hotel composed of two towers, there's an Italian marble open–air lobby with fountains, and each room features a lanai, in–suite jacuzzi, complete stereo system, and the executive suites have full kitchens. There's a cafe and restaurant where complimentary breakfast is served, fifteen person private karaoke rooms, and a sauna and small pool downstairs as well. Close to the old gay Kuhio block. 320 Lewers, Honolulu, HI 96815. (800) 922-7866, 923-2300

Non–Dorothy Digs

Coconut Plaza Hotel is a mainstream all–suite boutique hotel that is gay– and lesbian–friendly. A bit smaller than other Waikiki hotels, all eighty rooms are conveniently equipped with refrigerators and microwaves, and a complimentary continental breakfast is served downstairs every morning. Each room has a lanai, and views cost extra. The service is great; they go out of their way to make you feel that aloha spirit, which adds to the charm of the place. 450 Lewers Street, Honolulu, HI 96815. (800) 882-9696, 923-8828.

Waikiki Grand has an advantage that no other Waikiki hotel can offer: you can take the elevator home after whopping it up at Hula's bar downstairs. The small rooms (over 170 in all) have TV, phone, and refrigerator but are nothing spectacular. The noises from the nearby zoo (no not Hula's) can get a bit much, but with a roof top sundeck and pool, not to mention good discount packages, this isn't a bad deal for Waikiki. 134 Kapahulu Avenue, Honolulu, HI 96815. (800) 535-0085

The Royal Hawaiian is world–renowned as the Pink Palace of the Pacific. This amazing glance into old Hawai'i was the traditional getaway for wealthy travelers and Hollywood elite since its opening in 1927 (with the nearby Moana Surfrider being built in 1907!). The tasteful if tiny rooms harbor four–poster beds, high ceilings, and massive closets made for ship loads of luggage. Everything matches the salmon

Spanish–Moorish stucco exterior, right down to the pink bathrobes and towels, not to mention the phones! The koa wood elevators take you down to the historic lobby, and there's a more modern but less fascinating tower addition on the eastern end of the property. 2259 Kalakaua Avenue, Honolulu, HI 96815. (800) 325-3535, 923-7311

Bar Crawl ❖

For Sure Queer

Angles is located above Kuhio Avenue, with a fun lanai overlooking the street action, New Orleans style. Two small separate bar counters are on either side of the stairway leading in, with a neutral tone interior. A friendly young staff makes you feel at home, and an inside dance floor borders the lanai (live DJ Thursday through Sunday). Tuesday night is Country night – the closest thing you'll get to a gay Western bar in the whole state! You will find a decent mix of the homo world here as with most Honolulu bars, with a leaning towards the youthful and possibly straight crowd. 2256 Kuhio Avenue, Honolulu, 96815. 926-9766, 923-1130 www.gawhawaii.com/angles

Dis N' Dat Lounge is a fun, casual hang out for Hawaiians, *haoles,* and locals, with Hawaiian singers and live bands drawing in a fairly gay and lesbian crowd, with a few straights thrown in for good measure. The former site of Punani's, there's a newly remodeled carpeted interior that makes for a cozy lounge feel, but with an informal "hang loose" neighborhood atmosphere. Dis n' Dat is more for sitting around "talking story" and listening to music than for dancing and cruising. 1315 Kalakaua Avenue, Honolulu, HI 96815. 946-0000

Fusion Waikiki, spitting distance from Angles, is the most clubby gay dance place in Waikiki. The second floor is a dark cavern with pounding music and a stainless steel dance floor, and upstairs a smaller dance floor with railings peers over. Because of an older liquor license that lets them stay open 'til four a.m., Fusion gets busy after two in the morning when most other bars close. Certain Sundays are Kids Club (over 18), where the downstairs becomes non–liquor, and their All Male Revue strip shows happen on certain nights of the week, as well as Paper Doll drag revues on weekends and amateur strip nights. 2260 Kuhio Avenue, Honolulu, HI 96815. 924-2422 www.gay-hawaii.com/fusion

Hula's Bar & Lei Stand ripped itself up from its two decade–old (almost twenty-five years) roots under a massive banyan tree on Kuhio, to the second story of the Waikiki Grand Hotel. Now indoors with views of a banyan tree and the zoo across the street from the seventy feet of open windows, it is still a unique place. Housed in a formerly huge Japanese restaurant, there's a dance floor, DJ, video

screens, and a casual lounge feel that attracts a daytime beach crowd. Most importantly, you'll find Basket & Buns or Wet Underwear Contests happening here, so don't worry. Although gay tourists in tank tops can at times outnumber locals within its walls, this bar is probably the most popular in Waikiki for *kama'aina* (island residents), with a mix of ages and backgrounds, since everyone always ends up here anyways. Hula's is a good place to have your first sweet and tall rum Mai Tai, an island visitor tradition. Different nights have changing themes (Shirtless Sundays, for instance), and Happy Hour is a good long 10 a.m. to 8 p.m. daily. 134 Kapahulu Avenue, Honolulu, HI 96815. 923-0669

In–Between (formerly CC's Bar) is Waikiki's "friendliest and only neighborhood bar," where locals and visitors meet without attitude. A small cozy bar with a low counter and private lounge feel, the entrance is down a side street off Lewers (behind Moose's), making for a personal and secluded feel. The walls are painted with dolphins and underwater scenes, and there's a karaoke machine, free *pupus* (appetizers) daily, drink specials, a Sunday brunch, and the location in the center of Waikiki makes for a convenient stop. A good place to relax and converse rather than standing around eyeing people. 2155 Lau'ula Street, Honolulu, HI, 96815. 926-7060

Michelangelo at the tucked–away Eaton Square has recently transformed itself from a karaoke spot to a "guys" bar, complete with Monday night football. The interior is sporty, with a pool table, jukebox, darts, low lighting, and no dance floor. Drink prices are some of the best in Honolulu, with a constant happy hour every evening. A full kitchen serves hot sandwiches, BBQ burgers, hot dogs, and other male chow. Club P–10A is right next door with its own private entrance and admission fee, and there is a door that connects the two establishments, now owned by the same proprietor. So you can cruise, play darts, and eat dinner all under one validated parking pass! 444 Hobron Lane, P8, Honolulu, HI 96815. 951-0008 www.gayhawaii.com/michelangelo

Punani's is a fun local queer bar, in a new location downtown, near Indigo restaurant. Known for its great array of Hawaiian and local singers, there's lots of seating around a small stage, with a private patio in the back. Large windows overlook the street in front, and there are cute bartenders and an interesting mixed crowd of races, sexes, and sexualities – a great slice of Honolulu life. There's a *pupu* menu of island favorites, and try their house specialty Punani Juice: rum, vodka, Amaretto, Southern Comfort, and three types of juices, a liquor bargain for about $4! 1041

Nu'uanu Avenue, Honolulu, HI, 96815. 526-9395

QM II is a strange, dark place that some of you may feel more at home in than others. Just down from the more genteel Dis N' Dat, this homo bar seems like it's been around the block a few times. Once your eyes adjust, you'll make out a small horseshoe–shaped bar, plastic chairs, a sticky floor, and large carved plaque along one wall. Definitely not a posing bar, the crowd here has been described as "looking like they're waiting to cross the River Styx." 1401 Kalakaua Avenue, Honolulu, HI, 96815. (no phone)

A COMMUNITY LEADER

Jack Law

Owner of Hula's, founder of the Honolulu Gay and Lesbian Film Festival and Cultural Festival

"When you think of all the wars and the hate being caused all over the world in the name of race, religion, and sexual orientation, you realize how special Honolulu is, the very fact that we can all get along on this little island."

Venus has the same ownership as Michelangelo in Eaton Square, but quite a different feel. Housed under a parking structure behind the Ala Moana Shopping Center (below China House Restaurant), a valet parks your car and a shiny hallway takes you inside a large carpeted dance club. There's a small bar on one end, with plenty of couches around the place, a glassed–in "private" room, and a dance floor where live entertainment like male strippers or drag shows take the stage five nights a week. The crowd varies from gay boys to lesbians to straight girls depending on the night, and the predominately young and Asian crowd has a good time getting down to the DJ dance mixes that last until four a.m. 1349 Kapi'olani, Honolulu, HI 96815. 955-2640

Not Queer, But Oh Well

The Mai Tai Bar at the Royal Hawaiian on Waikiki beach is a gay favorite for sipping colorful, expensive drinks, listening to music, and watching Honolulu's tannest, buffest bods float by in skimpy suits on "Dig Me" beach (as is the nearby Halekulani Hotel's white–pillared outdoor lounge called House Without a Key). It's a nice beach setting without the sand in your suit, for exhibitionists and their admirers. 2259 Kalakaua Avenue, Honolulu, HI 96815. 923-7311

Eating Out ◀▶

Happy for Queers

Caffe Giovanini is an exquisite little gay–operated coffee shop in the grand Italian style. Large windows overlook Kalakaua Avenue, with The Wave club across the street. The upscale atmosphere has classy tables and expensive local art on the walls, making for a Euro getaway in the middle of Waikiki. The deli sandwiches are made with only the finest cuts of roast beef and beef pastrami, and the Italian expressos and ice cream mochas are delicious. There's air–conditioning inside or seating outside under umbrellas. 1888 Kalakaua Avenue, Honolulu, HI 96815. 979-2299

Kahala Moon is a gay–owned restaurant located next to the Kahala Mall. The place has been a big hit since it opened in 1995 to uniform praise for its Pacific Rim and Hawaiian regional cuisine. Try the signature Portobello Mushroom dish or the fresh island Moi served whole, Chinese style. An on–site pastry chef whips up things like chocolate ginger essence cake and warm mango sweet bread pudding. The white stucco exterior gives way to an upscale island–style interior with *koa* wood accents, fresh tropical flowers, and local art on the walls. Valet parking, reservations recommended. 4614 Kilauea Ave, Honolulu, HI 96815. 732-7777

Keo's is a chain of restaurants throughout Honolulu, which includes the Mekong I and II, began by gay restaurateur Keo Sananikone. The latest addition to the chain is this flagship 250–seat eatery with a classy bistro feel that includes walls of teak doors that open to the outside and orchids grown on the North Shore by Keo himself (not to mention the herbs, bananas and other produce). Chosen by both *Bon Appetit* and *Gourmet* magazines as "America's Best Thai Restaurant," Keo's offers an enormous menu including Evil Jungle Prince (a blend of chicken, lemongrass, coconut milk, and red chilies), green papaya salad, and prawns in sweet peanut sauce. Reservations recommended. 2040 Kuhio Avenue, Honolulu, HI 96815. 951-9355

Not Queer, but Oh Well

Cha Cha Cha is Mexican/Caribbean restaurant authentic enough that you'll be afraid to drink the water, or so the owners claim. This funky, yummy eatery in Waikiki serves up Caribbean and Mexican fare, like tart Jamaican jerk chicken, tamales steamed in banana leaves, and rum and chocolate flan. The bright tropical setting above the street includes patio seating, fake parrots, cute waiters, a Reggae soundtrack, and a massive pail of tortilla chips served to your table. 342 Seaside Avenue, Honolulu, HI 96815. 923-7797

Eggs n' Things has been a late night institution for the famished party crowd for over twenty years. This fast–paced, clanky diner overlooking Kalakaua has menus on wooden boards and gay–friendly waitresses, not to mention lemon crepes, mahimahi and eggs, or macadamia nut pancakes. Often there's a wait for seats, so you can practice "Hawaiian time." Be sure to pick up one of their note pads disguised as a match cover for handing out phone numbers. Validated parking at the Hawaiian Monarch Hotel. 1911-B Kalakaua Avenue, Honolulu, HI, 96815. 949-0820

Indigo is a spiffy restaurant in downtown, right near the Hawaii Theatre and Punani's. The tasteful Chinese interior includes red calligraphy lanterns, or ask for an outside table in the back, where you can listen to a gurgling fountain along the old brick exterior. The menu is Eurasian, with offerings like Mahogany Tea–smoked Glazed Long Island Duckling with Peking Pancakes, Pagoda of Ahi, or Broth of Prosperity seafood soup. Live jazz accompanies your dinner. Voted one of the top lesbian–friendly restaurants by *Girlfriends* magazine. 1121 Nu'uanu Avenue, Honolulu, HI 96813. 521-2900

Irifune is a purely original Japanese restaurant on Kapahulu. In the same family for years, what used to be the entire restaurant is now a waiting room filled with snapshots of friends on the walls. The main dining room is an eclectic mixture masks, fishing nets, posters, and a ceiling with glow–in–the–dark stars and planets. The food is excellent value, with dishes like seared sashimi, pork katsu, and the house specialty garlic ahi served in a variety of styles, explained to you by the amiable wait staff. And don't miss the TV in the bathroom. 563 Kapahulu Avenue, Honolulu, HI 96815. 737-1141

A Pacific Cafe is a pricey but rewarding example of new trends in local cuisine. This elegant restaurant at Ward Centre is a must for the financially endowed, with a menu full of Asian and Mediterranean hybrids, with an emphasis on fresh island ingredients. Try the Japanese pear Riesling broth, or the crispy taro–crusted salmon with tomato and white bean compote. The large windows quietly look on to Ala Moana Beach Park. Reservations required. 1200 Ala Moana Boulevard, Honolulu, HI 96815. 593-0035

Spending the Gay Dollar ☉

80% Straight is still *the gay* store for Hawaii - not only do they have racks of club clothes (Body Wear) and tight-fitting things (Speedo) any good homo would have to buy, but they also act as the gay book and magazine store (yes, they carry *Rainbow Handbook Hawai`i!*), card shop, lube shop, naked calendar shop, rainbow towel shop, and more! Although they are now in slightly smaller digs than before on the Kuhio gay block, this is still the place in Honolulu where you run in for the leather hand cuffs on your way back to your hotel. 1917 Kalakaua Avenue, Honolulu, HI 96815. 941-9996

PERMISSION TO PAINT

Douglas Simonson

Originally from Nebraska and innately knowing he needed to be in a warmer climate, Douglas had been plotting to come to Hawai'i since he was eight years old, and finally did so at age nineteen. In the early '80s, after publishing best–selling books such as Pidgin to da Max, Douglas committed himself to drawing and painting the male body in a variety of forms. "I had always been an artist, but when I finally gave myself permission to paint naked men, I realized I had something to say …I think O'ahu has the most beautiful men in the world, even better than Brazil!" Simonson's world–renowned works are collected in two autographed book versions, or you can arrange for a private showing at his studio on Date Street in Honolulu. 4614 Kilauea Avenue #330, Honolulu, HI 96816. 737-6275 www.douglassimonson.com

PERMISSION TO PAINT – CONT.

Bay Sport Blue does not have an actual store front, but they sell awesome gay/lesbian pride activewear (T-shirts, tanks, caps, shorts, polos, henleys, longsleeve t-shirts and sweatshirts) out of Angle's bar in Waikiki as well as on the Internet. Their unique and colorful embroidered designs range from the subtle to the OUT. The intent of the company is to increase awareness of the GLBT community through visibility towards equality. 1090 A Kumukumu Street, Honolulu, HI 96825. (808) 395-7853 www.baysportblue.com

Diamond Head Video is Hawai'i's premier gay and lesbian video store, with over 30,000 mainstream and special interest titles, mainly crammed into their expanded back room. They offer everything from magazines, lube, and toys, to all–male CD–Roms and other one–handed necessities. Besides things for your crotch, they also have gay documentaries, foreign and hard–to–find movies. There are no booths or anything like that, but plenty of free cruising down the aisles, on the house! Free membership with credit card, free parking and VCRs available for rent. 870 Kapahulu Avenue, Honolulu, HI 96815. 735-6066 www.diamondhead-video.com

Island Treasures is an overflowing antique mall made for shopping hounds, next to the Hotel Honolulu. This triple–level store has anything and everything in Hawaiiana and Victorian, and you could easily spend half a day getting lost in its corridors. Over thirty dealers offer an array of items, from collectible toys to depression glass to tribal art! They proclaim to get about thirty pieces every day,

FOR THE FAITHFUL

Francis Duran

President of *Diginity* (Gay Catholics)

"Dignity helped me know what's right and wrong, within the Catholic faith and also in my own con-science. Although the church won't let us meet on their grounds, we feel the need to affect change within the church. If we break away, we won't have the influence."

and nobody doubts it. They will pack and ship anywhere, taking any form of payment. 2145 Kuhio Avenue, Honolulu, HI 96815. 922-8223

Newt at the Royal is a classy and distinctive gay–owned shop at the Royal Hawaiian Hotel. They feature the legendary highly–prized Montecristi Panama Hats hand–woven in Ecuador, as well as fedoras and plantation hats, and '40s and '50s retro–print tropical shirts, ties and belts. This neat little store run by Fred Newton holds some of the finest Hawaiiana apparel in the islands. 2259 Kalakaua Avenue, Honolulu, HI 96815. (800) 508-HATS, 922-0062

Waikiki Video is a jam–packed shop tucked behind the ABC store on Kuhio, with more gay and straight porn tapes crammed into its little aisles than you

THE ALOHA SPIRIT

Tania Jo Ingrahm

Former editor of *Island Lifestyle* magazine

"Hawai'i is not a large place, only one million people statewide, and our communities are spread across five major islands. Overall, the local people are accept-ing. Hawai'i is laid back…people don't get upset as easily about things as Mainlanders do, and that is also seen in relationship to gays and lesbians. For many people in the non–gay community it's just not a big deal. The aloha spirit is here."

can shake a, well, stick at (almost 600 to be exact). Included is a section of very rare Asian titles only available at this store. Besides Colt, Falcon, and Catalina, they also carry mainstream Hollywood vids, magazines, lotions, and five different types of legal Herbal Ecstasy! The clerks are courteous and will help you find any title you desire. 2139 Kuhio Ave #108-B, Honolulu, HI 96815. 926-3613

Pump You Up ⚑

24 Hour Fitness, in the tourist area of Waikiki, is not really cruisy but gay–popular with locals and tourists alike. The treadmills, bikes and cardio equipment face the large windows on to one of the best sunset views of Waikiki on the island. The atmosphere is more laid back than serious power–lifting, and there is no steam room nor jacuzzi, but a co–ed sauna. Ask about their weekday aerobics class right on the beach! Yes, your Mainland membership will work here too. 2490 Kalakaua Avenue, Honolulu, HI 96815. 971-4653

The Gym is a warehouse–style gym close to Downtown, with three large, well–lit sections with the works: lots of free weights, treadmills, upright bikes, stair climbers, and aerobics. Mainly local straight weight lifters frequent the place, but The Gym is partly gay–owned, and helps out at gay fundraisers. But with no steam room or sauna, and no cruising, you either work out or get out. Short term membership available. 435 Keawe Street, Honolulu, HI 96813. 533-7111

Max's Gym and Health Club is actually two facilities in one. The small gym would please any gay body builder with heaps of free weights, sports trainer equipment, and lots o' mirrors to admire oneself in. But most guys go there for the adjoining "health club," which has both a sauna and a steam room, lockers, private video rooms, one public one, and guys with hard–ons. You can either get a health club membership, which includes access to the gym, or you can opt for a gym–only membership for a day or longer. The thing is, you can't waggle your weenie as you wander in from the health club: the gym requires shoes and shorts so those BB's won't lose concentration! Located on the fourth floor of Eaton Square. 444 Hobron Lane, Honolulu, HI 96815. 951-8232

P–10A is not really a gym at all, but I guess one could get "pumped up" here. This private club for men located next to Michelangelo at Eaton Square offers a pool table, coffee and tea (no alcohol), inexpensive private video rooms and two public ones, and a relaxed atmosphere – meaning you don't need to take *all* your clothes off when you walk through the door. Basically a bathhouse without the bath, with a more genial (but still horny) clientele. Call ahead for live male erotic show schedule. Suite P–10A, 444 Hobron Lane, Honolulu, HI 96815. 942-8536

You've Got A Friend ◆

Life Foundation Volunteers with safe sex kits.

AA Gay/Lesbian Group offers daily meetings in the heart of Waikiki with free parking. 946-1438

Affirmation is a group for gay and lesbian Mormons that meet at members' homes. Call Jim at 941-0578.

The AIDS Hotline on O'ahu is 922-1313, and the Honolulu AIDS agency, the Life Foundation, offers help at 521-2437.

Aloha Metropolitan Community Church holds Sunday evening meetings in Makiki. 223-5715

Blazing Saddles is a gay country line–stepping group that meets at the clubhouse on the Ala Wai Golf Course. Call Calvin at 941-4769.

Dignity Honolulu holds Sunday socials for the GLBT Catholic community. 536-5536

The Gay and Lesbian Community Center has some recorded visitor information and a volunteer staff who can return query calls at 951-7000.

Gay Community Directory is offered by the Gay and Lesbian Education and Advocacy Foundation and can return collect query calls at 532-9000.

Frontrunners at the annual AIDS walk.

Honolulu Frontrunners meet twice weekly at Kapi'olani Park, and welcome visitor joggers, walkers, and runners. David at 922-3252 or Joanne at 843-8121.

Honolulu Gay Support/Rap Group meets weekly on the third floor of the Hotel Honolulu, with guests welcome. 532-9000

Honolulu Men's and Women's Choruses hold two public performances a year, usually around Pride and World AIDS day. Call conductor Andrew at 524-0935 for info. ♀

***Ke Anuenue O Ke Aloha* Metropolitan Community Church** meets every Sunday evening at the Church of the Crossroads. 924-3060

Lesbian Support Group meets weekly at the Fernhurst YWCA Teahouse. ♀

289-8811, pager.

Likehike does minor to major gay hikes and camping around the island and around the state. Call Ed at 455-8193.

Marriage Project Hawai'i is a group supporting the legalization of same–gender marriage. Call 942-3737, or make a donation at 1-900-97-MARRY.

Mary Magdalene Society is a gay Lutheran group that meets for potlucks and social events quarterly. Call Thomas at 926-1944.

Men's Drop–in Massage Group is a nurturing non–sexual get together in Waikiki on the third Saturday of each month. Visitors welcome. Call David at 922-3252.

Na Mamo O Hawai'i (Hawaiian Lesbian and Gay Activists), is a group dedicated to fighting racism in the gay community and homophobia in the Hawaiian community (see sidebar in Chapter One). 595-0402

Our Family Christian Church is a gay–positive Christ–centered congregation that meets in Makiki on Sundays. 926-3090

Out In Paradise, Hawai'i's only Gay, Lesbian, Bisexual & Transgendered TV Show, can be viewed on Channel 52 on Sunday nights (see sidebar). 923-8829

Pacificare promotes the well–being of persons living with HIV/AIDS. 521-0344

PFLAG's O'ahu chapter meets on the second Wednesday of the month. Call Carol at 672-9050.

Task Force on Sexual Orientation is a university organization located on the UH campus at Manoa. 956-9250

Transcendence is an O'ahu organization for transgenders and transsexuals. Call Lee at 534-0008, or Pam at 922-4787

UH Gay, Lesbian, and Bi 'Ohana is a supportive group for college–age people that meets twice monthly. 955-6152

Weekly Meditation Group is an outreach to the GLBT community held at the Unity Church of Hawai'i. 922-3252

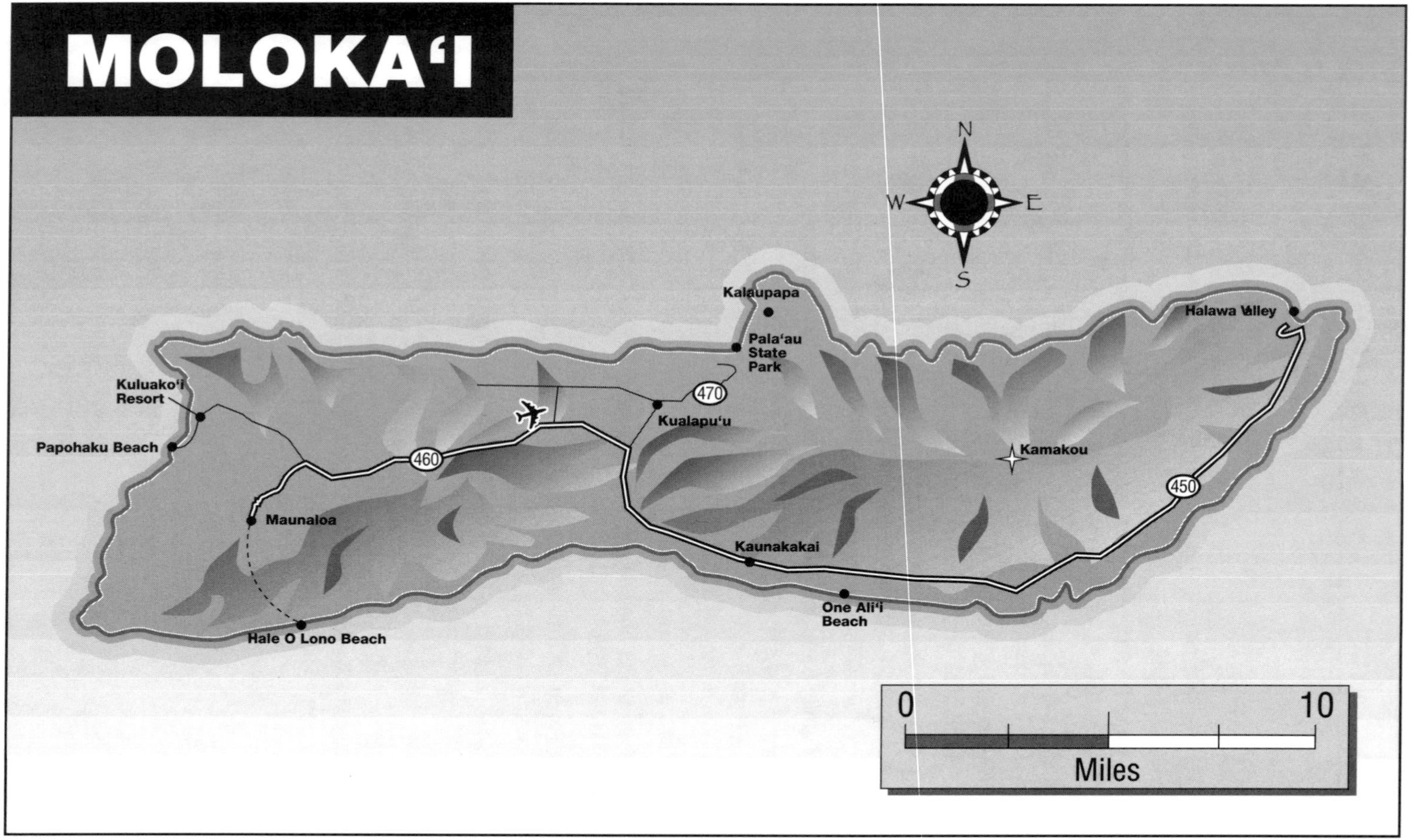

MOLOKA'I

Halawa Valley

450

Kamakou

Kalaupapa

Pala'au State Park

Kualapu'u

470

One Ali'i Beach

Kaunakakai

460

Maunaloa

Hale O Lono Beach

Kuluako'i Resort

Papohaku Beach

N W E S

0 5 10

Miles

CHAPTER 6

M O L O K A ' I

Moloka'i's staggering North Shore.

Island Facts for Trivial Queens

Moloka'i is nicknamed: "The Friendly Isle"
Island color: Green
Flower: White Kukui Blossom
Land mass: 260 sq. miles/676 sq. km
Population: 7,000 est.

Highest point: Kamakou at
4,961 feet/1,512 m
Rainfall: 27 inches/69 cm at the
Moloka'i Airport

Moloka'i has Hawai'i's highest named waterfall, Kahiwa, at 1,750 feet. Some of the world's highest sea cliffs are on the island's north shore at 3,300 feet with a 58–degree slope. World's largest rubber–lined reservoir is near Kualapu'u, holding 1.4 billion gallons of water.

Why Bother?

Visiting Moloka'i is like stepping into a time machine. This is *not* the place for glamorous parties or fancy shops: unhurried farmers and horses easily outnumber the tourists on any given day. The people here talk *slow* and drive *slow* since there's tons of Hawaiian time for everything. Besides the island of Ni'ihau, Moloka'i's residents have the highest percentage of Hawaiian blood than on any other island. Residents take pride in the fact that there are no traffic lights on the island, and no building is taller than a palm tree. If you want to see how Hawai'i was, and perhaps was meant to be, then Moloka'i's the place to head.

At first glance there seems nothing queer at all about this rural island. But little Moloka'i is not only known, but *renowned* for its resident transvestites, simply called *mahus*. Many live and work in drag, being accepted for who they are, and are affectionately called Auntie or Tutu. *Mahus* tend to be unassuming rather than glamorous in small–town Moloka'i, and it's hard to get across the island without bumping into one. They often work as wait help at the restaurants, so keep a lookout for a hairy arm with painted fingernails handing you that lunch special. By far they are at the forefront of the hula renaissance on the island, which many traditions say is the birthplace of hula. They stage local performances and win awards internationally.

The resident *mahus* are some of the nicest, most pleasant people you will be fortunate to meet on Moloka'i, and usually quite friendly despite the Molokaians' wariness of outsiders. The local populace is completely respectful towards the *mahus*, since they are an acceptable way to be "gay" here, and many *mahus* are integral members of the family. In fact, there are stories of certain Moloka'i police officers settling down and setting up house with *mahus*. Talk about approval!

Popular pastimes on quiet Moloka'i are cock–fighting (say what?), taro growing, and of course "talking story," since unemployment here is the highest in the state. New industries like coffee and eco–tourism on Moloka'i Ranch are being developed to curb the unemployment rate. And for a balmy island in the middle of the Pacific, there's an unfortunate widespread drug problem with *ice* (a smokable form of crystal meth) being the main demon.

Moloka'i was left on its own for a good portion of its history, perhaps due in part to stories of famous sorcerers who resided here. They were said to have carved poisonwood idols and concocted incantations to keep visitors at bay. Nowadays the residents are a tad more friendly, although perhaps not always as kissy–feely to tourists as the island's motto will have you believe. Don't forget you are a guest on this island, one of the least developed and least touristy in the chain.

This Town

Even the word *town* might be stretching it for **Kaunakakai.** If you blink you'll miss it, even if you're walking. The settlement has the distinct feeling of old rural Hawai'i. A quaint **town wharf** is near town, where teenagers hang out, ships unload, and the foundation remains of King Kamehameha V's vacation house sit nearby. If you

A "busy" day in Kaunakakai.

stood at the main intersection of Highway 460 and Ala Malama Street, you'll spot the **tourist information office** on your right. Walking up Ala Malama into town, you will see the snazzy little civic center and public library on your left.

Ala Malama curves around to the main drag into the heart of Kaunakakai, which lasts a whole whopping three blocks, complete with aged western store fronts. There are a few Filipino variety stores selling everything from local vegetables to shiny purses, a couple of places to eat, and some grocery stores. Whether it looks like it or not, this *is* the commercial center of the island. On the north side of the Ala Malama is the amazing **Moloka'i Island Creations,** a store that sells original Moloka'i glassware, coral jewelry, hunting gear, fishing hooks, cowboy hats, mounted animal heads, and anything else somebody might possibly want to pay money for. Next door is the small **Rabang's,** a divey and very ethnic Filipino diner.

A few doors further is a must–stop: the '50s–style **Kanemitsu Bakery,** which bakes *the* Moloka'i bread. Famous throughout the islands, pick up a round loaf of raisin–nut or onion–cheese, or their handmade crisp lavosh flatbread, for a delectable local experience. The bakery also has a small coffee shop that serves sandwiches and breakfast, with tacky painted murals of hula girls and a large relief map hanging on the wall. On Moloka'i, you can't get more local than this.

Moloka'i in a Mac-nut Shell

From Kaunakakai, head east towards the airport on Highway 460. You will spot the **Kapuaiwa Coconut Grove** just one mile from town. Ten acres of coconut palms planted by the young Kamehameha V make up one of Hawai'i's last surviving royal groves, where locals enjoying killing time and "talking story." Kapuaiwa translates as "mysterious taboo" – could it have something to do with all those enigmatic sorcerers way back when? Across the highway is another enchanted sight, **Church Row,** where various denominations are given a plot of land to set up shop right next to one another, side by side like reverent dominos.

As the highway begins to climb up from the dry grasslands, continue on to Highway 470 and make a left on 480 into the micro–town of **Kualapu'u.** The town

Kalaupapa from above.

was built by the Del Monte Corporation, who ran the pineapple plantations here until pulling out in the early '80s. The area is now trying its hand at coffee growing under the brand name Malulani Estate and Mule Skinner. You can buy coffee bags, carvings, gourds, flavored macadamia nut oils, and sample their 100% Moloka'i coffee at the **plantation store** – the green buildings on the right after you turn on to Highway 480. Further up the road is the **Kualapu'u Cookhouse** (see listing). If you really felt like it you could keep on driving through the dry, spread–out community of **Ho'olehua,** known for its ethnic Hawaiian population living on homestead lands.

Back on Highway 470 heading north, the scenery becomes a bit greener. You will soon pass the **Meyer Sugar Mill.** An admission fee gets you into the two buildings, one that houses

The rock hard phallic stone.

the last mill of its kind, with restored machinery and a century–old steam engine, the other with videos and displays on Molokaʻi's history. Further up are pasture lands and mule stables, then the road ends at **Palaʻau State Park.** This over 200–acre reserve offers remote picnicking and camping. You'll hit the dead end parking lot, and there's a choice of two trails. One leads to the **Kalaupapa Overlook,** where you gawk across the sheer cliffs to the leper colony of Kalaupapa below. The other trail leads up a wooded hill to the **Phallic Rock** (Kauleonanahoa) in a little clearing within an ironwood grove – not to be missed by any lover of prominent protrusions. The thrusting rock looks like it's been helped out by human hands a little. It has been said that women who spend the night here could become pregnant, but nothing's mentioned about men who slumber here (I dare you guys to try).

One thing the visitor to Molokaʻi should really try to do is visit the **leprosy colony of Kalaupapa**, one of the most soul–stirring journeys you can take in Hawaiʻi. A vertical, switchback hike down to the peninsula that takes about an hour and a half. But of course one should try to go by mule, since this is the fashionable mode of transportation to the colony (despite the erosion problems and mushy poo–poo on the trail). For you lazy bones, an air tour can zip you straight down into Kalaupapa, or show you the north shore cliffs. Any way you get there, you must hook up with **Damien Tours** to be able to see the colony. They take you around in a school bus and give you the all lowdown.

The quiet village holds fewer than 100 generally elderly people. Most are technically afflicted with leprosy, which is now called Hansen's Disease and is treatable by sulfone drugs (which means don't freak, you can't catch it.) For decades, the sick were forced to swim from offshore boats and fend for themselves at this remote outpost, completely disowned by family and burying each other in unmarked graves.

The four–hour tour includes a stop by **Father Damien's Church.** The building was named after the self-less Belgian priest who built the *entire* thing by himself, then died of leprosy shortly after in 1889. A true Christian, he devoted his life to bettering the lives of the colony's sufferers, and has become a much loved and revered figure in Hawaiian history. At

The church that Damien built.

CHICKEN–HAWK OF HAWAIIAN YESTERYEAR

Stoddard in front row with legs crossed and a hand on King Lunalilo. (Picture courtesy Bishop Museum)

Charles Warren Stoddard

An interesting footnote in American literature is the story of writer and poet Charles Warren Stoddard. A one–time secretary to Mark Twain and friend of queer poet Walt Whitman, this "Boy Poet of San Francisco" in 1864 at the age of twenty–one took off to Hawai'i for adventure. He found much more than he bargained for.

Corresponding with Mr. Whitman, he explained that among the islands he could act out his "nature" in a way he couldn't "even in California, where men are tolerably bold." Stoddard had not only fallen in love with Hawai'i's beauty and culture, but with many "coffee–colored," frequently nude teenage boys. His descriptions of rapturous evenings spent with island youths fills his stories with blatant homoeroticism, like passages from this story about a visit to Moloka'i in 1869:

"I was taken in, fed, and petted in every possible way, and finally put to bed, where Kana–ana monopolized me, growling in true savage fashion if anyone came near. I didn't sleep much, after all. I must have been excited."

and:

"Again and again, he would come with a delicious banana to the bed where I was lying, and insist upon my gorging myself…He would mesmerize me into a most refreshing sleep with a prolonged and pleasing manipulation."

Although racy enough to make modern readers blush, in the 1800s **homosexual escapades** were not even considered a valid reality, and many critics brushed Stoddard's work off as colorful and even silly. Stoddard traveled a number of times to Hawai'i and Tahiti, each time falling for "untrammeled youths," calling them by the intimate phrase "*aikane* – bosom friend." Usually Stoddard departed in an agonizing ending of impossible love.

In the autobiographical story "Chumming with a Savage," which took place in one of Moloka'i's lush north shore valleys, Stoddard slips out in the middle of the night by canoe, only to have his "little sea–god" Kana–ana rushing madly after him, compress time, a major movie was in production about the father's life, to be filmed in and around Kalaupapa.

From 470, backtrack and turn west on 460 towards the airport. You'll see the slumbering Maunaloa mountain range on the south side of the road. It was here that the goddess Laka is said to have learned how to dance, giving birth to the hula. The highway ends amid cattle land and the old Dole pineapple plantation town of **Maunaloa.** The bordering Moloka'i Ranch has recently been bought by a New Zealand company. The town's new huge face lift includes matching buildings and roofs, an actual paved road, cute shops (including the great **Big Wind Kite Factory**), the island's only movie theater, and yes, a Kentucky Fried Chicken! The spiffy town is also trying to attract an upcountry residential population with rows of quaint rustic homes.

On the right as you enter Maunaloa is the **Moloka'i Ranch Outfitters** Center (see listing). They arrange adventure tours on ranch land with mountain biking, horseback riding, and/or kayaking and gourmet lunch included. Who says there's nothing to do on Moloka'i?

If you really want to get off Moloka'i's beaten path (if you can find one), you can trudge down the dusty, red dirt road right next to the Outfitter's Center. The road progresses over cattle guards and past rodeo grounds with white cranes sitting on cows, and on down to the island's unpopulated southwestern shore. At the end of the road, you will find a small boat harbor and past that, the **Hale O Lono Beach,** which has been newly opened to the public by the state. Now popular with

Remote Hale O Lono Beach.

campers and fishermen, not to mention the odd jet ski, the beach and harbor also serve as the starting point of the annual Moloka'i-to-O'ahu outrigger canoe races. Further west from here are said to be more huge deserted beaches that are not on ranch land, awaiting the right adventurous explorer (is that you?).

Before you reach Maunaloa town on 460, you will find the turn-off at the 15 mile marker for the **Kaluako'i Resort** area. This is the island's only "touristy" spot, which isn't saying much. Originally, a much larger complex was planned to be built here, but the pleasant if aging redwood and *'ohi'a* structures of the Kaluako'i Hotel and adjoining condos fit well into Moloka'i's molasses atmosphere. In front of the Kaluako'i Hotel is the eighteenth hole for the golf course, as well as the lovely **Kepuhi Beach**, that unhappily presents often bone-crushing waves and killer currents.

Footprints on Papohaku Beach.

Sweet little St. Joseph's.

South of the Kaluako'i Resort along Kaluako'i Road is **Papohaku Beach.** This vast white stretch of beauty is one of Hawai'i's longest and most deserted beaches. Calm summer days are better for swimming, since the wind can get intense and there are rocky outcrops. The empty Papohaku offers some small sand dunes in the back which could be used for some discreet nude sunning, since there are few footprints on the sand, even on busy days. The beach cove at the very end of the road, **Dixie Maru,** is one of Moloka'i's better snorkeling spots, and popular with local families. Although it sounds like it, the beach wasn't named for a drowned tourist but a ship that sunk nearby.

Near Kaluako'i is the unique **Moloka'i Ranch Wildlife Park.** Antelope were originally brought over to control the spread of *kiawe* trees, and did so well that giraffe, eland, oryx, zebras, cranes, sika deer, and other exotic species were subsequently raised here for zoos and game parks. Sound neat? Well you can't visit it. Public tours of the park have been recently halted due to nasty insurance regulations.

Making your way back to Kaunakakai town again, head east on Kamehameha V Highway (450). You'll pass island homes along the shore, with views of fisherman knee–deep in water throwing nets along the shallow mud flats. There are a number of beach parks on this road, such as the pretty **One Aliʻi Beach Parks I and II,** good for picnicking and viewing the island of Lanaʻi. A few miles later on the right hand side of the road is a sweet one–room church built by Father Damien called **St. Joseph's,** with an unflattering statue of the father and a quiet graveyard.

A mile or so later is a soggy swamp where the **first Mainland to Hawaiʻi flight** safely crash–landed in 1927 (they were trying to get to Oʻahu – oh well). The Wavecrest condos are your last chance to buy groceries, since the houses peter out after awhile. Keep a careful eye out to the coast, since you will see a number of rock–walled **aquaculture fishponds** along the highway. The adept Hawaiians built them in order to have a constant supply of fish.

Don't be surprised if you can't make out the town of Pukoʻo, the former local seat of government. The road begins to wind onwards past the small serene **Murphy's Beach,** once the site of the local dump! Past Murphy's, the road quickly turns into blind curves as you pass popular surf spots around rocky points, with views of Kahana Rock off the coast. The highway will begin to head upwards

HULA COMING BACK

Auntie Moana
Kumu hula and florist

"Everyone is courteous here – there is no name calling or anything like that, and the teenagers are respectful towards you. The culture and hula are coming back full force, and the kids want to be involved."

God's Country: Halawa Valley.

and become more forested as you approach the jungled **Halawa Valley.** Just when you think the road can't curve any more, you will descend into the lush gorge, with views of different waterfalls in the back. After being hit by two tsunamis in the '40s and '50s, only a handful of permanent families live here now.

The valley has a pretty beach cove and one of Moloka'i's best trails, the **Moa'ula Falls Trail.** It lies on disputed land, so find someone to get permission from before you tread on it (most everyone on Moloka'i is nice if you *ask*). The hour hike starts on the dirt road next to the church, and is muddy and slippery (no heels, baby). Your sweet tender flesh will act as the perfect attraction to the armies of mosquitos awaiting your unique human taste. Follow the markers through the stream and up to a nice pond below the 250–foot falls. Legend has it you should place a *ti* leaf on the surface of the water before entering. If it floats, the giant *mo'o* lizard monster that resides in the water will welcome you in. If it sinks, well, let's just say I warned you.

Tell Me When You're Coming

A good chunk of Moloka'i's population turns out for the **Makahiki Festival** held at the Kaunakakai park in January. Competitions in traditional Hawaiian games take place such as lawn bowling, wrestling, and spear hurling, as well as lots o' good food and music. Originally an ancient four–month event honoring the god Lono, the festival now lasts for two days in January. On the third Saturday of May is the popular **Moloka'i Ka Hula Piko** festival, in celebration of Moloka'i as the traditional origin of hula. Papohaku Park comes alive with food, music, crafts, and excellent displays by proud local hula groups. **The Bankoh Na Wahine O Ke Kai** (Women Against the Sea) takes place on the last Sunday of September, while the men's race **Bankoh Moloka'i Hoe** (Bank of Hawai'i Moloka'i Paddle) takes place on the second Sunday in October. Both depart from the Hale O Lono Harbor on Moloka'i's southwestern shore. Founded in 1952, the race is a grinding forty–plus miles through the turbulent Moloka'i Channel to the finish line at Waikiki. Come down to the harbor to cheer on the paddlers in an old island sport that has become super popular and is now televised state wide.

Things for Homos To Do (well, actually anyone) ◈

Moloka'i Air Shuttle is the most reasonably priced of the shuttle planes that takes you to the Kalaupapa colony. Leaving from the Moloka'i Airport, the four–passenger plane zips you down the steep cliffs to the colony's little airfield. Or they can take you on a jaunt around the island's spectator north shore cliffs and valleys, with over a hundred waterfalls visible by air (try to go before the afternoon clouds). You have to arrange your own ground tour of Kalaupapa with Damien Tours (567-6171). 99 Monkey Place, Honolulu, HI 96819. 567-6847

The Moloka'i Mule Ride into the old leper colony of Kalaupapa is, despite the steep price, the traditional tourist outing on the island. You sit on your ass as it makes its way down perilous cliffs and precarious switchbacks to the quiet village, where you board a Damien Tour bus (567-6171) and see the sights. Although it was briefly closed down for awhile, Moloka'i without the mule rides is like San Francisco without the cable cars. P.O. Box 200, Kualapu'u, HI 96757. (800) 567-7550, 567-6088

The Moloka'i Ranch Outfitters Center runs a number of unique eco–friendly activity tours on ranch land. Tours include camping in large wooden–framed tents, complete with queen beds and mosquito netting, full gourmet meals, cooler with snacks and candy, and oh yeah, activity stuff like fishing, kayaking, surfing, mountain biking (Moloka'i has held international competitions), and horseback riding. Their little gift shop in their barn–style building also sells cool belt buckles, hats, and T–shirts. P.O. Box 259, Maunaloa, HI 96770. (800) 254-8871, 552-2791 www.molokai-ranch.com

Place To Put Your Head ◈

For Sure Queer

Blair's Original Moloka'i Vacation Rentals, run by the same gay owners who rent out Blair's Hana Plantation Houses on Maui, are two newly–decorated, deluxe private beachfront condos in the peaceful resort area of Kaluako'i. They are complete with full kitchens, private lanais, and a nearby pool. The views overlook the last hole of the adjoining golf course and the beach, and out towards beautiful ocean sunsets. The verandahs can be opened to join the two units together. P.O. Box 249, Hana, HI 96713. (800) 228-HANA, 248-7868.

Non–Dorothy Digs

Kaluako'i Hotel & Golf Club is the main resort on the western coast of the island. It's popular with golfers because of its scenic eighteen–hole course overlooking the beach and the PGA professionals on staff. All the tasteful rooms on the low–key, condo–lined property feature an outdoor lanai with views. There's a large swimming pool overlooking the ocean and surfers, as well as the Ohia Lodge restaurant and a handful of shops. P.O. Box 1977 Maunaloa, HI 96770. (888) 552-2550, 552-2555 aloha.net/~kmkk

Eating Out

Not Queer, but Oh Well

Kualapu'u Cookhouse has quite a country feel, with a wagon in the front, wooden tables and benches, cowbells, yokes, and hand plows adorning the walls. At one time the cafeteria for the Del Monte plantation, the restaurant now calls itself the headquarters of "the slow food chain." The menu has speciality omelettes, *mahimahi* burgers, homemade tropical chili, ribs, and chocolate macadamia nut pie. Patio seating is on the side, and the indoor pane windows look out on to the countryside. On Highway 480, P.O. Box 174, Kualapu'u, HI 96742. 567-6185

Ohia Lodge at the Kaluako'i Hotel is the biggest "real" restaurant on the island, and the prices prove it. Their continental cuisine includes duck, lamb, and prime rib, as well as yummy local pies and desserts, not to mention *kalua* pork potstickers, tempura prawns, Moloka'i baby back ribs. Try the Moloka'i bread french toast for breakfast. Extensive views of O'ahu are presented through the tall glass doors and windows, the ceiling is high and open beamed, and there's an adjoining bar overlooking the pool. A little aged for most places, but fancy for Moloka'i! P.O. Box 1977 Maunaloa, HI 96770. 552-2555

Spending the Gay Dollar

Big Wind Kite Factory is an incredible kite store featuring Hawaiian designs by owners Jonathan and Daphne that include tropical fish, cows, hula girls, and different island scenes. There are also boat kites, dragon kites, kites shaped like birds, and more. Ask for a tour of the crafts room in the back. The jam–packed gift store carries everything from Indonesian wood carvings, scrimshaw from local deer, pottery, quilts, and the island's largest selection of books on Moloka'i. 120 Maunaloa Highway, Maunaloa, HI 96770. 552-2364 www.molokai.com/kites

Melchor Ruiz Photography creates some of the best images of Moloka'i anywhere, from girls in leis learning to hula, to fisherman casting their nets, to the wild beauty of deserted beaches, to lots and lots of buff local boys on surfboards or in traditional Hawaiian dress. His models and locales are all on Moloka'i, lending an organic quality to his prints. Private showings can be arranged, and you will notice his *Visions of Moloka'i* cards at many of the shops and tourist spots around the island. HC-01 No. 851, Kaunakakai, HI 96748. 558-8167

You've Got A Friend ◆

Maui AIDS Foundation has a Moloka'i office for education and advocacy. 553-9086

LANA'I

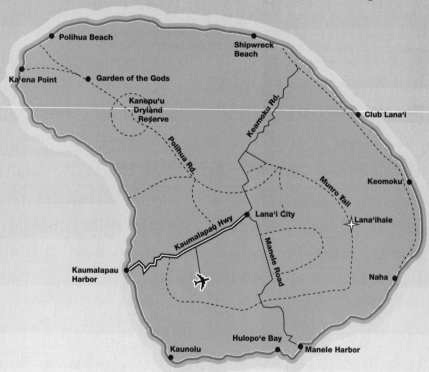

Polihua Beach

Ka'ena Point

Garden of the Gods

Kanepu'u
Dryland
Reserve

Polihua Rd.

Shipwreck
Beach

Keamoku Rd.

Club Lana'i

Keomoku

Munro Trail

Lana'i City

Kaumalapau Hwy

Manele Road

Lana'ihale

Naha

Kaumalapau
Harbor

Kaunolu

Hulopo'e Bay

Manele Harbor

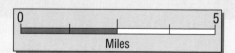

0				5

Miles

CHAPTER 7

L A N A ' I

Time keeps floating by at Lana'i's Manele Harbor.

Island Facts for Trivial Queens

Lana'i is nicknamed: "The Pineapple Island"
Island color: Orange
Flower: Kauna'oa
Land mass: 141 sq. miles/367 sq. km
Population: 3,000 est.

Highest point: Lana'ihale at
3,366 feet/1,026 m
Rainfall: 37 inches/94 cm in Lana'i City,
12 inches/30 cm on most coasts

Why Bother?

Lana'i is a small dry island in Maui's rain shadow, with only a couple of major resorts, a picturesque village–town, a mere thirty miles of paved roads, and no traffic lights to be had. For centuries, Hawaiians avoided the place because of stories of evil spirits that dwelled here. It wasn't until a mischievous son of one of Maui's kings was sent to Lana'i and killed them all that people began to populate the island.

Lana'i holds an old organized plantation feel to it, ever since Jim Dole bought the whole darn thing in the early 1920s for a little over one million dollars to grow pineapples. David Murdoch, under the name of Castle & Cooke, still owns 98% of the island. This includes the two plush resorts, the shuttle service, many homes, and anything else not bolted down. Pineapple production was phased out in the early 1990s, but the company eased the majority of the island's Filipino–dominated population into the tourist era with the construction of two mega–luxury resorts, not to mention three golf courses. What used to be a sleepy chunk of land with one, ten–room hotel now offers a *Lifestyles of The Rich and Famous*–style vacation for those who can afford a personal butler with their room. Some call the company too paternalistic, but with subsidized rent, high wages, and a wealthy visitor base, Lana'i has a somewhat brighter economic outlook than many other parts of the state.

Despite its pockets of luxury, Lana'i is really made for the adventurous. The one and only rental car company offers four–wheel drive jeeps and maps to remote beaches on the northern coast, the forested spine of the Munro Trail, and the "Garden of the Gods." You'll be coated by the island's red dust by the end of it, but you will be rewarded by having a glimpse of an old, interesting island many tourists never get to explore. (Oh, by the way, I hope you realize there's nothing even remotely gay about Lana'i beyond the odd waiter who will be thankful you and your "friend" sat at his table.)

You will understand the class of tourist Lana'i is looking for by the outrageous airfare to the island, so choose instead the only inter–island passenger ferry service in the state: *Expeditions* from Lahaina, Maui. It can roll you across the waves at nearly half the price of flying, offering whale and dolphin sightings in the process. This makes Lana'i an excellent day trip or overnighter if you are already on Maui. The fifty–foot, sixty–passenger vessel sails every day of the year, regardless of sea conditions! Call (800) 695-2624 for reservations.

This Town

Calling **Lana'i City** a "city" is something like calling Dolly Parton mammary–deprived. It just ain't right. However, this is where almost all of Lana'i's population resides in trim multi–colored plantation–style blocks, amidst huge Norfolk and Cook Island pines. The mood is of a peaceful, rustic mountain town. This tidy upland village becomes cool and misty in the afternoons and is so unhurried and mellow that you feel like you're walking in molasses half the time. Shops even close for a noontime siesta.

Relaxin' at Dole Park.

The straight–lined streets surround the main center of town, **Dole Park.** Large trunks jut up from six uninterrupted grassy blocks as kids play baseball and parents sit under the whistling pines. Around the park, a handful of idyllic shops and eateries face the grass. Along the north edge of the park on Seventh Street stands the **Lana'i Playhouse** movie theater on the corner. A few

Lana'i's best snorkeling at Hulopo'e Beach.

doors down is the **Blue Ginger Cafe,** as well as the **Lana'i Art Program** and other small shops.

Along the west edge of the park is the island's only school, some recreation buildings, and churches. Along the south edge of the park on Eighth Street are all the island's grocery stores and **Pele's Other Garden** health food eatery (see listing), and along the east end is the town's hot social spot: the Post Office. The **Hotel Lanai** (see listing), built in 1923 to house visiting executives of Dole, sits just southeast of the park on a grassy slope. And that is about all there is to say for Lana'i City.

Lanaʻi in a Mac-nut Shell

The road south out of Lanai City to **Manele Bay** is a nice smooth piece of pavement that only takes twenty minutes from start to finish – quite a luxury for Lanaʻi. You will pass the wide fields that were once chock–full of pineapple, and after you descend down the open hillside, views of uninhabited Kahoʻolawe Island appear on the horizon.

The first major right is the site of the posh **Manele Bay Hotel** (see listing) with an adjoining golf course. After that you will see the cliffs surrounding **Manele Boat Harbor,** where scuba and snorkel boats and *Expeditions* (the ferry to Maui) leave from. The road soon loops around at the popular **Hulopoʻe Beach Park,** a white sandy beach with Lanaʻi's best snorkeling and swimming in crystal waters, tucked away in a cove with the resort watching over.

You can hike around the east corner to see some pretty lava cliffs, tide pools, maybe some visiting dolphins, and the chunk of rock called **Puʻu Pehe** – also known as Sweetheart's Rock or Kissing Rock. Go on, get your picture taken sucking face with your loved one here!

Backtracking to Lanaʻi City, take the rougher Highway 44 north out of town. You can't miss the **Lodge at Koʻele** on your right – a cross between an English hunting lodge and a Ritz–Carlton wet dream. Deluxe suites with verandahs overlook the perfectly manicured lawns where croquet, lawn bowling, and miniature golf is played. The beautiful grounds in the back present a large pond and atrium. The grand lobby called the Great Hall is sumptuous with dark rich wood, sky lights, soft couches, *objets d'art,* and the two largest stone fireplaces in Hawaiʻi. There's also a fine restaurant within the Great Hall, not to mention lovely reading and sitting rooms in the wings that will make you feel like a hunter

Jeeping on the Munro Trail.

coming in for rest (feel like one or feel like having one, either way). The eighteen–hole championship golf course rounds out the picture of one of the most distinctively tasteful resorts in Hawaiʻi.

A mile past the lodge is a paved road on the right, which will take you to a colorful Filipino cemetery with brightly decorated tombstones (who says death can't be pretty?). This road quickly becomes dirt and turns into the **Munro Trail.** The trail is either a full day's hike or a couple hour four–wheel drive past muddy and slippery ravines (I vote for the jeep personally). The red potholed road rocks its way through thick foliage and pines, past views of the encircling neighbor islands and the ocean beyond. You feel like you are miles away from any form of civilization. For Lana'i, it's quite remarkable.

Rusting away at Shipwreck Beach.

The Munro Trail will ultimately descend back down to the highway, passing some petroglyphs on the way.

Further on Highway 44, past the turn–off for the Munro Trail, the road floats past horses in green pastures and then descends to the dry rugged coast line. Right after the paved road ends near the coast, take the sharp left fork for the dirt road to **Shipwreck Beach**. Past a few fishing huts will be a narrow deserted beach lined with gnarled driftwood, where you'll find almost anything washed up from condoms to sandals. You can't really swim here, but the view of the tilted cargo ship rusting away offshore makes an interesting souvenir photo.

If you turn around and head southeast along the coastal dirt road, you will see great views of Maui and five miles later, the ghost town of **Keomuku.** All that really remains of the failed sugar venture here is an empty wooden church house dating back to 1903, now maintained by volunteers. Look inside at the sweet altar where people leave cash offerings (hands off!).

Further down the dusty road is a small jetty for **Club Lana'i.** Appearing as a bizarre oasis amid all the dry abandoned scrub, a boat drops Maui tourists off at this remote spot, but not without offering them all the food, drinks, kayaking, and sunbathing they could possibly demand. There are No Trespassing signs everywhere, but you do have public access to the thin strip of beach. If you play your cards

Keomoku Church – 1903.

Divine wonders at Garden of the Gods.

Seldom-visited Polihua Beach.

right, you may be able to purchase something at the snack bar.

The dirt road goes further down the parched coast to the desolate and empty fishing spot of **Naha,** but I have no idea why you'd even bother.

Back at Ko'ele Lodge, there's a dirt road leading to the west just past the resort with a sign for Garden of the Gods on your left. Red dust flies around you as you head northwest to the fenced–in **Kanepu'u Dryland Reserve,** some of the last remaining Hawaiian drylands not devastated by wild goats and cattle. There are a couple of marked trails if you feel like wandering.

Right after you exit the reserve's gate, you will begin to spot the weird rock formations that make up the **Garden of the Gods.** You'll immediately wonder why it's called a garden. The sparse, eerie landscape that stretches all the way down the mountain side has ghostly rock configurations and stacks in hues of red and beige, with the bright blue of the ocean as a contrasting backdrop. There's not much green anywhere. Looking like it has been shipped in from some desert in Arizona, the barren ravines and stark boulders are a divine sight to behold. Keep your eyes peeled in this whole region for the famous Lana'i Axis Deer.

The dirt road will have a major fork soon, with signs for either Ka'ena Point or Polihua Beach. The descending road to the beach feels more like a jagged empty creek bed, complete with boulders and gullies. How driveable it is depends on your butt tolerance and whether they have cleared the road lately.

If you make it to the **Polihua Beach** without expiring, you will find an amazingly wide, windswept piece of sand devoid of people, making for a perfect nude picnic spot. At times there may be fisherman here, since the rough waters are known for their large fish (read: sharks) that swim nearby. Since it's such a hassle getting there, plan on spending the day, but don't even think of driving on the soft sand unless you want to spend a few more days there. If you took the Ka'ena Point fork, a road you technically aren't supposed to be on, you would bump and grind all the way to some dark sea cliffs on the northwest shore, with some *heiau* remains nearby.

Starting again from Lana'i City (does every road lead out of here or what?), you can take the well–paved Highway 440 out to the Kaumalapau Harbor, where the supply ship comes in from O'ahu weekly. There are some steep cliffs along the coast and local fisherman standing on the jetty, but that's about it. Further south down the coast is the scenic remains of the old Hawaiian settlement of **Kaunolu.** King Kamehameha used to spend his summers here fishing and enjoy making freshman warriors plunge off a sheer cliff called Kahekili's Jump. The road to Kaunolu is fairly awful, and the rental car agencies will probably torture and kill you if you try it, but don't let me stop you!

Things for Homos To Do (well, actually anyone)

Besides the usual rough road driving, beachcombing, hiking, and snorkeling, there are few organized activities on Lana'i besides, you guessed it, golf. The two resort hotels offer tennis, scuba, horseback riding, and sporting clays to their guests, but no telling what they'll charge *you.* You can always try sitting around and talking dirty gossip about the other tourists. If you get desperate, the Lanai City Service (565-7227) will drive you around for a fee and tell you what's up – they may have better gossip than you do.

Place To Put Your Head

Not Queer, but Oh Well

Hotel Lanai, dating back to 1923 and recently renovated by new owners, has quite a homey feel to it, with hardwood floors, pedestal sinks, a few four–poster beds, and patchwork quilts. Ask for one of the rooms with porches in front at no extra cost, overlooking the pine–filled town. There's a country restaurant offering pricey goodies by chef and owner Henry Clay (that's his Hummer parked in front). A reasonable place to stay, especially considering breakfast is included as well as complimentary snorkel

EVERYONE KNOWS EVERYONE

Shelia Bacalso
....
Filipino HIV/AIDS Prevention
Project

"I can count on two
hands the number of gay
people we have on Lanai,
but I perceive that people
are pretty open towards them, since everyone's
family and knows each other. Maybe people are
more tolerant here than in the Philippines even."

equipment and miniature golf
at the Lodge at Ko'ele. P.O.
Box 520, Lana'i City, HI 96763.
(800) 795-7211, 565-7211

Manele Bay Hotel offers 250
luxury Mediterranean villas
and suites with private lanais
and views of the sparkling
Hulopo'e Beach. There's a
dark wood library with
leather–bound books and chess
boards, a comfortable if ritzy
Asian–motif lobby with deep
couches, painted murals, sculptures, and vases, a number of
theme gardens, and tons of Italian marble everywhere, including the suite's bathrooms. An all–out spa and exercise center beckons, and the nearby eighteen–hole
oceanfront golf course was designed by Jack Nicklaus. If all this isn't enough, butler suites are also available (just don't call him James). P.O. Box 774, Lana'i City,
HI 96763. (800) 321-4666, 565-7700

Eating Out 🔶

Not Queer, but Oh Well

Pele's Other Garden is a spiffy little health food eatery on the south side of Dole
Park. Offerings include organic whole–wheat pizzas with vegetarian pepperoni,
thick sandwiches, homemade soups, and fresh apple, beet, or carrot juices. There
are salads and picnic goodies galore, as well as outside seating on their porch overlooking the going–ons of the shaded village. There's also a health food store in the
back, needless to say Lana'i's only. Corner of Eighth and Houston Streets, Lana'i
City, HI 96763. 565-9628

Tonigawa's is a very local old–fashioned 1950s soda fountain fronting Dole Park,
complete with swivel chairs and a general store. The interior is sparse to say the
least, but the burgers here are thick and juicy and full of bad stuff for you (that's
why they taste so good). Be sure to come early since they are only open for breakfast and lunch (despite the dinner sign stating otherwise). It's kind of nice to watch
your bacon sizzling in a pool of heavy fat from your seat across the counter, just
like in the old days. 419 Seventh Street, Lana'i City, HI 96763. 565-6537

Dining Room at the Lodge at Ko'ele is only open for dinner and offers some of the most sumptuous meals in the state (and the prices prove it). The menu continuously evolves, but hopefully you can try the Thai black rice dyed with squid's ink, barbecued Lana'i venison meat loaf, pan roasted Tiger Prawns, or opakapaka caught locally that morning. You can sit back in the tall wooden chairs and listen to the soothing piano music, gazing out into the large pond and dark green lawns. You might want to head to the Terrace Dining Room for afternoon British high tea as well. Oh, and try to lose that nasal American accent while you're at it. P.O. Box 310, Lana'i City, HI 96763. (800) 321-4666, 565-7300

Spending the Gay Dollar $

Lana'i Art Studio is located next to the community college building in town and offers local arts and crafts designed through the Lana'i Art Program. Items continually rotate, but you may find tapa cloths, carvings from local wood, lauhala weaving, fused glass, ceramics, paintings, silk scarves and bowls. Lana'i's got culture! 339 7th Street, Lana'i City, HI. 565-7503

You've Got A Friend ◆

Maui AIDS Foundation has a Lana'i office for education and advocacy. 565-6722

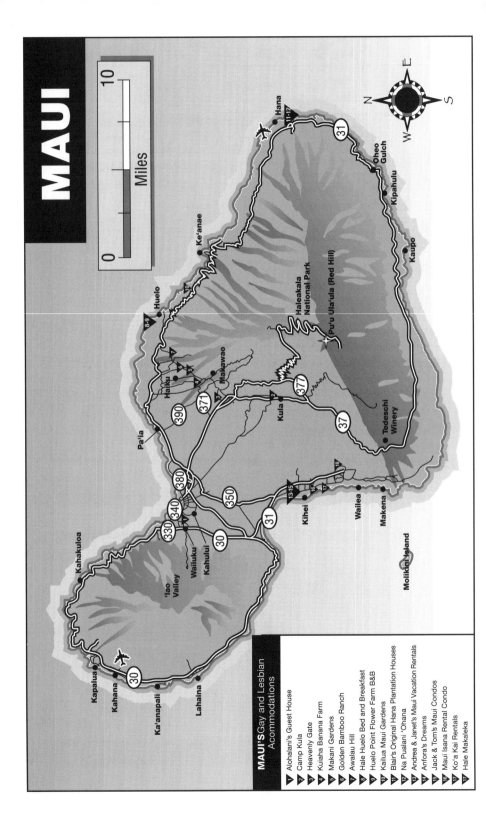

MAUI

MAUI'S Gay and Lesbian
Acommodations

1 Alohalani's Guest House
2 Camp Kula
3 Heavenly Gate
4 Kuiaha Banana Farm
5 Makani Gardens
6 Golden Bamboo Ranch
7 Awalau Hill
8 Hale Huelo Bed and Breakfast
9 Huelo Point Flower Farm B&B
10 Kailua Maui Gardens
11 Blair's Original Hana Plantation Houses
12 Na Pualani 'Ohana
13 Andrea & Janet's Maui Vacation Rentals
14 Anfora's Dreams
15 Jack & Tom's Maui Condos
16 Maui Isana Rental Condo
17 Ko'a Kai Rentals
18 Hale Makaleka

Kahakuloa
Kapalua
Kahana
Ka'anapali
Lahaina
'Iao Valley
Wailuku
Kahului
Pa'ia
Huelo
Ke'anae
Haiku
Makawao
Kula
Kihei
Wailea
Makena
Molokini Island
Haleakala National Park
Pu'u 'Ula'ula (Red Hill)
Tedeschi Winery
Hana
Oheo Gulch
Kipahulu
Kaupo

30
330
340
380
350
390
371
37
377
31

Miles
0   10

CHAPTER 8

M A U I

Maui's most popular "Big Beach."

Island Facts for Trivial Queens

Maui is nicknamed: "The Valley Isle"
Island color: Pink
Flower: Lokelani
Land mass: 737 sq. miles/1,916 sq. km
Population: 117,000 est.

Highest point: Mt. Haleakala at
10,023 feet/3,055 m
Rainfall: 83 inches/211 cm in Hana,
15 inches/38 cm in Lahaina

Maui is the only county in Hawai'i to include four islands (along with Moloka'i, Lana'i and Kaho'olawe). Haleakala is the largest dormant volcano in the world, and the island holds the last major pineapple and sugar production in the state. The largest banyan tree in the U.S. is in Lahaina, and Maui has the best winter humpback whale viewing in Hawai'i.

Why Bother?

Maui as a word conjures up all the mystic allure of the Hawaiian Islands as a whole. After Oʻahu, it is the most frequently visited of the islands, and you will know it by the unending stretch of abominable hotels elbowing the strip of beach in Kaʻanapali. Cheesy condos and mini–malls do the same thing in Kihei, leading to what some call the "California–zation" of the island. Now having made that ugly statement, don't be scared – the power of the raw island still surges through. There's a rustic upcountry, remote and pristine Hana, and a rugged and unpopulated southeastern coast, and enough good ole' fashioned aloha to make up for all the Embassy Suites and Westins they throw at the place! Maui may seem more homogenized than the other more pastoral neighbor islands, but its infinite beaches, dramatic valleys, twisting roads, and funky towns feel oh–so–true to what the essence of Hawaiʻi really is.

The gay and lesbian scene on Maui is the second largest in the state, although still tiny compared to Oʻahu's. The island seems to attract a constant influx of our gay family, with most of the socializing happening at the nude beach and numerous community events. Sadly, both of Maui's gay bars, Hamburger Mary's and Lava Bar, closed their doors in 1998. Mirroring the closures in Honolulu's gay center, Maui is now without an official gay bar. However, Lava Bar is apparently searching for a new home in Kihei, so stay tuned.

The Kihei area tends to be where most gays reside and play. There's a gay following upcountry around Makawao as well. A chunk of gay B&Bs are located east of Kahului, in the pretty Haʻiku and Huelo areas. The island has its own drag group, lesbian–owned surfing school, and a number of same–sex wedding services to choose from. There are all sorts of potlucks, video nights, and informal meetings held all around the island – check the *Out in Maui* newspaper for all the listings. Also, the Maui AIDS Foundation frequently hosts events, including the largest AIDS dance–a–thon in the state.

Hanging with the homies from Both Sides Now.

Frank Crouse, the seventy–seven year old president of the local gay organization Both Sides Now, is spearheading the formulation and fundraising of a future gay and lesbian community center upcountry near Kula. He is donating a forty–two–acre parcel for (hopefully) a meeting hall, offices, a ball park, campgrounds, a Metropolitan Community Church, a pool, guest lodges, and more. This center would completely overhaul and invigorate the island's gay community. So keep an ear out for developments and pitch in – dreams are known to come true!

MAUI Wailuku & Kahului

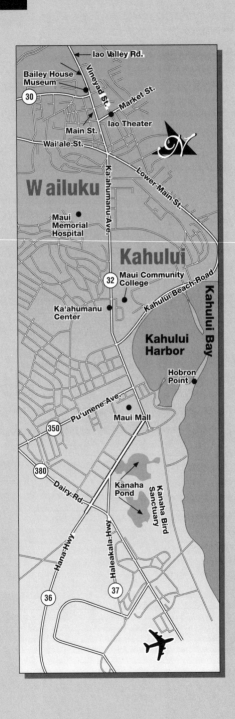

This Town

Wailuku and **Kahului** sit next to each other on Maui's northern shore like kissing cousins. You will be forgiven if you can't tell where one ends and the other begins. Nearly all of Maui's visitors fly into the Kahului Airport, and 40% of the island's population resides in these two towns. Where Kahului has the K–mart and Costco, Wailuku has the antique stores and funky restaurants. Although the towns are not that touristy, most visitors go through one or the other at some point during their stay.

From the airport heading west towards town, you will pass the **Kanaha Bird Sanctuary** on your right, and then come to the Hana Highway. This road goes through town and becomes Ka'ahumanu Highway after it veers left near the Maui Mall. A long strip of shopping malls and businesses line the area, including the humungous three–tiered **Ka'ahumanu Center** shopping mall across

The funky Iao Theater along Market Street.

from the Maui Community College. It's complete with a Gap store and multiplex theater that will make you *not* miss the Mainland. Past some sports fields and the Baldwin High School, a bridge takes you into Wailuku. Here the aesthetics suit the gay genes better, with charming shops and an old–town feel, the steep green West Maui Mountains presenting an eloquent backdrop.

For an island often accused of being "touristy," Wailuku, the county seat for Maui, Moloka'i, and Lana'i, is a very *un*–touristy town. You'll spot the old spot for Hamburger Mary's on the corner of Main and Market as you drive up the hill. Stroll just further north from here on **Market Street**, and you will be rewarded with a collection of little antique and pawn shops crying out to be explored,

The Queen's Church.

HAWAIIAN MUSIC

Many outsiders with little exposure to Hawaiian music assume it is a cheesy brand of archaic, monotonous, or unrefined melodies that act merely as back–up for smiling hula girls. They may only think of it in terms of camp value, along with plastic grass skirts, toy ukuleles, or Don Ho. Nothing could be further from the truth. Hawaiian music is a varied, evolving, and **rich art form** that is central to the ongoing renaissance of the island chain's unique culture.

Hula and *mele* (chants) were of immense importance to a people without a written language, and the islands' emphasis on music as a cultural core is still strong today. Certain instruments evoke Hawai'i in themselves: the ukulele (correctly pronounced ook–oo–lay–lay) translates as "jumping flea" due to the fast finger movements. It was originally derived from the braguinha, an instrument brought over by Portuguese laborers, and is supposed to be the easiest instrument in the world to learn. The steel guitar was invented in 1889 by a native Hawaiian, Joseph Kekuku. It is said that the steel guitar and banjo are the only two major instruments to have been invented in the U.S.A. The steel guitar is usually played with slack–key tuning, hence the name slack–key music. The light, melodic twangs of the strings sound uniquely Hawaiian. The late Gabby Pahinui, credited with bringing the instrument back into distinction in the '70s, is still probably the most famous slack–key guitarist in the world.

Like the islands themselves, contemporary Hawaiian music is a "mixed plate." Most performers have quite a range of styles, from love ballads sung in Hawaiian to modern folk–rock numbers to ancient chants. Men sing some or all of their songs in high–pitched falsetto. Jamaican reggae is also popular in Hawai'i, and a local hybrid version has emerged dubbed "Jawaiian."

As with hula and other island art forms, gays are prominent in the local music scene. The only out lesbian singer in Hawai'i, O'ahu resident **Kim Char Meredith's** first popular release was a lesbian–tinged, country/pop CD titled A *Slender Line of Lavender* (she had previously recorded four contemporary Christian albums). Hawai'i's biggest–selling artist to date, Maui resident **Keali'i Reichel,** climbed Billboard's world music charts with his albums *Kawaipunahele* and *Lei Hali'a,* and his 1997 album *E O Mai* included a song about the AIDS quilt. The **Brothers Cazimero** are a duo (one gay, one straight) that have been popular on the island scene for years, and most of their work includes a traditional Hawaiian flavor. Hometown favorite **Matt Yee** is an attorney by day, but dons some fabulous dresses for his fun piano lounge act at Honolulu night spots. **Nathan Kalama** on Kaua'i founded the Mokihana Festival and has produced a CD of Hawaiian favorites. Hawai'i has also given birth to some world–renowned dancers: island–raised **Jill Togowa** started up the Purple Moon Dance Project in Berkeley, California.

HAWAIIAN MUSIC — CONT.

Other mainstream island singers worth catching for their unique and individual sounds are Sistah Robi Kahakalau, the female trio Na Leo Pilimehana, the late Israel Kamakawiwoʻole, Bruddah Waltah, the Peter Moon Band, and many others. And don't forget gay icon Bette Midler was also raised on Oʻahu. The Hawaiian music industry is taking off, so keep watching those charts!

Kealiʻi Reichel

"Not everyone will like our music, but my job is to educate as well as to entertain…to make people think about who we are as Hawaiians. We don't run around naked, we don't live in grass shacks. We are modern. We are educated. We are a living, viable, important culture with a voice."

Kim Char Meredith

"My music is my therapy to process emotions, to focus on the essence of what I really feel. The record companies don't want me to narrow my niche and become a 'lesbian' singer, but I have a very strong women's following, and I'm proud of it."

including the **Abused Books** store and the amazing Gottling Ltd (see listing). A few doors down is the gay–managed **Iao Theater,** a wonderful piece of Maui architecture with plays, musicals, and a lovely outdoor cafe on the second level. Here you can dig into an inexpensive meal with a view of the tall mountains beyond. The next intersection is **Vineyard Street,** and walk westward up the hill to view more old western–style buildings, funky restaurants, and the **Northshore Inn hostel.**

Meander back to Main and begin walking up Main towards the mountains. You will notice some government buildings on your left, and at the intersection for Honoapiʻilani Highway you'll spot the **Kaʻahumanu Church,** built in 1876. In her always modest style, Queen Kaʻahumanu pointedly requested the church bear her name. Check out the old clock in the steeple that was brought around the Horn and still keeps good time. Treat yourself to hymns sung in Hawaiian on Sunday mornings.

'Iao Needle: ancient Hawaiian phallic symbol.

West Main now turns into 'Iao Valley Road, and five minutes' walk up the hill is the **Bailey House Museum** tucked away in a residential area. Built by another missionary family from Boston in the early 1800s, there are Hawaiian artifacts on display, a decent gift shop, and none other than one of Olympian Duke Kahanamoku's 150-pound surfboards. If you're lucky, you will also catch Uncle Sol Kawaihoa teaching ukulele and slack-key guitar here – can't beat that!

Enough walking – now get in your car and keep driving up **'Iao Valley** Road. Yep, as you may have guessed, there's a valley called 'Iao up here and what a valley it is. Sheer walls of green drama slice into this deep gorge, where King Kamehameha drove the Maui armies up into the valley during his conquest of the island in 1790. It is said the battle that ensued choked the streams red with blood and bodies.

The scene is a lot prettier now. You will pass the **Heritage Gardens** and **Kepaniwai Park** with Chinese and Japanese pavilions, a New England missionary home, a Polynesian *hale,* and a Portuguese garden (sounds like Hawai'i to me!). The state park at the end of the winding road will literally take your breath away. Towering sheets of rock drip down around you, with thin waterfalls making their way to the beautiful stream below. It feels as though you are actually inside an artist's painting. Take the walkway across a small bridge to view the 1,200-foot tall **'Iao Needle** (Kukaemoku). This interesting hump was formed by the erosion away of what used to be a volcano in these mountains. The phallic needle was originally a large virility symbol of the god Kanaloa – go ahead and praise it if you need to.

A short drive back down the valley and you are right back in the middle of town, even though it feels like you just went to heaven and back.

Maui in a Mac-nut Shell

Head out of Wailuku town north on Highway 340, and you will begin the counter-clockwise crawl around the northwest corner of the island. The road gets progressively twisted and decrepit as you snake up into dry ranch land in the boondocks. You have to drive something like one mile-per-hour around blind curves that hide tourist drivers, but the scenery is generally worth it.

HAWAI'I'S SUPERMAN

Maui is named after a Herculean figure in Hawaiian mythology: a half man, half god who possessed great *mana* or spiritual power. His legend is known throughout Polynesia. Even in far away New Zealand there are many stories about Maui. His traditional home is the Haleakala crater. It was **the heroic Maui** who pulled up the very islands of Hawai'i from the depths of the ocean with his magic fish hook. It was also he who lassoed the sun with fiber ropes in order to slow down its procession across the sky so humans might have a longer working day (which seems to be getting longer by the minute!). A cunning trickster, he stole the knowledge of fire–making from the mud hens of O'ahu, and gave the knowledge to humans. Maui is also credited for using his strength to raise the sky up to its current position.

Obviously not one to shy away from a challenge, there's a tale of Maui attempting to conquer death itself. A New Zealand myth tells of a nude and muscled Maui, spear in hand, jumping into the mouth of Hinenuitepo, the guardian of life, in order to rip out her heart and thus bring immortality to the world. Unfortunately, she awoke and bit Maui in two as he tried to escape and thus came the dramatic, operatic finale of Maui, Hawai'i's Superman.

You will pass the microscopic town of **Kahakuloa** which sports both a Catholic *and* Protestant church for the dozen or so houses (talk about Northern Ireland!). Keep on the road and near the 20 mile marker, there is a blowhole (no, not *that* kind) where you can pull off and see if the ocean is performing for you that day. You will soon pass a light house and the road will begin to get better.

You will know the surf is good when you pass **Honolua Bay** because everyone will pull over to watch the near–perfect sets of waves ridden by the near–perfect bodies on boards. On the southern section of the bay is the picturesquely named **Slaughterhouse Beach** (there used to be one on the cliffs above), which offers some nice sunbathing and bodysurfing.

Now you've reached a reality checkpoint, as the quirky road transforms into a super highway and luxury condos start popping up around you. Brash shopping centers line the road and traffic becomes

A bit o' history – Front Street.

SPIRIT OF MAUI

Lorenzo Ross

"There's a nice spirit throughout the gay community here; there's lots of 'ohana. You may not see someone for months, but you can always pick right up where you left off."

an actuality. **Ka'anapali** is a planned resort, with uninspired and insipid architecture and run-of-the-mill resorts crammed along the narrow beach. And it doesn't really end until you get to **Lahaina.** Ah, a simple whaling village, you figure. But the **Planet Hollywood** sitting along historic **Front Street** shouts out otherwise. Lahaina is tourist central, and most people trip upon it at some point during their stay. All the tourists simply cram themselves up and down Front Street, but there are some nicer places tucked away on the town's back streets, including **Lahaina Coolers** and **Gerard's** (see listings).

Lahaina, once the former capitol of the islands and a bawdy whaling center in the early 1800s, still holds its charm with antique buildings to explore like the **Wo Hing Temple** on Front Street. Next to the temple is an adjoining cookhouse showing early Edison films of Hawai'i. There's also a restored ship, the *Carthaginian* in front of the historic Pioneer Inn. Next to that is the old Lahaina Courthouse and fort remains, and an astonishing **Banyan Tree** that covers two-thirds of an acre nearby.

Lahaina offers some decent art galleries and boutiques, not to mention remarkable views of Lana'i. Lahaina is also the place to catch the great **Old Lahaina Luau** (see listing), submarine rides, parasailing, fishing boats, whale watching cruises, and the tacky Sugar Cane Train to Ka'anapali (whoopee!).

The Carthaginian.

For an excellent, highly-recommended day trip or overnighter, take the passenger ferry *Expeditions* to explore quiet yet interesting Lana'i island across the channel (see Lana'i chapter).

The stretch of road south of Lahaina to Kihei tends to be heavily used since no one wants to drive the slothful Highway 340 from Wailuku. This area offers parched views of the back of the West Maui Mountains, or more aptly their valleys. There's a string of small beach parks, and this section of Highway 30 presents some of the most intense winter **whale watching** ever. Huge mothers give birth and nurse in the shallow waters straight off the road – watch out for freaked–out motorists slamming on their breaks!

Turn south when you hit Highway 31, and you will be headed towards **Kihei.** This coast line of Maui offers six miles of unbroken beach and near–perpetual sunshine, as well as some of the most tangled growth in the state. Twenty years ago, Kihei was a scattering of houses, with a church or two thrown in. Now it is an unbroken chain of generic condos and mini–malls, traffic lights, and cars – a living example of "pave paradise and put up a parking lot." Having said that, there are a

A CASUAL ATMOSPHERE

Stan Houk
....
Former owner Hamburger Mary's, Wailuku

"I liked the casual atmosphere of doing business in Maui, and the fact that people don't try to mow you down trying to get ahead. I like the aloha spirit . . . Mary's had always been a place for everybody. I always felt like I was having friends over to eat and party."

The gay–owned Maui Rainbow Factory near Makena.

plethora of reasonably–priced condos and vacation rentals (many gay–owned), and the beautiful sand and sun could be a lot worse. At press time the very gay **Lava Bar and Grill** was looking for a new home in Kihei, so keep your ears out.

South of Kihei is the arid resort area of **Wailea.** Its manicured and formal atmosphere stands in stark contrast to Kihei's mishmash of growth. Wailea is where you will find the *la–de–da* hotels like the **Four Seasons, Grand Wailea Resort,** and the peculiar, Arabian–style **Kea Lani Hotel,** complete with white domes and tents and an *Aladdin* ambience. Just south of Wailea the road turns and peters out near the excellent, undeveloped Big Beach and Little Beach at **Makena** (see listing). Around this area you'll spot views of the crescent–shaped **Molokini**

HONOR THY CHILDREN

In 1997, Maui residents **Jane and Alexander Nakatani** published an incredible autobiographical account of their family called *Honor Thy Children,* written by Molly Fumia. Having started their family in California, the Nakatanis imagined an idyllic future with their three sons. However life is never that simple. Sadly, each one of their three young sons died tragically before his time. The eldest and youngest sons, both of whom were gay, died of AIDS while the middle son was shot to death in Los Angeles. Their powerful story of overcoming tragedy and shame was not easy to share, and since publication they have become beloved supporters of gay and lesbian causes in Hawai'i

Island offshore. The remains of this ancient crater make an excellent snorkeling spot, and the hoards of tourist catamarans from Lahaina prove it.

Dude–riding waves at Ho'okipa.

Rewind your way back up toward Kahului again on the Mokuele Highway (350), and you will spot one of Hawai'i's last sugar mills at **Pu'unene,** complete with small museum. Drive east towards Hana on Highway 36, and you soon hit the cool surf town of **Pa'ia** amid the sugar cane fields. Earthy restaurants and shirtless guys with dreds fill the place, with offbeat boutiques and store fronts painted in bright colors. Pa'ia is an old sugar plantation town, now reformed by the hundreds of windsurfers and surfers who come to the incredibly windy and wavy beaches nearby. Only experts or blockheads would venture out into the powerful currents and jagged shore break of **Ho'okipa Beach Park,** just past Pa'ia. Here, half a dozen international windsurfing tournaments are held throughout the year that make for awesome spectating of athletes.

Highway 36 quickly turns into 360, and you are officially on the road to Hana. The scenery becomes greener as you pass the Ha'iku area, and the highway more and more twisted. Not far from Ha'iku, there's a sign for the Kaulanapueo Church on the ocean side of the road. This is the turn–off for the spread out community of

Huelo, home to a few nice gay B&Bs.

Past Huelo the road becomes famously contorted with over 600 bends as you creep your way to Hana, and your stomach will count every one. Waterfalls gush down the steep cliffs, pools of all sizes await you on the side of the road, and signs for tropical gardens beckon you on. You will be amazed that the road exists at all, being cut directly into the cliff sides. With an endless number of one–lane yield bridges, roadside viewpoints, tropical fruit stands, and a parade of tourists making the trek daily, the driving pace is leisurely to say the least (more like molasses). Allow at least two hours one way, and know that the trek is not for the rushed or impatient. Plan on stopping a lot so you don't get dizzy (if you aren't already like that naturally).

The little village of **Keʻanae** is about half way there, and you can spot its cozy homes on the peninsula from above. A lush arboretum is just past the town's turn–off, with a pretty nature trail to stretch your legs out on. You will know you are almost in **Hana** when you see the sign for the **Gardenland Cafe and Nursery,** complete with rainbow flag (see listing). Your next stop is the **Waiʻanapanapa State Park** where you'll be awed by a black sand beach, lava arches, and a short loop trail that will lead you to some amazing ocean–filled caves where a princess is said to have died. The shrimps turn red here in remembrance of her spilled blood.

A section of the dizzy road to Hana.

If you follow the highway straight ahead without turning you'll see **Hana Bay,** a salt and pepper beach with local folk hanging out and kids jumping off the pier. On the other side of the rocky southern point is **Red Sand Beach,** approachable

Tranquil Hana Bay.

from around the south (see listing). As you meander down the peaceful streets, you will know you are in Hana. It is the exact opposite of tourist–ridden Lahaina and Ka'anapali. The sleepy village is full of neighbors waving to each other, island homes with *choke* (lots of) personality, and little tucked away coves.

Do yourself a favor and don't zip into Hana and then turn back like most silly tourists. Plan on spending at least one night here to savor the beauty and allow your butt a rest from the topsy–turvy road. **Blair's Original Hana Plantation Houses** offer inexpensive local studios and homes (see listing). The days are long and lazy in Hana, and if you want a sober and unwinding holiday, this is the place to head (many celebrities own relaxing homes nearby). And for those of you with lots of cumbersome excess money, check into the **Hotel Hana Maui.** This elegantly renovated inn has an enchanting restaurant and bar, ocean views, and adjoining local art gallery.

Instead of winding back to Kahului on the north shore's Hana Highway with everyone else and their mother, be an adventurous queer and drive the southern route on the **Pi'ilani Highway** (31). Some people simply describe the highway as "Hell," with rocks, gullies, dust, and potholes adding hearty character to this stretch, which can be washed out by flash floods perhaps twice a year. But it's actually a lot safer than people think. The rental car companies usually threaten to kill you if you drive it, but don't let those words stop you! Give the public works people a jingle beforehand (248-8524) to see if they know anything about conditions; the road has been greatly improved in recent years.

Once out of Hana's residential area, the highway will get even *more* twisted as you hug blind corners and sheer cliffs. Keep your eyes on the road and not on the nice views of the Big Island! The terrain slowly becomes drier as you approach the thin tail end of the Haleakala National Park, where the seven sacred pools (which never were sacred and are more like twenty–five) reside at the **Ohe'o Gulch**. Waterfalls pour down into the cascading rock ponds, and there's a loop trail starting from the unexciting ranger station that will take you to the main ones. You can hike and swim in the upper pools too, but keep the undies *on!*

A little way past the pools, the landscape opens up to sparse desert, and you may miss the **Palapala Ho'omau Church** sitting by itself on the shore. The cute aviator Charles

Hanging at Ohe'o Gulch.

Lindbergh is buried here, since he lived nearby during the last few years of his life. Now comes the fun part – if all the prior road wasn't bad enough, the highway now turns to nasty dirt and gravel. You crawl behind other tourist cars for four and a half grueling miles. Luckily, there's the wonderful **Kaupo General Store** along this stretch, there since 1925 and it looks it. Check out the help–yourself refrigerators and antique camera collection inside.

Thank God it's only forty–five minutes from the Kaupo Store until your next drink at the **Tedeschi Winery.** But first you will be treated to long reaches of desolate road with stoical, cud–chewing cows under trees, deep lava rock formations, dramatic views of Haleakala's craggy back side, and barely any sign of human intervention anywhere. The road will finally lead you to verdant upcountry. You

LOVE THE COMMUNITY

Frank Crouse
....
President of Both Sides Now

"I love the gay community here – they have done so much for me. I want to give something back. That's why I'm donating land for a future gay community center upcountry. I want to try to do the right thing, by supporting the community and also supporting the Hawaiian people. I've never seen a group as empathetic towards gay people than here."

Killing time along the Pi'ilani Highway.

will see the winery's tasting room in what used to be an old jail (the colorful King Kalakaua held killer parties nearby). Their pineapple, grape, or passionfruit wines are enticing to repulsive, depending on where your palate happens to be.

You'll pass a few country villages before the turn–off for highway 377, which takes you through Kula. Turn up Highway 378, and you are headed towards **Haleakala National Park** (hopefully you aren't trying to do this all in one day!). A winding road rapidly ascends past pasture land to the volcano, which last erupted in 1790. Haleakala means "House of the Sun," and this is where the studly demigod Maui lassoed the sun itself with fiber ropes (see sidebar).

BETTER THAN SEX?

Andrea Thomas

Owner Maui Surf School, Andi's Bed and Breakfast, and Royal Hawaiian Weddings

"I was a self–taught surfer, even though I was a klutz and not comfortable in the water. If you can walk, I can teach you how to surf. Anyone can learn – standing on a wave is a thrill to people. It's fun, easy, and better than (most) sex."

The mystifying Haleakala Crater.

Watch out for the mother duck and duckling bicycle tours, where tourists dressed in bright matching outfits speed down the slope, followed by a bored guy in a truck. After forking over some cash to the feds at the park entrance, the land will become a barren moonscape. There are some high and impressive lookouts before you get to the main visitor center, which gazes down 3,000 feet into the crater's eerie and awe–inspiring floor. It is said the whole island of Manhattan could fit into this crater, with no building tops poking over the rim. Drive up to the octagon building at the **Pu'u Ula'ula summit.** This is the highest point on the island at 10,023 feet. On a clear day, you might be able to see every island but Kaua'i from here.

It's a multiple–day hike around the crater, and there are campsites and cabins for use within the park. The park is also home to the rare *nene* goose (the state bird) and Hawai'i's own intriguing silversword plants. The park is open twenty–four hours, and many make the pilgrimage to view the delicate colorful sunrise, but be sure to bring something (or someone) warm and call ahead (572-7749) for weather conditions.

One of Maui's main upcountry towns is along Haleakala's north slope, off Highway 365. **Makawao** is a New Age/cowboy hybrid of a village, with holistic healers passing ranch hands in the streets, and revamped western store fronts accommodate health food stores and feed shops. **Cassanova** is the restaurant to hit here (see listing). Take Baldwin Avenue (390) back down the hill heading north, and you are right back in the heart of surfer town Pa'ia. Now you have done the whole darn island.

Tell Me When You're Coming

The winter **whale watching season** usually runs from December through March. Although the whales frequent other islands, Maui is a primo spot to catch 'em (which is exactly what those dirty whalers did in the 1800s). Lahaina is where whale watching cruises depart from, but your feet don't have to leave dry land to see them frolicking in the ocean offshore. The annual **James Manness Memorial Dance Party** (242-4900) in April is a popular fundraiser for the Maui AIDS Foundation, and a good chunk of the community shows up for it, since it's the largest AIDS dance-a-thon in the state. Tourist haven Lahaina is the spot for the **Halloween – Mardi Gras of the Pacific**, where even more drunk people than usual stumble around the place, the streets get packed, and the drag queens come out to play. There's a *keiki* (kids') parade in the afternoon before the debauchery. **The Maui County Fair** (243-7230) in Wailuku also occurs in October and is quite a site, drawing over 90,000 spectators. There are livestock shows for you 4Her's, rides, great arts and crafts, and live entertainment but no guys in dresses, since the island's drag troupe **The Cosmetix** was banned from performing one year, causing a local uproar.

Queer Pages ⚓

Out in Maui is a newspaper published by Both Sides Now and offers insight into gay Maui establishments and personalities, international briefs, photos from gay events, local business ads, and a generally good idea of what it's like to be gay and lesbian on the Valley Isle. P.O. Box 5042, Kahului, HI 96732. 244-4566 www.maui-tech.com/glom

Island Lesbian Connection is a creative newsletter for Maui and the whole state, encompassing articles, poems, community calendars, ads for womyn–owned businesses, a statewide directory, and helpful advice. Suite 171, P.O. Box 356, Pa'ia, HI 96779. 575-2681 ♀

Manpower Maui is a newsletter focusing on HIV prevention for men who have sex with men, put out by the Maui AIDS Foundation, with sexy pics, articles, and listings of monthly gay community events. P.O. Box 858, Wailuku, HI 96793-0858. 242-4900

Things For Homos to Do ⬧

Both Sides Now hosts a monthly gay and lesbian potluck picnic at a beach park in Kihei on the last Saturday of the month, from late morning to sunset. Visitors are most welcome. Bring something to eat and "talk story" and hang out island style! A great way to meet Maui's friendly queer community. Both Sides Now also puts on dances, boat trips, regular meetings, and is spearheading the effort to open up a gay community center upcountry near Kula, so get involved! Call 244-4566 for recorded info, or Frank at 248-8935. Check out their award–winning web site at mauinet/~pattie/glom.html

Gay Hawaiian Excursions specializes in activities tailored to your interests, including naked waterfall hikes, gay volcano tours, beach bonfires and commitment ceremonies, for gay and lesbian travelers to Maui and the other islands. They also offer air, room, and car packages ranging from five star to budget, and can arrange to have a car meet you at the airport. 256 Front Street, Laihaina, HI 96761. 667-7466 www.gayexcursions.com

Liquid Crystal Divers is run by the experienced dive team of Lynn and Rene, who have lived on Maui for over a decade and have done over 6,000 dives in Maui waters! They offer unique underwater adventures for women visiting Maui including introductory dives, four–day diver certification, shore dives, night dives, boat dives, and any other kind of dive experience you can think of! Liquid Crystal Divers is committed to sharing the beauty and serenity of the underwater world with women. P.O. Box 628, Makawao, HI 96768. 875-0183 www.home.sprynet.com/sprynet/aquaŞong

Married on Maui is a same–sex marriage business run by the enjoyable Reverend Susan Osborne. Ceremonies come in many forms running from "minister only" to "all the frills." Taking advantage of Maui's extraordinary beaches as a natural setting, services are moral, spiritual, and romantic commitments, with a wide choice of vows and Susan's personal touches to make them unique. Susan declares, "I love what I do and I guess it shows – it's such a joy to work with people in love!" 2162 Kahoʻokele Street, Wailuku, HI 96793. (808) 244-7400 maui.net/~revsuzio/union.htm ♀

Maui Dreamtime Weddings offers same–sex weddings on Maui by the island's only openly gay minister. Traditional and non–traditional rites at exclusive, remote locations are available in packages starting from less than $400. Champagne, limousine, and photographer may be added, and they specialize in sunset ceremonies on Maui's beautiful secluded beaches.

The stated goal of Maui Dreamtime Weddings is to enhance the lives of committed lesbian and gay couples by providing a loving, spiritual commitment ceremony. P.O. Box 246, Pukalani, HI 96788. (800) 779-1320, 573-4010 maui.net/~randm/mmw.html

Maui Surfing School teaches at Lahaina Harbor, and specializes in beginners, cowards, and klutzes, even non–swimmers! The gay–friendly instructors use Andrea Thomas' "surf in one lesson" technique, and swear you can stand up and catch a wave the first time out. The school offers group or private sessions for one, three, or five days, and even has a surf camp package. You can finally hang out at the beach and act like the cool surf dude or babe you always wanted to be. The innovative Andrea also owns the Royal Hawaiian Weddings and Andrea & Janet's Maui Vacation Rentals to boot (see listings). P.O. Box 424, Pu'unene, HI 96784. (800) 851-0543, 875-0625 maui.net/~andrea/mauisurf ♀

Open Eye Tours and Photos is run by Barry, an extremely knowledgeable guide and teacher who will reveal the unseen Maui to you on privately–guided tours. Barry tailors educational hikes and nature outings to each individual's needs, covering the island's evolution, medicinal and cultural plants (with seasonal sampling of fruit and other edibles), language, history, and legends. It's a great way to get a unique glimpse of Hawai'i you may have never seen. Barry is also a published professional photographer, and can take excellent photos of you in dramatic natural settings. P.O. Box 324, Makawao, HI 96768. 572-3483 www.mrlucky.com/openeye/aloha.html

Royal Hawaiian Weddings is a lesbian–owned company that has been performing same-sex unions since 1985. They offer a variety of tropical settings for your ceremony, including private beaches and pleasant gardens, and different packages ranging from the less expensive, to deluxe horseback or helicopter adventure weddings! Andrea and Janet also offer condo rentals in Kihei, and Andrea runs the Maui Surfing School in Lahaina (see listings). P.O. Box 424, Pu'unene, HI 96784. (800) 659-1866, 875-8569 ♀

Sachin Hazen is a sensitive, knowledgeable guide who will help you experience the hidden places of Maui. Hikes include a hidden temple and ritual pool in `Iao Valley, the extraordinary upper pools at Ohe`o Gulch, as well as the birthing pools at Ha`iku. Sachin is a certified tour guide for the state of Hawai`i, and a licensed massuer specializing in a spiritual, rejuenvanting thearpy called Spiritfire . P.O. Box 574, Kula, HI 96790. 573-2225, 573-3384 www.maui.net/~keikanan

Letting it All Hang Out ✧

Little Beach at Makena, is about one mile south of the Maui Prince Hotel in Wailea. Turn into the first paved parking lot, taking all your little valuables out of your car, and trek towards the water to behold the splendid Big Beach. No buildings spoil the 3,000–foot stretch of yellow sand, which is everyone's favorite beach on Maui. The beach used to harbor a large hippy encampment before the Health

Department closed it down in the '70s. Climb north to your right, up the trail on the rocky outcrop and you'll spot Little Beach resting peacefully along the ocean. Not at all large (duh!), gays place their towels to the north, with the fags and dykes usually slightly outnumbering the breeder sunbathers. Nudity is the norm, although technically illegal. It's quite a social spot, with locals and tourists alike meeting and  gawking. There are some trails, but Little Beach is more social than heavily cruisy. The beach also offers a good shore break for boogie boarders, who keep their shorts on and are indifferent to the weenie–waggers. Weekends are busiest.

Red Sand Beach (Kaihalulu) in Hana is one of the most scenic pieces of sand you will ever set eyes on. The remains of a small caved-in cinder cone, the beach is turned red through oxidation (rust for those of you who flunked Science). Park near the Community Center on Ua Kea Road, and find the dirt trail along the side of the back lawn. The trail soon curves around a tree and follow the flat coastal trail along the rocky shore to the hidden cove. You'll see a little crescent beach underneath rock walls with ironwood trees above. There's calm snorkeling in the bright, turquoise waters thanks to a rocky outcrop that makes a perfect natural salt water swimming pool. Red Sands is the unofficial nude beach for the Hana area, and may be clothed and/or straight depending on who got there first since the beach holds just a few people. But the pristine scenery is worth the effort in any event.

Place to Put Your Head ⬧

For Sure Queer

Alohalani's Guest House is a lesbian–owned and operated private compound for women only, conveniently located in Wailuku. There are spacious views from your breakfast porch of the ocean across the street, as well as a clothing–optional swimming pool. Both the tree house cottage and the apartment have four rooms (bed, living, bath and kitchen) and are equipped with cable TV and private entrances. The perfect place to renew romance or revitalize your soul. 122 Central Avenue, Wailuku, HI 96793. (800) 511-3121

Andrea & Janet's Maui Vacation Rentals offer two lesbian–owned condos for rent, a one–bedroom and a two–bedroom, with a pool, whirlpool, tennis courts, putting green, and yes, shuffle board. Beach equipment and an outfitted kitchen are also included. The condos' location in Kihei is prime for whale watching in the winter months. For a more personal experience, Andi also offers a B&B–style room in Wailea, with breakfast on the lanai and the benefit of her twenty years of knowledge as a resident of Maui. She and Janet also run Royal Hawaiian Weddings and the Maui Surf School, so you may as well get married on a surf-board while you're here too – it's possible! P.O. Box 424, Pu'unene, HI 96784. (800) 289-1522, 875-1558 maui.net/~andrea ♀

Anfora's Dreams offers over 100 one– or two–bedroom condo units in Kihei, from luxury two–story duplexes to economical single studios, most being gay or lesbian owned. All are completely furnished with full kitchens and most have ocean views, lanais, swimming pools, rattan furniture, and a clean tropical feel. Weekly rates are reasonable, and Dale furnishes you with a restaurant guide and a map to the gay beach. P.O. Box 74030, Los Angeles, CA 90004. (800) 788-5046, (213) 737-0731

Awalau Hill offers two self contained, lesbian and gay–owned redwood cottages, situated in the high country of Ha'iku. There's the studio with garden and ocean views, and the gazebo perched high on a gulch ledge with open–air kitchen and immense views of the North Shore. The property has complete privacy and seclu-sion, with a private pool as well as an organic vegetable and fruit garden. A wonderfully heal-ing and nurturing rental retreat. 635 Awalau Road, Ha'iku, HI 96708. 572-6204 maui.net/~liam/Awalauhill ♀

Blair's Original Hana Plantation Houses are situated in the remote town of Hana, where Blair and Tom also own the Gardenland Cafe (see listing). They've acquired over a dozen pri-vate rentals throughout the area, some with hot tubs, horses, and nearby ocean beaches. Houses range from two–story buildings to quaint cot-tages and studios, all with the serene and away–from–it–all atmosphere that Hana exudes. About half of their clientele is gay and lesbian, and they offer condos on Moloka'i too (see Moloka'i chapter). P.O. Box 249, Hana, HI 96713. (800) 228-HANA, 248-7868 www.kestrok.com/~hana

Camp Kula was the first gay B&B to ever open on Maui in 1989. Taking advan-tage of the 3,000–foot cool elevation, this five–bedroom, seventy–five year old

home offers seven secluded acres. A campfire pit, hammocks and a four person koa wood swing (for swingers, as the host puts it) are available, with nudity allowed. Recently reopened, the Camp's healing environment attracts those looking for some peace, and HIV–positive people are encouraged to visit. A good chunk of the clientele are repeats, and the Camp also has a large lesbian following as well. D.E., the Camp's warm and wonderful "counselor" frequently uses the motto: "Where the happy campers come to play!" P.O. Box 111, Kula, HI 96790. 876-0000

Golden Bamboo Ranch is not far from Makawao, on a seven–acre estate nestled on the lower slopes of the upcountry, with a newly renovated cottage and rustic plantation house broken into three suites. They have an on–site massage therapist and horses you can get your naked picture taken on! Perfect for romantic couples who want privacy – not for the pool or hot tub crowd. Owners Marty and Al (together twenty–five years) had a noisy B&B in Key West, and wanted to make this a tranquil getaway instead. They also own the Ki'i Galleries in Kahului and Wailea (see listing). 422 Kaupakalua Road, Ha'iku, HI 96708. (800) 344-1238, 572-7824 maui.net/~golden

Hale Huelo Bed and Breakfast is a newly opened, very clean and very comfortable B&B/resort with all the amenities a gay man can dream up, including entrances from the pool directly to the private bathrooms, artistically etched glass shower doors, a hot tub with gorgeous valley and ocean views, and bright and cheery decor. One upstairs loft and two downstairs suites, all with kitchenettes, face the blue Pacific from the hilltop perch. Friendly owner Doug has created one of the best get–aways in Hawai'i. P.O. Box 1237, Ha'iku, HI 96708. 572-8669

Hale Makaleka is a friendly bed and breakfast for women that offers one light, airy private room overlooking a secluded garden, with private entrance and private bath. Jackie is great to visit with during breakfast on the upstairs deck, where whales can be spotted in the winter months, and shares her knowledge of living on Maui for over thirty years. She describes her set–up as a "win–win situation. We like having people, and they like staying here!" 539 Kupulau Drive, Kihei,

HI 96753. 879-2971

Heavenly Gate is a comfortable bed and breakfast as well as a newly renovated, two–bedroom 800 sq. ft. private cottage with fifteen–foot ceilings. Kitchenette, full laundry facilities, BBQ, and the hosts' organic vegetable garden are all included, and the location is in the cool upland with views of the West Maui Mountains. Tropical breakfast is served in the open–beamed dining lounge or outside on the lanai. Gay–owned, with both straight and gay clientele. 276 Hiwalani Loop, Pukalani, HI 96768. 572-0321 maui.net/~marct

Huelo Point Flower Farm B&B is a gay–owned cottage retreat on Maui's North Shore, with four separate house or cottage rentals. Accommodations range from a private glass–walled room overlooking the 300–foot cliffs, to a full–fledged home with baby grand piano, fireplace, and large kitchen. Rates are surprisingly affordable for what you get. There are three hot tubs on the property, as well as a sixty–foot pool with mini waterfall. Ask if you can have the bed Ann Margaret slept in (if you dare!). Owners Doug and Guy have been on the island for years, and were divinely led to renovate this lush property. P.O. Box 1195, Pa'ia, HI 96779. 572-1850 maui.net/~huelopt

Jack & Tom's Maui Condos are run by Jack and Tom (who else?), who own four of the condos they rent out in Kihei, and manage forty–five others, both gay and straight owned units. One– and two–bedroom fully furnished and equipped condos are available (minimum five night stay) in the larger complexes, most with pools and tennis courts, fronting Kihei's long stretch of beaches. Be sure to book ahead, especially for winter months. P.O. Box 365, Kihei, HI 96753. (800) 800-8608, 874-1048.

Kailua Maui Gardens is on the way to Hana with a three–bedroom house and three adjoining cottages for rent with ocean views. They are all set amid two acres of ornate and beautifully manicured gardens. A swimming pool comes with the house rental and there are two other private hot tubs and a BBQ area. Dan, the caretaker of the immaculate and scenic property, also offers personal tours of the interesting nooks and crannies on the twisting road to Hana. SR Box 9 (Hana Hwy), Ha'iku, HI 96708. (800) 258-8588, 572-9726 maui.net/~kmg

Ko'a Kai Rentals are owned by Cloy and John, who have a unit at the Island Surf Building. Recently refurbished, the studio apartment sleeps two and includes light cooking facilities and beach equipment. Other units in the building are also gay–owned, and the studio is walking distance to beaches, shops, and restaurants. They also operate other condo units, from inexpensive to luxurious, throughout the island of Maui. 1993 South Kihei Road, #401, Kihei, HI 96753. (800) 399-6058 ext. 33, 879-6058.

Kuiaha Banana Farm and Guesthouse is a private two-acre organic banana farm with over 1500 plants, just downslope from Makawao. The property has a

A LENS ON THE COMMUNITY

Jon Fujiwara

Photographer

Raised in Kona on the Big Island, Jon's work has appeared in a myriad of venues, including Men of Hawaii calendars, the *Honolulu Weekly,* the Life Foundation's AIDS education ads, and covers for the *Gay Pocket Guide to Hawaii.* His funded exhibit of various portraits of gay Asian and Pacific Islander men and their response to AIDS, titled *From Pakala to Kealakekua: Being Gay in Hawai'i,* has been exhibited across the state. Jon says, "There's a lot of groups and sub–groups and different crowds in Hawai'i, but eventually you get to know every-one and you realize you are deeply within the community." 419 Waiakamilo Road #204, Honolulu, HI 96817. 578-4776

A LENS ON THE COMMUNITY – CONT.

two-room guest suite made entirely from New Zealand cedar: a bedroom with a queen-sized bed, down pillows, and mosquito netting; a sittingroom with daybed, breakfast table, microwave and refrigerator; and a private bath with jacuzzi bathtub. Sliding doors lead to a 900 square-foot deck for private sunbathing, complete with an outdoor shower amid potted palms. The farm has nearly an acre of lawns with rope swing and hammock, and their six-person spa is perfect for an evening soak under the stars. 1515 West Kuiaha Road, Haiku, HI. 573-9100

Makani Gardens is a studio guest house with small loft and kitchenette, available on a two week or longer basis. Located in rural and tranquil Ha'iku, the lush two–acre gardens have views of West Maui and Haleakala. There's also a fully equipped main house, with a yoga/meditation sidehouse, for month long rental. Gordon and Gerard live on the property and are involved with a tree nursery and forestry restoration. They will gladly take interested individuals or small groups on a tour of their gardens by appointment. 1625 West Kuiaha Road, Ha'iku, HI 96708. 572-6337 maui.net/~makanig

Maui Isana Rental Condo is across the street from the beach in Kihei, on the fourth floor with ocean views to the west and views of Mt. Haleakala to the east. The beach is excellent for swimming and walking and, when trade winds are blowing, the ocean below the condo is filled with windsurfers. The fully equipped two–bedroom condo can sleep up to six, and it's located in a quieter area of town. About half of the building's tenants are gay or lesbian. 515 South Kihei Road, Kihei, HI 96573. (800) 414-3573, (360) 321-1069

Na Pualani 'Ohana is located in rural Hana, just above the Gardenland Cafe. Owned by Frank, the president of Both Sides Now, the homey suites in the two–story house sleep up to six. There's a large living room with grand piano, fully equipped kitchen, two bedrooms, two private bathrooms and front and rear lanais overlooking the property's four acres and ocean and mountains beyond. Fruit trees and lush growth encircle the island–style property and your hosts can provide directions to hidden caves, black sand beaches, and crystal blue pools. P.O. Box 118, Hana, HI 96713. (800) 628-7092, 248-8935 www.randm.com/nuapalani97.html

Non–Dorothy Digs

Grand Wailea Resort, Hotel, and Spa has a price tag of over 600 million dollars with 40 acres, 767 rooms, 5 restaurants, 12 lounges, 50,000 square–foot health spa, and a 15 million–dollar water playground. Oh, and every minimum 640–square foot room has three telephones. This addition to the Wailea resort area is as grandly extravagant as America gets (only outdone by the ostentatious Hilton Waikoloa on the Big Island). By the way, its not cheap. For an odd chuckle, check out the strange, anatomically–correct Buddha–esque sculptures on the lobby level.

3850 Wailea Alanui Drive, Wailea, HI 96753. (800) 888-6100, 875-1234

Royal Lahaina is an ample resort well north of Lahaina in Ka'anapali. Over 500 rooms sit in a twelve–story tower and surrounding cottages, with tons of swimming pools and tennis courts on twenty–seven acres. Although echoes of Waikiki ring through its corridors, it's still a pleasant, if somewhat enormous affair. The place is also known for its popular nightly lu'au, run by the notable *kumu hula* (hula teacher) Frank Kawaikapuokalani Hewitt. You can also book the hotel as a package through the gay–friendly Hawaiian Hotels and Resorts at (800) 22-ALOHA. 2780 Keka'a Drive, Ka'anapali, HI 96761. (800) 447-6925, 661-3611

Bar Crawl ♥

At press time, with the 1998 closing of both Hamburger Mary's in Wailuku and Lava Bar and Grill in Kihei, there was no totally gay or lesbian bar on Maui. However, rumor has it Lava Bar is actively seeking to open a new establishment in Kihei (despite prior harassment by the unfriendly county Liquor Commission), so keep an ear to the ground! In the meantime, head over to Hapa's Brew Haus (879)-9001 at the Lipoa Center in Kihei for their Lava Nites that happen every Sunday from ten at night 'till two in the morning for dancing, drinks, and cruising the mixed gay, straight, and bi crowd. Also, call Cassanova's Restaurant (572-0220) to see if they are holding "Thursday Night Out", a weekly gay dance night. For gals, head over to the Upcountry Night's Women's Dance Club held on Saturday nights at the Heart Dance Studio in the Haiku Cannery Mall (573-4035).

Eating Out 🏮

Happy for Gays

Hana Gardenland is an interesting hybrid of plant nursery, arts and crafts shop, and charming cafe. You can buy dendrobiums, munch on a smoked turkey wrap, and paint a coconut to send home all in one visit! The outdoor cafe serves healthy fare like papaya halves filled with ahi salad, homemade pesto pizzas, and fresh vegetable soups. You can sip your Jungle Java amidst the nursery gardens (they ship many flower species), and the gift shop offers great local handiwork like musical bamboo instruments, kukui nut leis, and stunning pottery. This was Hillary Clinton's favorite lunch spot when she vacationed in Hana! Owners Blair and Tom also offer some great rentals in the area (see listing). P.O. Box 248, Hana, HI 96713. 248-8975

Not Queer, but Oh Well

Cassanova Restaurant and Deli is a great Italian eatery, run by "Real Italians," in the funky town of Makawao. One entrance takes you into a decent deli with all kinds of coffee, home–baked pastries, fresh pasta, and deli to–go for your upcountry picnic. Cool residents hang out in front to watch Makawao pass by. The restaurant, open for lunch and dinner, offers *kiawe* wood–fired pizzas, veal and local fish specialities. They claim to have the largest dance floor in Maui, with mini–amphitheater seating, where drag shows have been known to periodically take the stage, and the overall establishment is very gay–friendly. 1188 Makawao Avenue, Makawao, HI 96768. 572-0220

Gerard's is a classy, spiffy restaurant located at the elegant Plantation Inn tucked behind Front Street. You can sit in the garden, on the verandah, or in the downstairs of the old Victorian home. The wicker chairs and antique wallpaper evoke a bygone era. Voted "Best Chef on Maui" for three consecutive years, French owner and chef Gerard (who else?) offers sumptuous fare like shiitake and oyster mushrooms in puffy pastry, ahi steak tartare with taro chips, and fresh Kona lobster with avocado salad. And don't forget the award–winning wines and homemade mango and guava sorbets. Not badly priced for the quality. 174 Lahainaluna Road, Lahaina, HI 96761. 661-8939

Grandma's Coffee House is located on the western slopes of Haleakala in Keokea, the last real town on the southern route to Hana. Grandson Alfred uses his grandmother's 100–year–old–plus roaster to process the rich beans from the trees his family planted in the early 1900s. For the discerning connoisseur, their organic 100% Maui highland coffee is a rare treat, and they do offer mail order. A cheerful place with watercolors of cowboys on the walls, there's an outside porch with great ocean views, or you can take–out great java and homemade soups. Be sure to try the I–Am–Hungry sandwich, piled high with turkey, ham, and avocado. Off Highway 37 in Keokea. 878-2140

Old Lahaina Luau sits on the coast just north of Lahaina town, in a new configuration that opened in 1998. They take great pride in presenting an evening of authentic Hawaiian food (*kalua* roast pork, *lomilomi* salmon), and loving and reverent hula dances. You get the flower lei greeting, presentation of pork coming out of the *imu* underground oven, an open bar, and hosts and hostesses who help explain the buffet items to bewildered Mainlanders. The new setting is poetic, on the shore under palm trees, with traditional styled buildings and an open–air mood. Both the lu'au and its sister business, the Aloha Mixed Plate cafe down the road, are partly gay–owned. 1251 Front Street, Lahaina, HI 96761. 667-1998

Spending the Gay Dollar ⬧

Dave's of Hawaii is a novelty head shop hanging over the ocean off Front Street in Lahaina, where you can finally pick up your Colt Calendars, postcards of Prez Bill and pal Al in leather harnesses, and the indispensable six–foot inflatable punching–bag penis. A welcome break from the gooey art galleries and activity centers lining Lahaina, they also carry nasty toys, bongs, and yes, girlie magazines too. Not for the weak of heart. 815 Front Street, Lahaina, HI 96761. 661-4009 davidwww.sofhawaii.com

Gottling Ltd. is a classy, gay–owned antique shop just down from the old Hamburger Mary's in Wailuku, along Market Street's pawn and antique shops. A must for Asian antique freaks, the store brims with ornate wooden chests, carved furniture, rare jewelry, calligraphy scrolls, bird cages, statues and figurines, and museum reproductions of vases, animals, and china. Karl, the friendly Swedish owner, claims gift prices range from a mere ten dollars up to $75,000, so bring your checkbook! 34 North Market Street, Wailuku, HI 96793. 244-7779

Ki'i Gallery specializes in stunning black pearls and unique *objets d'art,* including exquisite vases and glass bowls "blown" by local artists. Also included are interesting knick–knacks the owners picked up from their overseas travels to the Mediterranean and Asia, and even refrigerator magnets of Michelangelo's David, complete with drag costume! Owned by Marty and Al (who also have the Golden Bamboo Ranch), there are two locations: one is at the Ka'ahumanu Center shopping mall, 275 Ka'ahumanu Avenue, Kahului, HI 96732. 871-4557. The other is located within the Grand Wailea Resort, 3850 Wailea Alanui Drive, Wailea, HI 96753. 874-3059

Tropical Artwear is a fascinating gay–owned shop in Lahaina's Wharf Cinema Center, chock–full of amazing items from across the world. Included are Buddhist paintings, tribal face masks from the Pacific and Africa, crystal art, hand crafted jewelry, and toe rings custom fit while you sit on their special wooden fitting chair. But the real show–stoppers are the hand–carved figures of manhood initiation rites performed by a tribe in Papua New Guinea, that includes young boys doing *certain things* to the older warriors. Just to make extra sure there's no doubt, a rainbow flag hangs on the counter. 658 Front Street, Suite 184, Lahaina, HI 96761. 667-7100

You've Got A Friend◆

Both Sides Now offers recorded info on gay events and happenings on Maui at 244-4566. Also check out their information–filled web site at mauinet/~pattie/glom.html

Bridges is Maui's only lesbian, gay, bi, and trans youth group, every Wednesday in Wailuku. Call Karen 575-2681, or Joe 573-1093.

Dignity Maui serves gay and lesbian Catholics and their friends in all of Maui. Call Ron at 874-3950.

Gay/Bi Men's Coffee Klutch is a community–building event that happens on the first and last Monday evening of the month at Borders Books in the Maui Marketplace Mall in Kahului. Call David at 242-4900.

Gay/Bi Men's Hiking Group explores different parts of Maui on the first Saturday of each month. Call David at 242-4900.

Gay/Lesbian AA Meetings are held twice weekly in Kahului and Kihei. Call Don at 874-3589.

Lesbian Video Night happens monthly for residents and visitors alike. Call Jackie at 879-2971. ♀

Marriage Project Hawai'i/Maui is a group supporting the legalization of same–gender marriage. Call Sandy at 879-7129, or make a donation by calling 1-900-97-MARRY.

Maui AIDS Foundation offers service and referrals, as well as great community fundraisers. 242-4900

PFLAG meets the first Friday of the month in Wailuku. 879-2971

Unity of Maui is a very gay–friendly church that holds services in the Iao Theatre in Wailuku. 242-9327

Women's Hotline of fun events and activities around the valley island. 573-3077 ♀

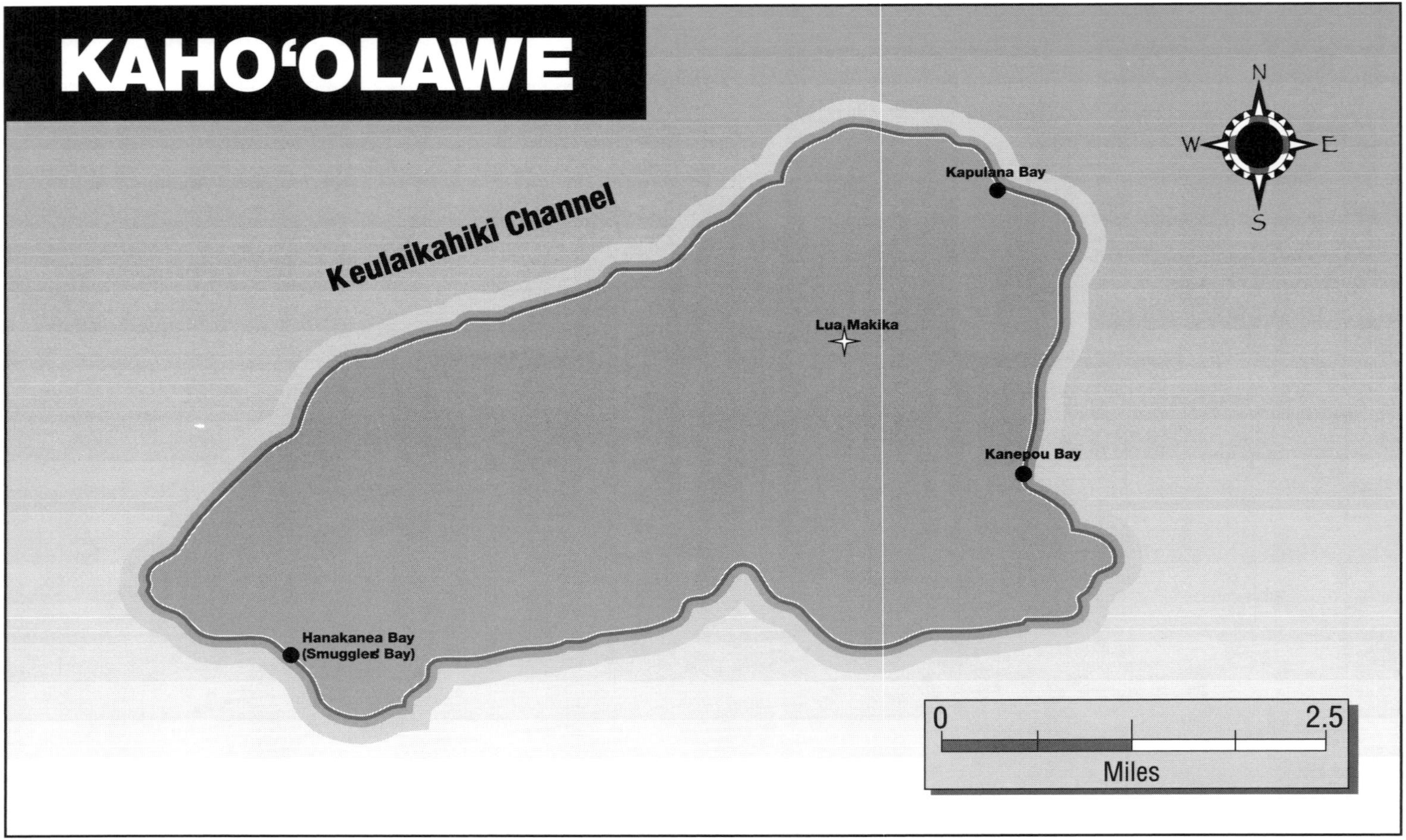

KAHO'OLAWE

Keulaikahiki Channel

Kapulana Bay

Kanepou Bay

Lua Makika

Hanakanea Bay
(Smuggler Bay)

N
W   E
S

Miles

0   2.5

CHAPTER 9

K A H O ' O L A W E

Dramatically desserted Kahoʻolawe. (Hawaiʻi State Archives)

Island Facts for Trivial Queens

Kahoʻolawe is nicknamed: "The Uninhabited Island"
Island color: Gray
Flower: Hinahina

Land mass: 45 sq. miles/117 sq. km
Population: 0
Highest point: Lua Makika 1,477 feet/450 m
Rainfall: 15 inches/38 cm

The only uninhabited of Hawaiʻi's eight major islands, and the only one ever solely used for military target practice.

Why Bother?

The answer to the question of visiting Kahoʻolawe is the same for the island of Niʻihau: *Don't even think about it*. The U.S. military used the island as a bombing target for over forty years. They even simulated an atomic blast here. This was regardless of the fact that the island is home to hundreds of Hawaiian archaeological sites and temples. It was actually the most bombed island in the *entire* Pacific during World War II (the lack of an enemy there didn't stop 'em).

In Hawaiian history, Kahoʻolawe was traditionally used as a place of exile for criminals and certain social misfits. It's been said that the god Kanaloa ruled the land of the dead from this island, and in the old days it was revered by dark sorcerers.

In the '60s and '70s, Hawaiian rights activists acted up and formed the Protect Kahoʻolawe ʻOhana group, which advocated for the return of the island by the military. At times the group illegally occupied the island for demonstrations. Their efforts paid off in 1980 when the Navy agreed to preserve the sites, but the bombing continued. It wasn't until 1990 that the bombarding was finally halted. In 1994, during a moving service that included Hawaiian chants and prayers, the Navy relinquished rights to the island and returned it to the state of Hawaiʻi. The island has since become a symbol for Hawaiian autonomy.

Kahoʻolawe is still heavily saturated with unexploded ammunition, and access is denied to all but government officials and members of the Protect Kahoʻolawe ʻOhana. There are no paved roads, ports, nor airfields on the island. A $400 million dollar fund has been established to clean up the ordnance on the island, which some estimate will take over a decade. Future plans for a cultural reserve are being discussed, but it may be many, many moons from now.

Kahoʻolawe in a Mac-nut Shell

If you have a good eye or can hallucinate easily, you'll see that Kahoʻolawe looks something like the profile of a crouching lion gazing east. The island's slopes, once a little greener, have been meticulously eaten away to a dusty brown by the left over goats and sheep. Successful and unsuccessful ranching efforts that lasted up until 1939, when the bombing commenced. Wild goats were finally eradicated in 1993, but field mice and cats still wreck havoc over the ecosystem. Soil preservation has been a main concern for the future, and efforts at replanting native species have taken place.

Kaulana Bay on the northeast shore was the site of an encampment for exiled prisoners in the 1800s (some of whom would swim back to Maui anyways). On the island's southwest corner is Hanakanea Bay, commonly known as **Smuggler's Bay,** since this is where smuggler's used to store illegal Chinese opium from the fuzz. It's also been used as a military encampment as well.

HAWAI'I The Big Island –Kona

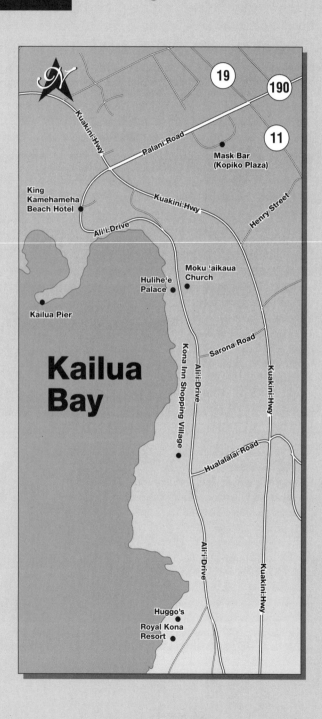

H A W A I ' I

One of Kona's black rock coasts.

Island Facts for Trivial Queens

Hawai'i is nicknamed: "The Orchid Isle" and more generally called "The Big Island"
Island color: Red
Flower: Lehua
Land mass: 4,028 sq. miles/1,047 sq. km (and growing!)

Population: 138,000 est.
Highest point: Mauna Kea at 13,796 feet/4,205 m
Rainfall: 25 inches/64 cm in Kailua, 145 inches/368 cm in Hilo

The island of Hawai'i is the youngest of the major islands, and the largest island in the U.S. It is home to the longest continuous volcanic eruption in human history at Kilauea (since 1983). It also has the largest mountain mass in the world, Mauna

Kea, measured at over 31,000 feet from its base 18,000 feet underwater. The island was birthplace of King Kamehameha the Great in Kohala in 1758, and Captain Cook was killed here in 1779.

NOTE:

Since the Big Island is larger than all the other Hawaiian islands *combined* (and almost four times the size of Rhode Island), we'll split it up into the Kona Side of the island and the Hilo Side. Even residents treat them like two separate islands (or perhaps separate universes)! You may want to fly into one side and fly out the other, to taste a little of each. Deciding which side of this contrasting island you fancy is a defining personality test in which you find your true self. Where Kona is dry and bright, Hilo is wet and tropical. Kona has *vog* (yucky volcanic fog); Hilo has mold and mildew. Kona has insipid tour groups; Hilo has marijuana traffickers. Kona has garish, Disney–esque resorts; Hilo has enough rain to water Mars. *Tomayto – tomaato,* I'll let you decide.

So without a hint of bias, we'll start on the side that most people land on, which is Kona (really!).

K O N A S I D E

Why Bother?

The Big Island is just that – big – and the wide, dry expanses and huge ranches of North Kona can make you feel like you are in any Western state (despite the palm trees). The Kohala Coast north of Kailua–Kona town, home to many monolithic resorts and black lava fields, is said to be the sunniest part of the state. The impressive slopes of Mauna Kea, Mauna Loa, and Hualalai are all easily visible along this coast, and you can meander up Saddle Road to get a closer look too. Kona overall has a well–lubed tourist infrastructure, lots of excellent diving (with manta rays no less), snorkeling, whale watching, horseback riding, golf, sports fishing, and kayaking. Day activities are plentiful while the night life is pretty much dead on arrival.

Since so much of the state's history is linked to the Big Island, Kona is also home to some of the largest, best preserved *heiau* (Hawaiian temples) and petroglyph fields (ancient rock carvings) in Hawai'i. The Pu'uhonua O Honaunau (Place of Refuge for you language–impaired) is an awesome pre–contact sacred site, located in the greener region of rural South Kona, where the famous Kona coffee is grown and roasted. There's a lot of driving involved, but be sure to spend enough time to explore all the differences along the Kona Coast.

The homo community in Kona is fairly hidden, and you will stand out as *the visitor* at the island's only gay bar, Mask. The nude beach at Honokohau Harbor also acts as a social spot to meet local queer residents (despite clothing crackdowns by rangers). Where the men's community in Kona is a bit fragmented, the women's scene is alive, with well organized get–togethers listed in the Lesbian Brunch Bulletin. Kona offers a nice selection of gay and lesbian B&Bs, many congregated south around the Honaunau area. There are also lesbian wellness retreats, gay kayak and dive companies, a couple of homo–owned restaurants, and a vigorous group of same–gender marriage activists. People in Kailua–Kona are some of the most gay–positive on the island and will make you and your S.O. (or S.O.B.) feel most welcome overall.

West Hawai'i AIDS Foundation volunteers at Ironman.

HAWAI'I The Big Island –Kona

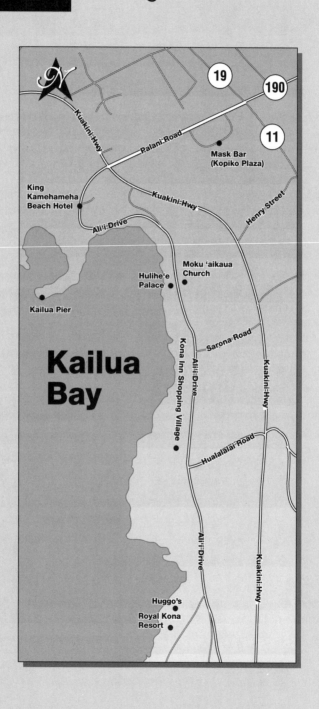

This Town

When you land at the **Keahole Airport** on the Kona Coast, don't freak out. Many tourists do. It's because they have spent thousands of their hard earned vacation dollars to land in the middle of a huge, barren, black lava field complete with sharp spears of ugly rock bordering the runway. *This is tropical Hawai'i?* Well, look at it this way – you've arrived at a unique historical spot. Close to the airport is where none other than King Kamehameha the First threw his regal garland crown into advancing hot lava that threatened to swallow up the town of Kailua, as an offering to the fire goddess Pele. The King always had fate on his side, and sure enough the lava stopped just short of the village. Pele plays favorites.

Heading south on Highway 19 from the airport, turn towards the ocean at the main drag through Kona, Palani Road. You will pass some busy shopping centers and end up by the sea on Ali'i Drive. You are now in the heart of **Kailua–Kona** village. The town had only one stoplight up through the 1980s. Now it is rated as one of America's Top 25 Boomtowns by Fortune Magazine (with a Safeway, a Denny's, and a Hard Rock Cafe popping up to prove it). Residents worry about the *wikiwiki* growth and many car bumpers don *Keep Kona Country* stickers. But fisherman still stand solemn on the seawall in town for hours, Aunties yawn and sell flower leis on the sidewalk, and kids scream and jump off the pier, just like in the old days. Compared to Waikiki, you're still in the 18th century.

The pier in front of the King Kamehameha Beach Hotel along Ali'i Drive is where diving, snorkeling, parasailing, and other cruises take off from. A little beach next door, **Kamakahonu Beach,** offers the only real sand in town. You will also spot the reconstructed **Ahu'ena Heiau** here, near where King Kamehameha spent the last years of his life. This historical locale is home to the best lu'au on the island called the **Island Breeze Luau** (326-4969), reenacting the King and court alighting on the beach in full pageantry, and lots o' dudes in *malo* (loincloths).

You can hit two of your easy tourist obligations right along Ali'i Drive, a short stroll south of the pier. The first is on your left: **Moku'aikaua Church,** the first Christian church in all of Hawai'i, was built with coral stone and koa

The Ahu'ena Heiau in Kailua–Kona.

Royal vacation pad – The Hulihe'e Palace.

Kayak studs near Kahalu'u.

wood by missionaries in 1837 (illustrated in the film *Hawaii* with Julie Andrews). Yes, the missionaries *were* against the suggestive hula and introduced the very un–sexy *mu'umu'u* tent dress to the islanders, but they did give the Hawaiian language a written alphabet and opened many beneficial hospitals and schools for the native born.

Across the street from the church is the **Hulihe'e Palace**, where the Hawaiian royalty spent their holidays in sunny Kona. A few bucks slipped to the Daughters of Hawai'i who run the place gets you in to look at the museum, that has beautifully recreated rooms and incredible *koa* furniture for you antique queens. There are great photos of the Hawaiian royalty, including the big–hearted Princess Ruth (I won't mention her size, which was somewhere around 6'2"–6'10," 400–450 lbs.), who slept outside in her own hut. The palace is a fascinating look into the lifestyle of the revered Hawaiian royal family.

Next to the palace is the historic **Kona Inn** (where Errol Flynn and Tyron Powers used to come for holidays, not at the same time mind you). It's now a shopping village with low–key boutiques along a boardwalk promenade. In front of the **Kona Inn Restaurant,** you can sit on the spacious lawns and watch the sea pass by and even nap without being mistaken for homeless. Head further south on Ali'i for more shops and restaurants.

A small **farmer's market** with delicious local fruits (although probably not the type of fruit you're looking for) happens in the not–so–sanitary parking lot across the street from the Hale Halawai pavilion.

A QUEER RANCHER

Richard Smart

Richard Smart stands as one of the better known gays in recent Hawaiian history. Smart was directly descended from the original John Palmer Parker, who jumped ship in Hawai'i as a teenager in 1809, made friends with King Kamehameha, married his granddaughter, and ended up owning what at one point was *the* largest individually–owned ranch in the U.S.A. with well over 500,000 acres. As an infant, Richard Smart became sole heir to this wealthy **Parker Ranch in Waimea** after his mother died of tuberculosis in the early 1900s. The ranch was run by trustees until 1960s, when the flamboyant Richard, fresh from a successful run as an actor and singer on Broadway and in Paris, took over the estate. His love of the theatre and lavish demeanor (not to mention his *artsy* friends) raised a few of the old–time *paniolo* cowboys' eyebrows on the ranch, but everyone eventually abided. Smart added an impressive art collection to his family's Pu'opelu Home, with work by Pissaro, Monet, and Kluge, and opened the Kahilu Theater in Waimea, named after his mother Thelma. His philanthropy made the town into the arts center that it still is today.

Richard Smart died in 1992, and as soon as the bucket was kicked, his two sons (from his one "marriage") became involved in a fierce lawsuit dispute over the inheritance of the estate. All was settled, and now Parker Ranch is peacefully owned by the Parker Ranch Foundation Trust. It's the first time in six generations that it has no single individual ownership.

Visitors can still visit the **Pu'opelu family home,** off Highway 190 near Waimea (885-5433). The family's Impressionist and Chinese art, statues, and antiques still adorn the scenic 1862 home, which sports a French Provincial interior, and a yellow Hawaiian Victorian exterior. Most of all, don't forget to pick up your cassette copy of Richard Smart singing the best of Broadway, available at the gift counter.

If you continued south on Ali'i Drive, it would lead eventually past the **Royal Kona Resort** (see listing) and onward past endless condos with names like Kona Tiki and Kona By The Sea until you reached the **Kahalu'u Beach Park.** There isn't much of a beach here, but plenty of turtles and "feed me, feed me" fish, not to mention a plethora of tourists who aren't really supposed to be feeding them (or to be touching the turtles either, even though it is said to be good luck). A van nearby rents snorkel gear, and there are usually some locals playing the ukulele and selling bracelets, a few Euro dudes in skimpy bikinis, and an insistent smattering of gays – probably due to the now boarded-up glory holes in the bathrooms (sorry, kids).

Kona Coast in a Mac-nut Shell

Head north out of Kailua-Kona town toward the airport on Highway 19, and you will find the sign for the **Honokohau Harbor** on your left (see listing). This is

the site of Kona's kind-of nude beach, as well as home to sports fishing charters. Beyond the harbor and the airport is lava wasteland for miles. Check out the Donkey Xing signs on the highway – if you're lucky you might be able to spot one of these local asses, called "Kona Nightingales." During the winter months, also keep your eyes on the coast since this region is celebrated for whale sightings. The Kohala Coast is also known for its scat-

Hawaiian rock art.

tered fields of petroglyphs (Hawaiian carvings in the lava rock).

The Kohala Coast stretches in the arid area north of Kailua-Kona. This is where a majority of the most out-of-control luxurious resorts in the state reside amid the stark lava rock. The show-stopper of them all is at the first turn-off you hit, near the 76 mile marker, called the Waikoloa resort area. Included here are two excellent golf courses, a nice beach (Anaʻehoʻomalu Bay), some classy resorts, and the amazing **Hilton Waikoloa Village** (see listing). A visual definition of the word *opulent* (not to mention *flamboyant*), you'll witness waterfalls plunging into swimming pools, water slides, a monorail system, a canal for passenger boats, gourmet restaurants, $5 million of Asian art (well, some are replicas), a wedding chapel (hetero only!), and a protected lagoon where you can pay to play with captive dolphins (if your name happens to get picked from a lottery). Picture *Gilligan's Island* on steroids and LSD. Amazingly, everything is open to the public, except the swimming pools.

Further north are more resorts lined up along the coast, including the **Mauna**

A PICTURE OF INNOCENCE

Raymond Helgeson

Having lived on and off Hawai'i for over two decades, a chunk of Raymond's work is inspired by the canoe club paddling team he belonged to on the Big Island. Many of his teammates show up as amateur models in his work. Although portraying the male form in most of his figurative work, Helgeson's real subject is light and its effect played out on the body. "My style is definitely not 'in your face', even when it shows full frontal nudity. My favorite poses capture an innocent shyness, or a moment of privacy when the model is not 'on display.' " (Send $5 for a color brochure) Bodies of Work, 11350 Alethea Drive, Sunland, CA 91040 (818) 352-0557 www.raymondhelgeson.com

A PICTURE OF INNOCENCE ~ CONT.

Lani and its famous golf course. The best beach on an island not known for its beaches is **Hapuna State Beach,** near the mile 69 road marker. Smooth white sand with an absence of rocks and coral makes for a postcard–perfect afternoon of sun-burnt memories. It also offers the best boogie boarding on the island when the waves are up in winter.

Palm trees swaying at Hapuna Beach.

At the junctions of 19 and 270, be sure to take a peek at the **Puʻukohola Heiau.** It was built to the war god Kukaʻilimoku after a *kahuna* priest prophesied that King Kamehameha would subdue all the Hawaiian islands upon its completion, which of course he went ahead and did. It is also said to be the last Hawaiian temple where routine human sacrifices were carried out (not pretty virgins but ugly slaves). Further up is the industrial **Kawaihae Harbor,** where the sets for the ill–managed film *Water World* floated (and occasionally sank) for over a year during shooting here.

Hawaiian cowboys rounding 'em up.

Head up on Highway 270 towards Hawi along the dramatic, spartan desert coast that looks like it was shipped in from Baja California. The scenery quickly turns green as you near the village of Hawi. Stop here and snoop the artsy little shops and galleries, and be sure to gobble something at The Bamboo Restaurant in an old hotel–like building with a very Hawaiian feel to it.

Further past Hawi is Kapa'au, where the nearly seven–foot tall King Kamehameha Statue stands, which is actually life size! Salvaged from a sunken ship, there are usually leis draped around the neck of the beloved king. At the very end of Highway 270 is the lush **Pololu Valley.** This is the little bookend sister of the seven valley system that ends to the southeast with big mama Waipi'o Valley. The lookout at the end of the road offers nice views, and take the time to hike down the rocky trail (less than half an hour – come on) to the bottom of the deserted valley. If you want to swim here, just know that island tradition describes a shark breeding ground close to the shore.

From Hawi you can drive south on Highway 250 on the green rolling hills of the Kohala Mountain range, which is frequently rainbowed. The cheerful road descends into the ranching town of **Waimea.** This *paniolo* (cowboy) village looks like it was imported from Montana and you may even pass some Marlboro Men in the pastures, albeit with shorts and sandals on. Headquarters of the 225,000–acre **Parker Ranch,** you can visit the Parker family home, **Pu'opelu,** off Highway 190 south of town. It has a French Provincial interior and an Impressionist art collection and was last owned by queer rancher Richard Smart (see sidebar).

If you continued south on Highway 190, you would encounter the turn–off for Saddle Road. The rental car people threaten to murder your mother if you drive on this potholed road but most tourists say screw 'em. There's not a heck of a lot to see up here except close–up views of Mauna Kea and Mauna Loa, which are

THE WORLD'S LARGEST SPEEDO CONVENTION

For those of you who can't wait until summer for a good ogle at all the guys in cute little swimming briefs, **The Ironman Triathlon** is the peak experience for you Speedo queens from around the world. Sleepy Kailua–Kona comes alive with thousands of extra visitors and competitors filling the streets from all over the world – something like the United Nations of Spandex. Up to a month before the actual Ironman date, you will notice swarms of dudes and dudettes making their way up and down the coast, frantically trying to acclimatize to Kona's hot, harsh terrain. On the third Saturday in October, get up early to watch the guys and gals take off from the Kona Pier just after dawn, swim 2.4 miles, mount their bikes for the 112 mile round trip ride to Hawi, then race 26.2 miles down to the finish line set up at the Kailua pier. Hundreds of visitors and residents alike cheer on the Iron people every step of the way, with aid stations set up all over the course.

Driving around the Kona Coast that day is complicated, with lots of detours, so stay put at your hotel or in town for convenience. By mid–afternoon, the quickest ones are past the finish line and into the arms of the waiting medics and massage practitioners. You will be amazed at the Ironmen who are missing limbs or race in wheel–chairs who finish quite early! (Bound to make the buffest of you feel out of shape.)

Of note: in 1996, Jim Howley was the first person to do the Ironman as a publicly disclosed HIV–positive person. Diagnosed with the virus in the early '80s and with full blown AIDS in 1989, he took up the Ironman as a way to "defy death." At thirty–five, Jim beat out many other competitors in the field. The West Hawai'i AIDS Foundation proudly set up a refueling station to support him and all the other non–disclosed HIV–positive people in the race.

dusted with snow in the winter.

The **Onizuka Visitor's Center is** up about 9,000 feet on the slopes of **Mauna Kea,** and is named after the Big Island astronaut who perished in the Challenger disaster. Call ahead (961-2180) to see if they'll be taking out their smaller telescope for public night viewing of the planets on the weekends. If you have a four–wheel drive and a lot of guts, take the ragged dirt road up to the top of the mountain for a splendid sunset. Since it is above 40% of the earth's atmosphere and far from continental dust, the surrealistic summit of Mauna Kea is home to the world's most powerful land–based telescopes. This includes the famous Keck Observatory, and none of them are open to the public. Needless to say, it gets mighty windy up here, and cold enough to freeze those *cajones* off you needed to get up here in the first place. Watch out for innovative skiers dodging rocks when the peak is snow–ladened in wintertime.

Near the tippy–top of Mauna Kea.

If you continued on Saddle Road going east, you would come the back way into Hilo town (see Hilo Coast in a Mac–nut Shell).

Making your way back down the Kona Coast to Kailua–Kona again, if you head south out of town on Highway 11, the Queen

The historic Aloha Theater in Kainaliu.

Ka'ahumanu Highway begins to ascend to nearly 1,000 feet as it enters Kona coffee country. The **Aloha Cafe** in the Aloha Theatre at the village of **Kainaliu** offers tasty local meals, as well as performances of various plays and musicals by local actors on weekends (hey, it's regional theater). A stone's throw down the block is the original **Bad Ass Coffee** cafe, with insignia Bad Ass T–shirts for sale to those who dare to wear them to a gay club.

Keep your eyes peeled for Napo'opo'o Road on the ocean side of the highway after the 111 mile marker. Follow this winding road as it descends past rural homes into drier country, and winds up at the remarkable **Kealakekua Bay.** Renowned as the spot where Captain Cook was killed, a small obelisk stands in his honor on the opposite side of the bay under the cliffs, near where large snorkeling boats come to dump tourists into the crystal water. Spinner dolphins often visit the bay, circling

A GAY MAORI

Phillip Hema

Board member of West Hawai'i
AIDS Foundation

"My personal experience about being a gay Maori probably has more to do with having a loving mother and family. I now recognize that New Zealand is way ahead of the U.S.A. in the area of rights for gay people. I remain here because I love Hawai'i and the U.S. I have decided the important battle is here, because when the USA moves so many other countries follow."

the astonished kayakers and snorkelers. There was once a large Hawaiian settlement here, as well as a sandy beach that is long gone. But the stark beauty of the bay remains.

Back on the upper highway, between mile markers 112 and 111, across from the turn-off to the local high school is the inevitable **Little Grass Shack in Kealakekua** (named after a song written before *my* time). The store offers handicrafts of varying quality and tourist take-me-homes. Once you go through the micro-town of **Captain Cook,** you will soon pass the **Mauna Loa Royal Coffee Mill,** which offers interesting historical photographs of the only commercial coffee region in the U.S., as well as free samples and tasting (guzzle the Peaberry blend, made from pods with half-beans, since it's the most expensive). In the back, get tubed by walking through the little lava tunnel.

Mean looking tikis at Place of Refuge.

Once you pass mile marker 104, turn *makai* (towards ocean) at the Honaunau Post Office, and you will be headed down towards the Pu'uhonua O Honaunau National Park. Before you hit the park, however, you will pass a turn-off for the **Painted Church** near mile marker 1. Stop by this genuine little church to behold the interior painted with trees and murals and stars on the ceiling, by the artistically inclined Father John Velge around the turn of the century. Bound to stir even the most atheistic.

One more lunch stop before you hit the Place of Refuge is **The Wakefield Gardens**. Ms. Wakefield (a former model) founded the eatery as a way of employing wayward hippies and artists, and the amusing patio restaurant offers yummy vegetarian fare made from local ingredients.

The actual **Pu'uhonua O Honaunau,** or Place of Refuge National Park for the tongue–tied, is at the bottom of the road and costs a few dollars to get in. It's worth an hour or so to explore the centuries–old ruins of huge temples and fif-teen–foot walls the Hawaiians built as a sanctuary for refugees of wars and *kapu* law–breakers. *Kahuna* priests here would exonerate the offenders of their official sins (cheaper than pris-ons, no?). Bordering the park to the immediate north is a decent snorkeling spot called Two Step. (Not much in the way of steps – more like lava rock). You know you're in the right spot when a group of underwater bricks spells out "ALOHA."

Back up on Highway 11, just past the Honaunau Post Office on the *mauka* (left) side of the road, you will spot the

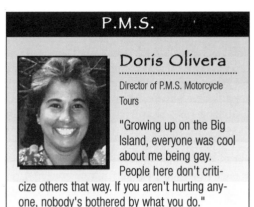

P.M.S.

Doris Olivera
···
Director of P.M.S. Motorcycle Tours

"Growing up on the Big Island, everyone was cool about me being gay. People here don't criti-cize others that way. If you aren't hurting any-one, nobody's bothered by what you do."

Where fruits can buy fruit.

South Kona Fruit Stand. Run by the friendly Michael and Dennis, a selection of incredibly exotic tropical fruits and plants are featured. Keeping on 11 further south, the road becomes more and more twisted and the population thins out a bit. You will pass through the largest macadamia nut orchards in the state before you hit **Hawaiian Ocean View Estates,** or for those in the know, H.O.V.E. Touting itself as the world's largest subdivision, this "neighborhood" stretches so far back up the banks of Mauna Loa that it nearly snows at the end of it. Everyone from million-aires to food stamp recipients (and many gays and lesbians at both ends of the spec-trum) seem to own a chunk of the lava back here, since land prices are still dirt cheap. Stop in the women–owned **Cafe Ohia** at the Ocean View town shopping center for local gossip (see listing).

If you continue on 11, you will pass the turn–off for South Point and then see the gentle town of Na'alehu (see Hilo Coast in a Mac–nut Shell).

Tell Me When You're Coming

The **Queen Liliʻuokalani Long Distance Outrigger Canoe Race** (326-4732) takes place in August at the beach in front of the King Kamehameha Hotel. It's the largest race of its kind in the world, attracting over 3,000 participants from seventy–seven international clubs. The weekend closest to the first full moon in October is when all eyes in Kona are on **The Ironman Triathlon** (329-0063) which begins at the Kailua Pier (see sidebar). A lot of fun, but it is hard to get rooms this time of year since thousands of people normally show up, so be sure to call ahead. The **Kona Coffee Festival** (326-7820) happens in early November around Kailua–Kona and Kealakekua, with coffee picking contests, coffee farm and mill tours, tasting competitions, and even a healthy baby contest!

Queer Pages

Lesbian Brunch Bulletin not only gives the time and place of the second Sunday of the month womyn's brunch (which attracts a big crowd with visitors welcome), it also includes a calendar of parties, potlucks, workshops, and classifieds for both the Kona *and* Hilo lesbian communities. Call Lori at 326-4065. P.O. Box 134, Mountain View, HI 96771

Outspoken is printed on the *other* side of the island (see Hilo chapter) and covers some random events in Kona, and it's the closest Kailua–Kona's gay male community gets to a queer periodical! 936-7073

Things for Homos to Do

Eco–Adventures is a gay–owned dive company offering some excellent diving opportunities, like the incredible Manta Ray night snorkel and dive in Keauhou Bay. These manta rays (some with a twelve–foot wing span) are related to the sting ray, but have no stingers nor teeth, making them more human–friendly than say, the shark? Feeding on the plankton attracted by the boat's flood lights, these creatures are a sight to behold. The Kona Coast is one of the world's major sites for manta ray viewing. P.O. Box 3033, Kailua–Kona, HI 96740. (800) 949-3483, 329-7116 www.eco–adventure.com

Tropical Tune–ups is a series of "Hawaiian Health Holidays" open to gay, bi, or straight women. Bette and Peggy, together for over twenty years, are musicians and certified Kripalu Yoga teachers, as well as a transpersonal hypnotherapist and massage therapist respectively. They organize periodical wellness retreats where like–minded women stay in an ocean side house and experience ocean sports, massage, meditation, and vegetarian meals together. They also customize intimate retreats for two or more people. P.O. Box 4488, Waikoloa, HI 96738. (800) 587-0405, 882-7355 www.tropicaltuneups.com ♀

Matt's Rainbow Tours is run by yours truly, where I take gay visitors for a half-day paddle up the rugged South Kona coast in a three-seat kayak, perfect for beginners. Then we alight on a secluded black sand beach, bordered by a hardened lava flow, where naturist sunbathing is possible. Here, you'll picnic under palm trees, then snorkel and swim on the nearby coral reef, where you'll likely encounter friendly sea turtles. During heavy swell season, hiking to secluded beaches is also available. P.O. Box 100, Honaunau, HI 96726. (800) 260-5528 http://members.aol.com/mrlinkk/kayak.htm

P.M.S. Motorcycle Tours (Pacific Motorcycle Sistahs) is run by the friendly Doris, Big Island born and raised, who takes adventurous riders for full– or half–day tours around the island. Doris helps you arrange cycle rentals, and customizes each private tour to fit your interests. Half–day tours include stops at Hawaiian historical sites, and full–day tours include trips to South Point, Saddle Road, and beyond. Doris will share her perspective of growing up on the Big Island and show you places only residents know about. 328-8721 ♀

Waves of Change offers healing and renewal retreats in Kapa'au, near Hawi. Three–day and seven–day retreats are available with lodging in the comfortable Chakra Suite, complete with gazebo, outdoor jacuzzi and shower. The Hawai'i Nature Fast happens three times a year, where participants fast for three days in the beautiful natural setting of North Kohala, with ceremonies and guided consultation. Waves of Change is run by the knowledgeable Tom, a massage therapist and consultant, who has also written a book on healing AIDS. P.O. Box 1360, Kapa'au, HI 96755. 889-0553

Letting it all hang out ◆

Honokohau Harbor Beach is the main nude beach on the Kona Coast, just north of the Honokohau Harbor off Highway 19. Follow the road to the marina and veer right (north) around the harbor shops and park along a rock wall. On the other side of the wall is a dirt trail leading to the ocean, and you'll see a small strip of yellow beach up ahead. You can sniff out the north end which (as usual) is mostly gay, with a few bushes. Don't expect much coverage or privacy (a hotel room offers a lot more, honey). The snorkeling's not bad here, and be sure to dip into the cool brackish water ponds behind the beach; these baths are found all along the coast, and were a favorite dipping spot for ancient Hawaiians. A word about wagging your weenie at Honokohau: in early 1997, an ordinance was passed that officially made this beach clothing *not* optional, even though it's been a nudist hang out for decades. Since it's on federal land, rangers have been known to do the awful work of scouring the beach for naked flesh, but usually beachgoers warn each other of ranger visits before anyone gets ticketed. For now, nudism is still going strong in the face of adversity.

Place to Put Your Head ⬍

For Sure Queer

Hale Aloha Guest Ranch is a large two–story home run by JoHann, a friendly German host, and is way up the mountain side with sweeping views of the coast. The large house works perfect as a B&B, with lanais on both levels, large and medium guest rooms, and lots of peace and quiet. The upstairs bath sports an whirlpool and the amazing two-headed shower stall is big enough for you and all your friends! Good place for romantic seclusion. 84-4780 Mamalahoa Highway, Honaunau, HI 96726. (800) 897-3188, 328-8955 www.halealoha.com

Hale Kipa O Pele is run by the friendly host couple Scott and Brent. Conveniently located in a quiet neighborhood up the hill from Kailua–Kona town, the spacious plantation–style house has an open atrium with lava rock waterfall and *koi* pond, wide lanais around the front views, bright rooms each with their own private tiled entrance, pleasant lawns and landscaped yard, and an outdoor hot tub. There's also a separate bungalow, with mini–kitchen and living room, for rent. P.O. Box 5252, Kailua–Kona, HI 96740. (800) LAVAGLO, 329-8676 http://home1.gte.net/halekipa

Ho'onanea Bed and Breakfast, is a lesbian–owned studio apartment rental in the cool upcountry of Waimea, near the Parker Ranch. Popular with women (with men welcome), the rental is private, and comes equipped with kitchenette and views of the gardens and nearby Mauna Kea and Mauna Loa mountains. A hot tub is in the back, overlooking a fresh mountain stream (the owners also have ducks). Barbara and Shay provide mountain bikes and snorkel equipment for their guests.

P.O. Box 6450, Kamuela, HI 96743. 882-1177
www.kamuela.com/lodgings/ho'onanea ♀

Horizon Guest House is a newly–opened, luxuriously tasteful bed and breakfast
resort that offers miles of uninterrupted views of
the huge Pacific. On over forty acres of upcountry land with goats and cattle, features include an
excellent Infinity pool and whirlpool, and both
solitude and a social atmosphere. The place was
built to order, with four classy rooms full of
antique Asian furnishings, private lanais and
bathrooms, and wonderful amenities like a laun-
dry room and outside shower. Clem, the owner, custom–designed the whole property from scratch, and his vision shows through. First class all the way, this is the
premier mini–resort on the Big Island. P.O. Box 957, Honaunau, HI 96726. 328-
2540, 328-8702 www.horizonguesthouse.com

Plumeria House offers a great location in the residential area off of Ali'i Drive, a
short jaunt from the renowned snorkeling beach of Kahalu'u. Owner Randy offers
two clean, roomy bungalow rentals adjoined to a large home, one with full kitchen
and one with kitchenette. They overlook the manicured Japanese gardens in the
back yard, which has a clothing–optional hot tub. Daily, weekly, and monthly rates
are available, and the locale is a perfect setting for long stays. 77-6546 Lani Drive,
Kailua–Kona, HI 96740. 322-8164

Pu'ukala Lodge is a guest house located in the cool residential area above

Kailua–Kona. A 1,400–square foot lanai wraps
around the main house, offering 180–degree
views of the coast line and spectacular Kona
sunsets. Besides the two cabin–like rooms
upstairs, there's a two–bedroom,
1,500–square foot *'ohana* rental in the base-
ment, and hosts Ron and Tom are known for
their entertaining and gourmet cooking. The
homey atmosphere includes a crystal and porce-
lain collection too. P.O. Box 2967, Kailua–Kona, HI 96745. 325-1729
www.puukala–lodge.com

Non–Dorothy Digs

The Royal Kona Resort is within walking distance to most of Kailua–Kona town.
You can't miss the weird ski–jump profile of the hotel on the town's horizon. With
three separate towers, most rooms come with lanais and views, and a salt water
swimming area, restaurant, and an adequate lu'au (if you don't mind sitting next to

Bill and Doris from Topeka). Actually once a
Hilton, it's slightly showing its age by the groovy
room decor and overall Don Ho atmosphere,
but it's a pleasant and comfortable hotel with a
gay–friendly management and staff. 75-5852
Ali'i Drive, Kailua–Kona, HI 96740. (800) 774-
5662, 329-3111 www.royalkona.com

The Hilton Waikoloa Village is the mother of all resorts with over sixty–two acres, a
monorail and canal boat system, waterfalls and water slides, hallways full of excellent
Asian and Pacific Rim artifacts, restaurants, shopping malls, and an overall

Disney–esque atmosphere, catering to lots and
lots of heterosexuals. But the *fabulousness* of it all
will make any queer feel at home. You might have
caught the *Regis and Kathy Lee* or *Wheel of
Fortune* broadcasts from the site? (Between taping
your *Bay Watch* reruns?) 69-425 Waikoloa Beach
Drive, Waikoloa, HI 96738. 886-1234
www.hilton.com/hawaii/waikoloa

Bar Crawl

For Sure Queer

Mask is the only official gay bar on the whole of the Big Island. It's of course in a
strip mall next to Domino's Pizza. It is tiny but clean, with the ever–present
Karaoke mike and a horse shoe–shaped bar. You get the feeling sometimes it exists
for novelty only, and on some week nights when less than a dozen patrons stare at
each other, you might want to bring a good book. But come late on a Friday or
Saturday night and the place will fill up with a friendly, predominately gay male
clientele, with some gals too. Also light meals and *pupus* are served. 75-5660
Kopiko Street, Kailua–Kona, HI 96740. 329-8558

Not Queer, but Oh Well

The Other Side is a simple bar owned by a gay male couple, and sports a neon
pink triangle on one wall, but its subdued location in the Old Industrial Area
draws hopelessly heterosexual, working class guys who have never ever heard of
Judy Garland. The interior is basic bar, with plastic chairs and dark carpet and
beer signs, and there are usually no gays to be found here at all. Still, it's a good
place to shoot some pool if you can handle the testosterone level. 74-5484 Kaiwi
Street, Kailua–Kona, HI 96740. 329-7226

Captain Bean's Dinner Cruise – now we're talking party! Take this booze cruise from the pier on a 150–foot mock Hawaiian vessel for its camp value alone, with *non–straight* acting loin-cloth–clad guys (and gals in coconut–shell bras) dancing right on top of your banquet table! A decent meal is served by the gay–friendly staff, and the obligatory Conga line they save 'til last. Good place to witness straight male tourists being forced to don grass skirts and wigs. All you drinkers will be glad to know all booze is included in the admission price! 73-4800 Kanalani Street, Kailua–Kona, HI 96740. 329-2955

On the Level

Skip Burns
Realtor and Same–gender Marriage Activist

"Marriage Project Hawai'i is busy building a community, one person at a time. We envision a Hawai'i where lesbian and gay people have gained their basic rights. A place where we can be open, honest and safe. When the marriage playing field is absolutely level, I will take a rest."

Eating Out

Happy for Gays

Huggo's, located right next to the Royal Kona Resort, offers seafood and steak dining over the ocean. Spot lights at night shine into the water, attracting fish and manta rays. There are nautical charts on the table tops, a roomy open–air bar, and live local bands on most nights (as well as karaoke of course). The restaurant has been owned by the same family for over twenty–five years, and is now run by Eric, one of the sons. Try the slow–roasted Black Angus prime rib, *mahimahi* with prawns, or the outrageous Kona Coffee Mud Pie – a three course meal in itself! 75-5828 Kahakai Road, Kailua–Kona, HI 96740. 329-1493

Edward's at Kanaloa is a gay–owned restaurant sandwiched (punny?) between a swimming pool at the Kanaloa condos and the ocean, which turns out to be a pretty nice and simple location in Keauhou, twenty minutes south of town. The food is made with expertise, with dishes like chicken liver *mousseline* and flourless chocolate cake. Open for breakfast, lunch, and dinner, there's also a good wine selection, and reservations are recommended for dinner. Oh, and Edward is currently single and looking! 78-261 Manukai Road, Keauhou, HI 96739. 322-1434

Cafe Ohia is an out–of–the–way gay spot near South Point. Owned by two enthusiastic women, this cute little cafe is located in a shopping center all the way out in Ocean View, about an hour south of Kailua–Kona, and serves great Kona coffee, tasty homemade soups and sandwiches, quiche (for real men), and assorted entrees, all reasonably priced. This is a place you need to stop at on your way to Volcano – there's said to be a sizable gay crowd living down here, where land is cheap and life isn't! 525 Lotus Blossom Lane, Ocean View Town Center, HI 96737. 929-8086 ⚥

Not Queer, But Oh Well

Sibu's is an Indonesian cafe tucked in the back of Banyan Court just south of the pier in Kailua–Kona town. A fountain gurgles on the sidewalk along the shops as you munch on excellent curries and vegetarian fare, including Balinese chicken marinated in tarragon with peanut sauce. The prices aren't a steal, but the portions are large, and everything tastes fresh and unique. The place is so popular there's often a wait for the few tables the restaurant holds. Cash only. 75-5695 Ali'i Drive, Kailua–Kona, HI 96740. 329-1112

Spending the Gay Dollar ⑤

Paradise Found is a lesbian–owned boutique that has been around for a couple decades, selling mainly women's apparel including sarongs, belts, hats, bracelets, necklaces, pearls, scarves, all with an distinct island flavor. They also carry Avanti men's silk shirts and aloha wear. Their main store is in the funky town of Kainaliu, just down from the Aloha Theatre, and they also have satellite stores at the Lanihau Center in Kailua–Kona town, and in the Keauhou Shopping Center. P.O. Box 949, Kealakekua, HI 96750. 322-2111, 329-2221 ⚥

Klystra is a Kailua–Kona mail order company that specializes in enema gear and related accessories for gay men and anyone else into it. Their custom–made vintage bags, colon tubes, water syringes, clamps, and hoses are based on antique designs, some bordering on the artistic! Klystra offers one of the most extensive and unique array of enema goods for the connoisseur, and a massive web site to boot! P.O. Box 5290, Kailua–Kona, HI 96740. 325-3157 (For orders call 1-800-708-0477) www.klystra.com

You've Got A Friend ◆

Marriage Project Hawai'i/Kona is a group supporting the legalization of same–gender marriage that regularly holds meetings in Kona, and they can always use the boost from visitors. Call Skip at 323-3296, or make a donation by calling 1-900-97-MARRY.

The West Hawai'i Aids Foundation (or WHAF) located in Kealakekua offers services and counseling to resident P.W.A.s, as well as fundraising and community functions. 322-1718

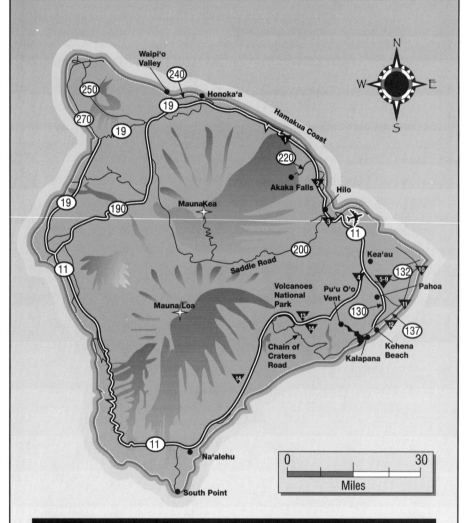

HAWAI'I HILO-SIDE

Waipi'o Valley
240
250
19
270
19
Honoka'a
19
Hamakua Coast
220
Akaka Falls
Hilo
MaunaKea
19
190
3
11
Saddle Road
200
Kea'au
132
10
5-9
Pahoa
Volcanoes National Park
Pu'u O'o Vent
130
11
Mauna Loa
13
12
137
14
Kehena Beach
Chain of Craters Road
Kalapana
14
11
Na'alehu
South Point

0   30
Miles

N
W   E
S

HILO'S Gay and Lesbian Acommodations

1. Pu'upuananiokawaihone
2. Our Place Papikou's B&B
3. Dolphin Bay Hotel
4. Butterfly Inn
5. Volcano Ranch Inn & Hostel
6. Lavender Boot
7. Peter's Bed & Breakfast
8. Rainbow's Inn
9. Village Inn Hotel
10. Pamalu
11. The Orchid House
12. Kalani Honua Oceanside Eco-Resort
13. Hale Ohia Cottages
14. Lokahi Lodge
15. Earthsong

CHAPTER 11

HILO SIDE

The stark beauty of Volcanoes National Park

Why Bother?

Hilo acts as the exact opposite of Kona, and for good reason. It rains here more than anywhere in the state except Kaua'i. And I mean *rain.* The kind of rain Noah prepared for. Hence, where Kona is browned and naked in the sun, Hilo is extraordinarily lush and green and thick. But don't be surprised if it is cloudy and gray during your *entire* time in Hilo. If you ask a resident they will say the rain and drizzle and deluge isn't that bad at all – in fact they wouldn't have it any other way. Given the old, colorful, rainforest feel of this side of the island, you'll understand what they mean.

On the up side, Hilo is very much local Hawai'i, undiluted by tourism and keeping its distinct flavor and character of a proud Hawaiian town. The Puna area, with its black sand beaches and steam vents and rich foliage, is as organic as the island chain gets. And don't forget, the volcano goddess Pele resides on this side of the island. Her fiery home at Volcanoes National Park is the site of the longest continuous lava eruption in *human history*. For you tightwads, now's the time to

Resident gays enjoying life on hiking trip.

splurge and spend the money to fly over Pele's turbulent furnace by helicopter or airplane. It's worth every penny to witness the lava's breath–taking outbursts.

Hilo residents are a bit tourist–shy (sometimes spilling into downright tourist–annoyed), but don't let their frosty demeanor fool you – they need the tourist dollar just as bad as anyone. Actually worse, since the last sugar plantation closed on the island a couple years ago, leading to high unemployment throughout the region. Hilo's gay community is not really centered around Hilo town, but south in the fundamental, bohemian Puna district, where a large number of gay B&Bs are to be found. Here the gay community is tight knit, with gays and lesbians coming out of the rural woodwork for miles to enjoy the large parties at people's homes promoted through the *Outspoken* newsletter.

The black sand nude beach at Kehena is quite social, and there's also a gay hiking group as well as various community events sponsored by the Big Island AIDS Project. The women's community is well organized island wide, with monthly brunches presented in the Lesbian Brunch Bulletin, and several women's guest houses are located on the Hilo side as well.

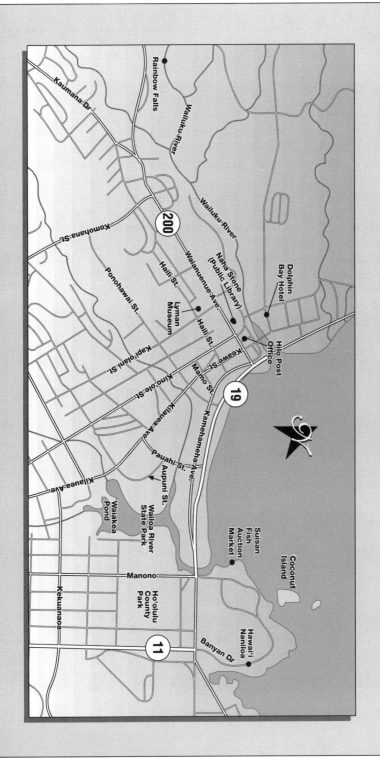

This Town

The **downtown** area of Hilo still has the feel of an old sugar plantation town which it once was. Store fronts dating back to the 1910s line the main drag of Kamehameha Avenue, overlooking the highway and ocean. The recent refurbishing of the old downtown area makes for a nice stroll among the handful of artsy shops and cafes.

Starting from the north end of Kamehameha along the bayfront, walk up Waianuenue Road and you will pass the most dramatic building in town: a lavish two–story **post office** with white columns and an outdoor courtyard. Across the street is **Kalakaua Park,** with a statue of the Merrie Monarch, an impressive banyan tree, and antique buildings lining the south edge.

Hilo's proud post office.

Walk a block further up Waianuenue and you will find the 7,000 pound **Naha Stone** in front of the public library, which is fabled to have been the one that King Kamehameha lifted when he was a lad of fourteen, helping to fulfil the prophecy of his conquering of the island chain. Go ahead and give it a try, but remember to bend with your *knees.*

If you drive up past the library for another mile or so on Waianuenue, you'll come across the turn–off for **Rainbow Falls**, a postcard waterfall that is best to catch in the rainy season (which I guess means most of the year). King Kamehameha is said to have buried the bones of his father in a cave below the falls. Although impressive, Rainbow Falls doesn't hold a candle to her sister Akaka Falls up the coast. You can even drive further up the hill to some

The gayly named Rainbow Falls.

MEN AND HULA

The lifeblood of the Hawaiian people...hula.

Hula has been called the lifeblood of the Hawaiian people, and stands as one of the most truly indigenous dance forms in the world. Hula along with *mele* (chants) were the main form of story–telling and handing down of information for the ancient Hawaiians, in place of a written language. Not only were legends and tales told by hula, but also important historical events and royal lineage. For years, students would train under a *kumu hula*, who would scrutinize with an eagle eye to make sure not one movement was off, which might alter the meaning of a dance. Although hula is known for its swaying hips, the dancers' hands, arms, feet, face and overall movement all convey meaning.

Interestingly, men were the only ones allowed to dance hula in the very old days. They were the only ones allowed at *heiau* (temples) to perform the religious dance, although it's speculated women had their own *heiau* and hula as well. Muscular males would enact the precise dance clad only in *malo* (loincloths); grass skirts were introduced to hula only about a century ago. Missionaries suppressed what they saw as a suggestive dance, leading many *mahus* (gay men), among others, to keep the dance alive in secret.

King Kalakaua (known as the Merrie Monarch for his love of dance and parties) resurrected the hula as a cultural art form in the late 1800s. Women had to wear skirts *and* tops, while men could still don skimpy *malo*. The dance also resurfaced in the '30s and '40s, thanks to popular radio and then TV shows that mixed orchestration and English songs with hula. This created *hapa haole* (half white) hula. *hapa haole* tends to be the watered–down form most Americans conjure when they think of hula as camp.

Nowadays, hula falls into two categories. The *kahiko hula* (ancient) is serious in tone and involves the *kumu hula* who sits on the ground drumming a hollow gourd and chanting an old *mele*, with the dancers also involved in chanting. The *'auana hula* (modern) is much freer and more jovial in style, and can depict topics as contemporary as airplane travel, surf meets, even basketball! *'auana hula* usually

MEN AND HULA ~ CONTINUED

includes a band of some sort, while *kahiko hula* never has modern instrumentation. In the 1960s, the **Merrie Monarch Festival** formed on the Big Island, which acted as a venue for hula competition and appreciation. Today the festival is broadcast live across the state starting Easter Sunday. Many *halaus* (dance troupes) compete from around the world. Ironically, women solely performed at the festival until the men's division was introduced in 1976. Today, a majority of hula's great teachers and performers are gay men, and their skill and love of the dance has helped to rejuvenate this truly Hawaiian art form.

other smaller waterfalls and **Boiling Pots** above Rainbow Falls, which is not hot water but turbulent ponds fed by the cool mountain river.

Back at the post office downtown, turn left on Keawe Street to **Bear's Coffee.** It's a good place to sip cappucino on the sidewalk with the hip Hilo crowd, which may included a smattering of gays (maybe even some cuddly big ones as the name implies). Keep walking up the block and hang a right on Haili Street (heading west), uphill past a stucco Catholic church to the **Lyman Museum.** Treat yourself to a succinct lesson in Hawaiian history with *poi* pounders, feathered cloaks, Korean dresses, and Hawaiian Bibles. Upstairs is one of the most incredible rock collections you have ever laid eyes on. (Although it is rare to use *incredible* and *rock collection* in the same sentence, you will see what I mean.) Visit the **Lyman House** next door, lovingly built by a die–hard missionary family.

Heading back down Haili Street to the bayfront, you will pass the grand, soon–to–be–remodeled **Palace Theater.** Then walk right along the stores on the bayfront until you reach some blue tarps at the intersection of Mamo and Kamehameha. You are now at the best **farmer's market** on the whole island. Fresh white pineapples, jackfruit, papayas, organic bananas, and any other tropical fruit you can think of sit next to a myriad of locally grown flowers, nuts, fish, as well as plants and clothing. Although Saturday is the big morning, there's usually someone there any day of the week hawking their wares.

Strolling further down Kamehameha Avenue heading east, you will hit the wide **Wailoa Park** with curved bridges and a shiny newly–erected statue of King Kamehameha. This was once the site of numerous businesses and homes of sugar workers, but on April's Fool Day 1946 a tsunami decimated this entire part of Hilo. It leveled most of the buildings and claimed almost 200 lives. After another tidal wave in 1960 killed thirty–eight people, the town's fathers wisely decided to keep the area as a green park instead.

Continue on Kamehameha over a bridge and you'll see the **Suisan Fish Auction**

Market on the ocean side of the road. The catch of the day is thrown out on to the decks for the hungry buyers in the morning, and it smells like it. Take a walk around **Banyan Drive,** dripping with huge cavernous trees, with the pretty Coconut Island as a backdrop – a favorite spot for fishermen and hetero family picnics. The nearby thirty–acre **Lili'uokalani Gardens,** complete with Japanese pagodas, arch bridges, and stone lanterns, makes a nice shot for the honeymoon album.

The fascinating Lyman Museum.

Hilo's small handful of hotels are along Banyan Drive, including the Hawai'i Naniloa and Hilo Seaside. At the other end of the crescent of Banyan Drive, at Reed's Bay, local keikis (kids) go jumping off into the brackish water and *mahus* (fags) carry on the tradition of *da kine* cruising at the icky restrooms nearby. Carry on past Banyan Drive and drive

Japan meets Hilo at Lili'uokalani Gardens.

to Kalaniana'ole Avenue and the best beaches around Hilo. The term beach is used loosely here, since there is usually no sand, but lagoons with swimming and snorkeling such as at **Leleiwi Beach Park**. Don't forget to stop by the very local, lesbian–owned **Puhi Bay Beach Store** nearby (see listing) to stock up on your beach goodies.

The rest of Hilo lies off Highway 11, past the airport. This is where you will find the older neighborhoods, industrial and commercial areas. For you mall chicks, there's the **Prince Kuhio Plaza,** a large, quintessential shopping center (including a Cinnabuns and Hot Dog on a Stick and Border's and a cineplex), which could be found in any American town, even one in the middle of the Pacific Ocean!

Hilo Coast in a Mac–nut Shell

Heading north on Highway 19 from Hilo, you'll pass some large ravines caused by the run–off from Mauna Kea, and some small villages. Keep an eye out on the ocean side of the road for the four mile scenic coastal route (past the 7 mile marker), and be sure to take this little drive which winds through rainforest, heavy streams, and old–time homes tucked away (don't worry, the road will curve back to the main highway). You don't have to be the flower–arranging type to appreciate **Hawai'i Tropical Botanical Gardens.** There's a hefty charge to get in, and despite the mosquitos and drizzle, the bay and gardens are full of over 2,000 exotic species and makes an attractive stop.

Back on the main highway, you will see the turn–off for the **Akaka Falls State Park** between the 13 and 14 mile markers. Turn up this road (Highway 220) and park your car fifteen minutes later at the park. Stroll along a nature trail with bamboo groves and lush foliage until you get to an easy

Going down at Akaka Falls.

lookout at the 440–foot drop waterfall slinking its way down a sheer cliff wall, one of the best photo ops in the state.

Back on Highway 19, you will snake up the **Hamakua Coast's** dense rainforest ravines and rich fields of abandoned sugar cane left from the now–defunct plantations nearby. Turn on Highway 240 and go through **Honoka'a,** which was once the old sugar town. Be sure to check out the homemade ice cream parlor and little stores and galleries.

The road through Honoka'a leads directly to the lookout for the **Waipi'o Valley,** one of the wonders of the Big Island. A huge open valley with high green walls greets the eye like something out of a dream. It is possible to get

The meandering river at Waipi'o Valley. down into the phenomenal valley with

THE GODDESS PELE

Pele, **the goddess of volcanoes and fire,** is one of the most honored and revered figures in Hawaiian culture. And the most famous. It was she who loaded up a bunch of her volcanic brothers and headed north from Tahiti in a canoe, in order to rid herself of her troublesome sister, the goddess of the sea Namakaokaha'i. They set foot on Ni'ihau Island first. As soon as Pele started digging her volcanic holes, her sister would promptly put them out with sea water.

Frustrated, Pele moved on to Kaua'i, then O'ahu, then Maui, and finally ended up on the island of Hawai'i, all the time thwarted by her meddling sister who destroyed every volcano Pele attempted to prolong. As with every great legend, there's a ring of truth: Ni'ihau is indeed the oldest of the main Hawaiian islands, formed by a volcanic hot spot in the earth's crust, and every island was geologically formed in the order that Pele was said to have inhabited them.

Some legends state that Namakaokaha'i finally killed Pele on the Big Island, but as always, Pele had the last laugh. Her spirit dug a hole far from the shore line and her sister's sea water, and thus the spectacular crater of Kilauea was formed. Halema'uma'u Crater at the Hawai'i Volcanoes National Park is still the sacred home of Pele, and park visitors may spot flowers and gin bottles (Pele's favorite drink) left as offerings there. Belief in Pele is as strong among the locals as it is with the tourists who won't dare take lava rocks off the island for fear of Pele's retribution (even though the national park is credited for having started that one).

If you see a glorious young woman with long black hair walking alongside a Big Island road, or perhaps an old woman with a white dog, be sure to look twice. There are many accounts of people giving the woman a ride, then she suddenly disappears. Thus, our goddess Pele.

four–wheel drive or four–wheel hiking legs (but the stroll back up is a killer). Hint: in the valley, the best trail is along the base of the northern wall. The valley used to be a major pre–contact settlement, and over fifty generations of islanders have lived here, adding to the *mana* or spiritual power of the place. It is also meaningful to Hawaiians since this is also where high chiefs would meet to make important decisions. Young Kamehameha was tucked away here as an infant, when his life was threatened by a king who heard he would someday conquer the island (fate was always on Kam's side!). A tsunami in 1946 wiped out a good chunk of farmers living down here, but taro is still cultivated on the ancient land as it has been for centuries.

If you kept going further north on 19, you'll hit the yee–haw cowboy town of Waimea, described in the Kona Coast in a Mac–nut Shell section.

Hippy Hollow: Pahoa.

Making your way back down the coast to Hilo again, if you instead head south out of Hilo town you'd be on Highway 11. It will take you past the airport and the industrial parts of town. The road transforms into a four lane highway, and between mile markers 5 and 6 is the sign for the **Mauna Loa Visitor Center** on the left. If you're really into it, they'll take you through their orchards and orchards of macadamia nut trees on a trolley. But watch out: the nut is said to be the most fattening in the world!

A few miles further south is the town of Kea'au and the turn–off for Highway 130, which will take you into the heart of **Puna.** This alternative, hippy refuge region is where a large chunk of the state's biggest cash crop, *pakalolo,* is grown in the rich and wet landscape. Government helicopters have been flying overhead for years, trying to shut down local production of the sweet–smelling illegal herb (that's supposed to make you dizzy or hungry or something? I forgot). Most of the gay and lesbian populace on the Hilo side of the island lives in and around the Puna district.

Pahoa is the very funky center of Puna (with two lesbian–owned eateries –(see listings), that has wooden sidewalks and old store fronts, where earth mothers and moonbeams congregate to smoke and "talk story." Also, check out the old–fashioned, gay–managed **Akebono Theater** that shows inexpensive classic films in a funky auditorium with couches and hand–painted murals. Next door to the theater is the funky gay–owned **Village Inn** (see listing), if you feel like crashing in town.

Driving out of Pahoa south on 130, you'll pass the **steam vents** about three and a half miles later (see listing). Before the end of the road, you will see the little

Star of the Sea church, which had to be moved from its site in Kalapana before the lava got to it. Highway 130 abruptly ends at some recent lava flows covering the pavement. The road used to continue from here along the coast to the Volcanoes National Park, until lava flows from eruptions in the '80s and '90s put an end to that. It's at this end of 130 where you may be able to take the long, multiple–mile hike or four–wheel drive to the present lava flows, depending on the course of the current eruption (sometimes the lava is closer to the national park end of the road). Although the park service shakes their tisk–tisk finger at the danger of it, many people hike across the crackling new lava to catch an up–close glimpse of the lava rivers emptying into the ocean. Of course a few of those hikers are no longer with us!

Follow the coastal Highway 137 until the road ends again at **Kalapana.** Here, almost 200 homes were slowly destroyed by encroaching lava from up the mountain side. You may be able to stand on top of the black lava rock and see the huge steam clouds from the lava flows hitting the sea in the far distance.

Vog–making clouds near Kalapana.

From the Kalapana dead end, if you turn around and head north on Highway 137 along the coast, you will go over a series of dips until you pass the gay–popular **Kehena black sand beach.** The **Kalani Honua Eco–Resort** is just a short ways up from that (see listing). The lush and quiet Highway 137 is called Red Road, and if followed further will take you past the **Ahala Nui Park.** Puala'a is the name of a warm soaking pond along the ocean here, complete with cute lifeguard and hand railings. The water hovers above ninety degrees and there's usually not too many people, except on weekends. Further

Soaking it up at Puala'a.

TESTING TOLERANCE

In 1993, one of the counselors at Pahoa High School, the openly–gay Tom Aikten, received permission to implement a **Project 10 counseling program.** The program was for gay and lesbian students to deal with topics of homophobia and other issues. However, a group called *Stop Promoting Homosexuality Hawai'i* (many of whom did not have students at the school nor lived in the district), protested at Board of Education meetings about this counselor who they claimed was actively recruiting students to homosexuality and "disgusting, filthy sexual acts." Despite the principal's support of the program, Project 10 was completely cancelled and scrapped in early 1994 due to pressure from the group, and no other like programs have been initiated in Hawai'i since then.

---

up, the road will meander into the rural and sunnier area of Kapoho.

After your adventure in funky Puna, head back to the main circle–island Highway 11 going south, and you'll pass the towns of Mountain View and Glenwood. Along the roadside you will spot a few **orchid nurseries,** most open for walking tours, since this is the major orchid growing region in the U.S. In fact, keep an eye out for species growing on the side of the road like weeds (not *weed,* mind you)!

A few more miles and you are at the entrance of the **Volcanoes National Park.** This is the main tourist draw of the whole island, and deservedly not to be missed. Most of the action centers around the Crater Rim Drive, with its older non–lava vents. When you pull into the park, the first thing you will hit is the **Visitor's Center.** Stop in for the latest viewing info posted on the wall, plus a cool twenty–minute film of past eruptions wrecking mayhem. The men and women in uniform here seem *very* gay–friendly, oddly enough.

Pele's hang–out: Halema'uma'u Crater.

Across the street is the **Volcano House,** rebuilt from the original 1800s structure. There's an overpriced restaurant offering excellent views of the crater, although afternoons tend to get foggy and almost cold up here. The Volcano House is a cozy accommodation lodge open to the public, and check out the longest burning fireplace ever in the lobby! Crater Rim Drive from here will curve around some sulfur banks and steam vents worth taking your picture next to. You will then hit the **Jagger Museum,** with seismographs, displays of lava–eaten boots, and a colorful mural explaining the different Hawaiian gods and goddesses, fire goddess Pele undoubtedly being the local star (see sidebar).

Further along the drive, you will cross incredibly stark lavascapes, some as recent as the '70s. They appear as mammoth rock brownies of varying shades stretching off into the distance. The whole place has a *feel* to it that is immense and indescribable. Stop and walk to the edge of **Halema'uma'u Crater,** the traditional home of Pele, and peer into a huge pit that was alive and bubbling for a good part of the 19th century. It still holds a quiet power to it.

The next turn–off will be at the **Chain of Craters Road** to your right, heading towards the ocean. It may or may not be worth the forty–five minute drive to the coast to witness distant steam clouds produced from the hot lava entering the ocean. Ask around to find out what the view is like first. But it's generally a dramatic drive through a massive lava wasteland, where the road will once again abruptly end, covered with old black lava like on the Kalapana end.

The big action has been taking place at the **Pu'u O'o Vent,** about eight miles east of the Crater Rim Drive, up on the mountain side. Active since 1983 with periodic lava spouts that have reached up to 2,000 feet, the spewing around Pu'u O'o Vent has been the longest eruption in human history. You may see red glows in the evening depending on what Pele's up to. If you have the time, by all means fly over it via aircraft. There are some trails that may get you kind of close, but believe me, you don't want to be walking around too much up there! The really tremendous views are from the air. The cheapest flights leave from Hilo, and will take you directly over the active vent. The sight of red liquid rock burping and spurting and cascading is nothing less than spiritually fantastic.

The eastern end of Crater Rim Drive will take you around some other non–active craters. Park at the **Thurston Lava Tube** (hopefully devoid of irritating tour buses), which is a huge damp cave that you could run a parade through. It opens up at the other end into the lovely fern tree grottos that surround this part of the park.

Across the street from the

Hell hath no fury like the Pu'u O'o Vent.

tube is one of the best easy hikes on the island (easy enough for city queens): the **Kilauea Iki Crater** trail. In 1959, this spot spewed with molten fountains thousands of feet tall, but now it is as hard as black ice. You are able to walk right along the bottom of the crater, cracked with steam fissures and sulphur fumes. The park is riddled with excellent hikes – ask those handsome uniformed officers for advice on others.

South of the national park is a straight–away stretch of Highway 11 where you can usually floor it past the vast openness along the flanks of Mauna Loa, one of the most remote regions on the island. Don't forget to pull into the **Punalu'u Beach Park** which, if you're lucky, will have some large hawksbill turtles on its shores (it's a major nesting site). Swimming's not terribly good here, but the black sand is nice for laying out, despite the tours that throng here. A run–down resort that never took off sits across the lagoon and looks like someone's expensive mistake.

Black sand beach at Punalu'u.

Head further south on 11, and you will ultimately hit one of the prettiest towns on the island, **Na'alehu.** Although recently depressed from the closing of nearby sugar mills, the town holds a certain charm, with a sweet bread factory and old theater/gallery and snug isolation from both Kona and Hilo. Be sure to check out the tree on the side of the road that Mark Twain planted way back when; it's massive now.

Past Na'alehu is the *makai* (ocean side) turn for **South Point,** the southernmost point in the U.S., about the latitude of Mexico City. Twelve miles of undeveloped road and an army of steel windmills later, you are standing on the edge of windswept cliffs, with one big hole where the ocean rushes up near the parking lot. I wouldn't try to be butch here and jump

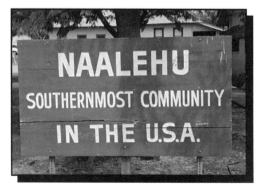

off the cliffs into the water since it's said the currents will whisk you straight out to sea.

If you take the easternmost fork of South Point road, it will end at a boat ramp area where you can park and walk a ravaged coastal dirt road north to **Green Sands Beach.** Be prepared for a wind–swept, hour–long stroll that will take you to a desert–like cove with a small olive colored beach (no you aren't hallucinating). It's made from the semi–precious olivine, a by–product of the lava hitting the sea. Just when you think it's safe to rip off your togs and body surf naked, a flock of German tourists will pop up with cameras; the beach is pretty busy despite its remoteness. Only in Hawai'i can you get red, black, white, or green sand in your swimsuit!

> ## ALL THAT MATTERS
>
>
>
> ### Keoni Castillon
> ....
> HIV Outreach Educator
>
> "I was fortunate to have loving, caring, and supportive parents and family, so being gay in Hawai'i was comfortable. I was just being myself. My parents and family always said if you're happy being who you are, that's all that matters."

Tell Me When You're Coming

Hilo always has a number of festivals year round, including **The Big Island Women's Gathering** (331-0336) occurring in late February and early March. The majority of events, including drumsong workshops, moon dances, and sunrise ceremonies, happen on the Hilo side. **The Merrie Monarch Festival** (935-9168) ignites the town of Hilo in April with hula and celebration, and it is usually a challenge to get tickets close to the date. Luckily, it's also televised state wide (see sidebar "Men in Hula"). **The Aloha Festival** (885-8086) kicks off in August and lasts until October, with numerous displays and parades island wide. Try to catch the reverent ceremony of the crowning of the annual queen and king of the festival and presentation to the goddess Pele at Halema'uma'u Crater at the Volcanoes National Park during the start of the festivities; it is Hawaiian culture at its finest.

Queer Pages ⬙

Lesbian Brunch Bulletin not only gives the time and place of the second Sunday of the month womyn's brunch (which attracts a big crowd and visitors are welcome), it also includes a calendar of parties, potlucks, workshops, and classifieds for both the Hilo and Kona lesbian communities. For info call Lori at 326-4065. P.O. Box 134, Mountain View, HI 96771 ♀

Outspoken, subtitled *A Queer Publication from East Hawai'i* is a newsletter published in Pahoa "seasonally – equinox and solstice." It's as organic as it gets, with articles, poetry, personal ads, cartoons, queer business ads, and calendars of upcoming community parties and events for Puna and environs. P.O. Box 1746, Pahoa, HI 96778. 936-7073 www.aesweb.com/out

Things For Homos To Do ⚑

Christopher Travel and Tours is proudly gay–owned and arranges car and air packages around the state, as well as offering local reservations for gay B&Bs and vacation rentals in Hilo and Kona. They're also the ones to call for gay–friendly four–wheel drive trips to the volcano and other sightseeing adventures around the island. Collin and Richard used to live on the other islands and are happy to call the Big Island home now. RR 2, Box 6261, 12-4272 Oceanview Parkway, Pahoa, HI 96778-9758. 965-1316 www.CTT-Hawaii.com

Gay Hiking Group is run by Ron in Puna, and has a loyal following of outdoor enthusiasts (mostly male), with visitors welcome given enough notice beforehand. Organizational meetings are held before the hikes, which may include overnight camping to remote waterfall valleys, hikes to the lava flows, secluded beach campfires, and the like. A great way to commune with resident gays and enjoy the beauty of the island. 961-3700.

Hawaii Men, put on at the Kalani Honua Eco-Resort in Puna, includes Pacific Men's Gathering in August, Body Electric (erotic massage) week in October, Gay Spirit (tribal and transformative camaraderie) week in late December. Adventure Hawaii also happens three times a year, which includes a week of hiking, swimming, and kayaking with gay brethren. For women, Kalani Honua also puts on the **Into the Womb of Pele** spiritual adventure in April. Don't miss any of these uniquely Hawaiian gatherings! RR 2, Box 4500-IP, Kehena Beach, Pahoa, HI 96778. (800) 800-6866, 965-7828 www.kalani.com ♀

Rainbow Excursions is run by the friendly Terrie (who also owns the pleasant Rainbow's Inn B&B) and offers bicycle, kayak, and camping gear rentals. Personalized tours are also possible, such as hiking to secluded beaches, telescope tours of the stars, and viewing the lava flows at dusk. Her other adventures, like snorkeling and surfing, await the eager explorer of the Hilo Coast. P.O. Box 983, Pahoa, HI 96778. 965-9011

Letting It All Hang Out ◈

Kehena Beach is the queer–popular nude beach in the Puna district, just off of Highway 137 near the 19 mile marker. Look for the cars parked on the side of the road and the trail down some steep cliffs. The beach didn't exist before the 1950s, when lava hit the ocean nearby, forming an alcove for black sand to collect. The cliffs and dark sand make for rustic scenery, and tall trees offer shade for the short beach. Like most of the beaches on the Hilo side, the strong trade winds create forceful waves and currents, so be careful swimming here. The

crowd is your typical Puna variety, with lots o' dreds and *pakalolo* and hairy armpits. (Keep a look out for the parrot man who is down here almost every day with his birds.) A camping community of naturists used to reside at the beach until an icky outbreak of hepatitis put an end to all that. The beach is still popular with local residents, even though it is often overcast, especially in the afternoons. Be sure to bring some kind of footwear since that black sand can get *hot*.

The steam vents off of Highway 130, past Pahoa at mile marker 15, are a hike *makai* (towards the ocean) from the scenic lookout pull–over on the road, and only for the adventurous. Formed by natural sulfur exhaust compliments of Madame Pele, these vents amid the foliage range from a small crawl–through cavern, to bowl–like structures you can climb down into, to one–man open–air sitting chambers. The steam is usually at the right temperature to enjoy a nice sweat. Popular with residents who normally use them nude, there's a following of gay users too. The protocol is to keep quiet and not disturb the other users in their respective vents. The trail gets muddy, and there are no public facilities, so bring water. A truly Hawaiian experience.

Place to Put Your Head ♦

For Sure Queer

Butterfly Inn is a wonderfully secluded women–only B&B, run for over a decade by the friendly Patti and Kay. Located about halfway between Hilo and the volcanoes, the house is on an acre lot, with a backyard bordering what used to be sugar cane fields. In the back you will find a hot outdoor shower, hot tub, and steam house with naturist sunbathing possible. There are two rooms upstairs, with common bath and kitchen. P.O. Box 6010, Kurtistown, HI 96760. (800) 54-MAGIC, 966-7936 ♀

Dolphin Bay Hotel is a small quaint hotel in a residential area very close to Hilo town, with sliding glass doors and lanais opening up to the surrounding jungle landscape. Rated the nicest small hotel in the Hilo area, all rooms have kitchens and private baths, and there are weekly rates available, and even one– and two–bedroom apartments for rent. Friendly owner John will recommend local restaurants, or you can arrange to have a home cooked meal brought to your room. 333 'Iliahi Street, Hilo, HI 96720. 935-1466 www.dolphinbayhilo.com

Earthsong is a healing women's sanctuary near South Point. Walking meditation paths meander throughout the three lovely acres, which also include a lava cave and Goddess temple. Most visitors come for the spiritual, psychological, and ecological retreats facilitated by Rashani, who lives on site. Simple, solar-powered cottages comfortably house groups of up to twenty. A marvelous haven for any woman visiting the Big Island. P.O. Box 916, Na`alehu, HI 96772. 929-8043 ♀

Hale Ohia Cottages, just a mile from Volcanoes National Park, are set amid sixty year old botanical gardens. There's one main lodge and adjoining cottages, one with a lava rock fireplace. A small, outdoor Japanese *furo* tub sits under Tsugi pines, where you can soak up the forest landscape around you. The rooms are personable and charming, complete with books and games, and it gets a wee chilly here at night, lending to the coziness of it all. The gay owners will help you out with info about current lava viewing too. P.O. Box 758, Volcano, HI 96785. (800) 455-3803, 967-7986

Kalani Honua Oceanside Eco-Resort is a gay and lesbian retreat on Puna's shore line, with a large hetero following as well. Bordering a lush and misty conservation area (Hawai`i's largest), the resort has a comfy and healing air about it. There are a pool and steam room (clothing-optional after dark), delicious buffet-style vegetarian fair, and regular week-long Body Electric Massage, Gay Spirit, and Pacific Men's Gathering workshops and retreats. Tents can be pitched on the grounds for a small fee. Most of the staff lives on the property as part of a work program, and nudism takes over for particular events. Perfect for those looking to retreat to Hawai`i's restorative nature. RR 2, Box 4500-IP, Kehena Beach, Pahoa, HI 96778. (800) 800-6886, 965-7828 www.kalani.com

Lavender Boot is a wonderful women-only "Make Your Own" bed and breakfast near Pahoa. Guests stay in the main three-story house that offers spectacular views of the ocean, full kitchen privileges, jacuzzi, and plenty of open space. The home-like rooms include shared baths, and the grounds are available for group workshops or retreats. One of the owners Ena is a professional chef who can whip up delicious Hawaiian meals for you, and her partner Rashida is a renowned musician. Camping and work exchange also available. P.O. Box 431, Pahoa, HI 96778. 965-0111 ♀

Lokahi Lodge is a B&B inn nestled in cool Volcano Village, near the Volcanoes National Park. A calming ambience with a country charm, each room has two extra long double beds, antiques, a private bath, and private entry from the wrap–around lanai. A cozy parlor with wood stove keeps you warm on the misty evenings, and afternoon tea is served too. Rates are reasonable, with a full continental breakfast included. P.O. Box 7, Volcano, HI 96785. (800) 457-6924, 985-8647

The Orchid House is a cozy getaway along the coastal Red Road in Puna. Ned, better known as Sparky, keeps a tidy and homey vacation rental. There's an ocean–facing lanai, bedrooms looking out on to the jungle foliage, a small lava tube in the back yard, an open–air shower, and views of the rugged black lava rock coast from the house. Room rates are some of the most reasonable on the island with daily, weekly, and monthly specials. The Kehena nude beach is not far away, and the active gay community in Puna is also close–by. 13-6768 Kapoho Kalapana Beach Road, Pahoa, HI 96778. 936-7480

Our Place Papi'kou's B&B is a lesbian–owned cedar home four miles north of Hilo town. The house's Great Room holds a library, a fireplace, and a grand piano, all under a cathedral ceiling. Four cozy, woodsy rooms with down–home decor share a lanai that overlooks the Ka'ie'ie stream, and there's a tree house loft that peers out over the Great Room. The setting is typically Hilo tropical, and the clientele is about half gay and lesbian. Your hosts, Ouida and Sharon, also practice acupuncture, herbalism, and Rolfing. 3 Mamalahoa Highway, P.O. Box 469, Papa'ikou, HI 96781. (800) 245-5250, 964-5250 www.best.com/~ourplace

Pamalu is a large two–story country home situated on five private acres of Puna's sun belt in Kapoho. There are upstairs and downstairs rooms, all with private baths, and the living room displays hardwood floors and a vaulted ceiling, not to mention a lovely piano. Breakfast is served on an ample screened–in lanai overlooking the lush, landscaped grounds. Tide pools and snorkeling are within walking distance, and the large private pool offers nude swimming (at the discretion of the other guests) and an adjoining cabana perfect for evening BBQs. All this accompanied by the personable host Randolf. RR2, Box 4023, Pahoa, HI 96778. 965-0830

Peter's Bed & Breakfast is located in 'Ainaola near the town of Pahoa, in a quiet country setting. Peter and Fred have been together for over thirty years, and their home is surrounded by lush gardens, with each cozy room having a private bath and French doors opening up to private lanais. You'll wake up to the sounds of chirping birds, and Peter's daily breakfast specials are served by the accommodating hosts. Ample parking is provided, and the location is convenient for both Hilo and Puna sightseeing. P.O. Box 1324, Pahoa, HI 96778. 982-5239

Pu'upuananiokawaihone is a vacation rental apartment on a gated, private estate north of Hilo, on eleven acres that harbor natural private pools and waterfalls. The bottom floor of the quiet, spacious house is decorated with Asian art, and includes two beds and a futon, a full kitchen, and a hot tub right outside the door, with gardens and statues from Bali that are lit up at night. The top floor is where breakfast is served by the friendly Dana and Kai to panoramic views of the Pacific. The whopper of a name means "house on hill with beautiful flowers near a sweetly rushing stream." P.O. Box 101, Ninole, HI 96773. 963-6789 www.members.aol.com/ninole

Rainbow's Inn is a women–owned B & B hideaway just outside of Pahoa. Guests are offered a private and comfortable king size bedroom, living room/dining room, a private bath and full kitchen stocked with fresh fruits and local Kona coffees. The ocean is a stone's throw away and visible from the wide deck, and you can stroll along the lava cliff coast line or simply relax in the double hammock. Owner Terrie makes sure there's fresh baked taro bread ready in the morning. She also runs Rainbow Excursions for snorkelers, kayakers, hikers, and surfers who want to explore the Hilo Coast. P.O. Box 983, Pahoa, HI 96778. 965-9011♀

Village Inn Hotel is an interesting former upstairs boarding house next to the Akebono Theater in Pahoa. This inexpensive gay–owned inn (with mainly straight clientele) has rooms full of antiques and old–fashioned furniture and beds, and there are both private and shared baths. An upstairs patio area serves as a place to hang out and read next to the colorful caged parrot, and the front desk is inside a musty antique shop of glass bottles, ceramics, pictures, plates, etc. A good place to stay if you really want to experience the true character of funky Pahoa. P.O. Box 1987, Pahoa, HI 96778. 965-6444

Volcano Ranch Inn & Hostel is located right next to the steam vents near Pahoa. The two-story complex includes rooms with private baths, as well as a cheaper bunk house/hostel to camp out in. There are views of the ocean, and the friendly owners will show you the trail that leads directly to the "public" steam caves, where you can shed your clothes and soak in the primordial vapor, care of Pele! 13-3775 Kalapana Highway, Pahoa, HI 96778. 965-8800

Non–Dorothy Digs

Hawaii Naniloa Hotel is the nicest choice out of the small handful of decent hotels in Hilo. The place has over 300 rooms in three wings, an admirable health spa, and a pool surrounded by black rocks bordering the pounding surf close–by. Views mainly look north on to Coconut Island and the Hamakua Coast beyond, and only the top floor rooms have balconies. The Japanese–friendly decor includes gobs of lavender–colored marble (making it gay–friendly as well one supposes), and rates are generally cheaper than the mega–resorts of the Kohala Coast. 93 Banyan Drive, Hilo, HI 96720. (800) 367-5360, 969-3333.

Bar Crawl ❖

At press time there was no gay bar operating on the Hilo side - try calling the guys at Outspoken (965-4004) to see there are any open parties going on in the gay community. Otherwise, you'll have to schlep on over to Kona and hit the island's only queer bar, **Mask** (see Kona Listings).

Eating Out ◀▮▶

Happy For Gays

Godmother's, owned by a female couple, is a decent eatery in the town of Pahoa, with good standard Italian fare including pizzas and pastas, and yummy country breakfasts. The seating is inside one large dining room with an adjoining outside patio, with the service tending to be casual. The three–seat bar sometimes attracts gays, and there are often queer community holi-day parties here, but the place has more the feel of a local diner, complete with the characters. Look for the cartoon logo of the mafia hit–woman on the sign. P.O. Box 1163, Pahoa, HI 96778. 965-0055

Mady's Cafe Makana, owned by the "goddess mother to all" Mady, is a vegetarian eatery open until the early afternoon, right in downtown Pahoa, next to the health food store. The food is tasty, with homemade cakes, muffins, soups, pizzas, curries, stir fry, and an inside store that sells batik dresses and wraps, lotions, and lovely *koa* wood pipes. The crowd is fun and alternative, with a fair share of groovy gay women and men. P.O. Box 183, 15923 Government Main Road, Pahoa, HI 96778. 965-0608 ♀

Not Queer, but Oh Well

Cafe Pesto is an airy, comfortable bistro with ceiling fans and a black and white motif, and windows overlooking Hilo's historic waterfront. Light, California–style personal pizzas are served, with local toppings like *kalua* pork and Hamakua goat cheese, poke (Hawaiian–style sashimi) salads, and numerous pastas. The wait staff are some of the friendliest and most helpful you'll find in Hilo (although let's say the competition's not too fierce). 308 Kamehameha Avenue, Hilo, HI 96720. 969-6640

Spending the Gay Dollar ⊛

Big Island Tropical Flower Farms is a gay–owned flower shipping company that can send, locally or world–wide, *fabulous* fresh–cut selections that include Big Island orchids and anthuriums. Their living plants and trees include bonsai and sprouted coconut palms. Gift baskets come complete with jams, salad dressings, cookies and more. All foliage is guaranteed fresh! HCR 2 Box 9593, Kea'au, HI 96749. (800) 32-FARMS, 982-5231 www.pocc.com/~bigisland

Puhi Bay Beach Store is a "Mom & Mom" general store along Hilo's string of swimming bays and small beaches on Kalaniana'ole Avenue. They fly the rainbow flag out front, and inside is a little local convenience store that sells lots of island goodies like laulau, poi, lomilomi salmon, *opihi* (non–tourist food!). You can also find fierce beer, glass and *koa* wood items, fancy water tobacco pipes, and of course, rainbow pride decals and jewelry. Pam and Elana also rent out an inexpensive vacation rental room in the back, as well as a rustic shack in Fern Forest. 1283 Kalaniana'ole Avenue, Hilo, HI 96720. 969-1434 ♀

You've Got A Friend ◆

Big Island AIDS Project offers services for resident clients, as well as local fundraisers and advocacy. 935-6711

Gay and Lesbian Ohana is a student organization at the University of Hawaii, Hilo. Call Lenard at 935-6711.

Marriage Project Hawai'i/Hilo is a group supporting the legalization of same–gender marriage that meets twice monthly in Hilo. Call Amy at 959-5784, or make a donation by calling 1-900-97-MARRY.

PFLAG holds meetings the first Wednesday of the month at the Hilo Hongwanji Buddhist temple. Call 965-0326.

Queer Networking – call the guys who put together the Outspoken Newsletter for info on gay events and things to do. Buck 965-4004.

PAU

Contented Hawaiian rod fishing, circa 1890.
(Courtesy Bishop Museum)

Aki, Sue L., *Attitudes Toward Homosexuality in Hawai`i*. Hilo, Big Island: Ph.D. dissertation for the University of Hawaii, 1995.

Bisignani, J.D., *Hawaii Handbook*. Chico, CA: Moon Publications, 1995.

Buck, P.F. (editor), *Outspoken*. Pahoa, Big Island, 1998.

Cunningham, Scott, *Hawaiian Religion & Magic*. St. Paul: Llewellyn Publications, 1995.

Department of Business, Economic Development, and Tourism, *The State of Hawaii Data Handbook 1997: A Statistical Abstract*. Honolulu, 1998.

Doughty, Andrew and Harriet Friedman, *Hawaii: The Big Island Revealed*. Lihu`e, Kaua`i: Wizard Publications, 1997.

Doughty, Andrew and Harriet Friedman, *The Ultimate Kauai Handbook*. Lihu`e, Kaua`i: Wizard Publications, 1995.

Flanagan, Christine (editor), *Essential Hawai`i*. Aiea, HI: Island Heritage Publishing, 1997.

Fumia, Molly, *Honor Thy Children*. Berkeley, CA: Conari Press, 1997.

Gunter, Gregg S. (editor), *Out in Maui*. Kahului, Maui: Both Sides Now, 1998.

Handy, E.S. Craighill and Mary Kawena Pukui, *The Polynesian Family System in Ka`u, Hawai`i*. Rutland, VT: Charles S. Tuttle, 1972.

Hobica, George, *Gay USA*. Chicago: First Books, 1995.

Hollon, John (editor), *Hawaii Magazine*. Honolulu: Fancy Publications, 1998.

Ingrahm, Tania Jo (editor), *Island Lifestyle*. Honolulu: Island Lifestyle Publishing Company, Inc., 1998.

Joesting, Edward, Hawaii: *An Uncommon History*. New York: W.W. Norton & Company, 1972.

Jordan, Freddie (editor), *Odyssey Magazine Hawaii*. Honolulu, 1998.

Kalakaua, King David, The Legends and Myths of Hawaii. 1888.

Kane, Herb Kawainui, *Pele: Goddess of Hawai`i's Volcanoes*. Captain Cook, Big Island: The Kawainui Press, 1987.

Kay, Joshua (editor), *Pocket Guide to Hawaii*. Honolulu: Pacific Ocean Holidays, 1998.

McMahon, Richard, *Camping Hawai`i: A Complete Guide*. Honolulu, University of Hawaii Press, 1994.

Malo, David, *Mo`olelo Hawai`i (Hawaiian Antiquities)*. Nathaniel B. Emerson, translator. 1898. Honolulu: Bishop Museum Press, 1976.

Maugham, W. Somerset, *The Trembling of a Leaf*. Honolulu: Mutual Publishing, 1990. University of Hawaii Press, 1992.

Morris, Robert J., Aikane: *Accounts of Same-Sex Relationships in the Journals of Captain Cook's Third Voyage*. Journal of Homosexuality, Volume 19(4), The Haworth Press, 1990.

Pukui, Mary Kawena and Samuel H. Elbert, New Pocket Hawaiian Dictionary. Honolulu: Reyes, Luis, *Made in Paradise: Hollywood's Films of Hawaii and the South Seas*. Honolulu: Mutual Publishing, 1995.

Stoddard, Charles Warren (edited by Winston Leyland), *Cruising the South Seas*. San Francisco: Gay Sunshine Press, 1987.

Tregaskis, Richard, *The Warrior King: Hawaii's Kamehameha the Great*. Honolulu: Falmouth Press, 1973.

Westervelt, William D., *Hawaiian Historical Legends*. Rutland, VT: Charles S. Tuttle, 1977.

Bold words are accompanied by illustrations